# Friendship Sloops

# Roger F. Duncan

**IM**

INTERNATIONAL MARINE PUBLISHING COMPANY
Camden, Maine

Typeset by Journal Publications, Inc., Camden, Maine
Printed and bound by Edwards Brothers, Inc., Ann Arbor, Michigan

Published by International Marine Publishing Company
21 Elm Street, Camden, Maine 04843
(207) 236-4342

**Library of Congress Cataloging in Publication Data**

Duncan, Roger F.
  Friendship sloops.


  Includes index.
  1. Friendship sloops. I. Title.
VM311.F7D86   1985     623.8'223     84-47757
ISBN 0-87742-172-2

*Illustrations by Kathy Bray*

*To Mary Chandler Duncan*

# Contents

# *F*oreword

*O* *ut of privation and a hard chance*, out of risk and danger, out of fog, winter gales, and summer sunshine, out of the sea amidst rocky headlands, sunken ledges, and many islands came a boat the Maine fishermen built themselves, a boat with the wings and power of the native osprey, the Friendship sloop.

The author's account of how this came about makes an absorbing tale, and one never fully told before. We can only marvel at how fishermen unschooled in naval architecture and self-taught as boat builders, with few and simple tools, were able to conceive and contrive a vessel of such perfection, grace, and functional capability.

With the passing of working sail, the Friendship lapsed into what was virtually a period of suspended animation that was to continue for upwards of half a century, although during that time a few surviving sloops were converted to yachting use and a few new ones were built. But by the 1950s new winds were blowing in the yachting world, the traditional watercraft revival was just getting underway, and the qualities that had distinguished the Friendship sloop as a working fisherman made it the natural choice of a special sort of sailor looking for a special kind of yacht.

Then in 1961 the Friendship Sloop Society was formed and its first regatta sailed. A new era dawned for the Friendship sloop, and since then its numbers have continued to grow and its fame has spread. In a world in which there is so much that is wrong, the Friendship sloop is one of the things that is right.

It is fitting that Roger Duncan should write this book. He was in on the Friendship revival from the beginning, and has been an active participant ever since. *Eastward*, the 32-foot, Class B Friendship built in 1956 for his family of growing boys, was designed by Murray Peterson. *Eastward* may have supplied the spark that fired the gun for the first Friendship regatta, and she has won her share of trophies, including the Governor's Trophy for the overall winner of Classes A and B (four times); the Lash Class B Trophy (five times); and the Anjaca Class B Overall.

In 1965 and 1968 Roger Duncan served as president of the society that he helped to build, high points in a record of continuing service. This book is yet another contribution, and one that promises to have influential and far-reaching effects, for it will be widely circulated. Roger writes with authority, affection, and pride, and he writes well. His book is a joy and an inspiration to read.

John Gardner
Mystic Seaport Museum
December 1984

# $P$*reface*

*The Friendship sloop is unusual* in that it was first a successful work boat and, after having been neglected for half a century, suddenly was reborn as a yacht. Why this remarkable revival? Why the Friendship sloop rather than the Hampton boat, the Block Island cowhorn, or the Chesapeake Bay bug-eye? The answer lies in the qualities of the boat and in the qualities of the people who built and sailed it in utility, beauty, and tradition.

In her day, the Friendship sloop was admirably adapted to her purpose. She was a good sea boat, capable of winter fishing in hard weather and fast enough to run home ahead of a gale. She was handy among the ledges and in the small harbors of Maine. She carried a good load of fish or lobsters and made a steady working platform for her crew.

As work boats go, she was not remarkably cheap or easy to build; but the inhabitants of Bremen Long Island were remarkably skillful, and they had an eye for style. They wanted handsome, fast boats, even if they took time to build. For instance, the clipper bow is largely decorative. The cutwater and trail boards do not support the bowsprit and add nothing to the seaworthy qualities of the boat. The lovely, elliptical counter is difficult and time-consuming to build; the vessel would lift as well to a following sea with a cheaper stern. One may claim that the graceful sheer is functional, for the boat must be high and flaring forward to throw the chop aside and low aft so fish and lobster traps can be hauled aboard easily. At any rate, the combination of clipper bow, quick sheer, and graceful stern is a joy to behold and a source of pride to the builder. Even when Wilbur Morse moved to Friendship and got into something like mass production of sloops, his boats retained their appealing appearance. Surely both the utility and the beauty of these boats attracted the fishing community, for out of every harbor from Eastport to Cape Ann sailed numbers of Friendship sloops.

When they became obsolete as fishing vessels, the sloops served for a while as yachts, but the trend toward lighter and faster marconi-rigged boats left most of the Friendship sloops rotting on the bank. With the foundation of the Friendship Sloop Society in 1961, however, the breed came back with a rush. Modern Friendship sloops have slightly smaller mainsails, larger staysails, auxiliary power, and sometimes luxurious cruising accommodations. They are ballasted with lead instead of beach rocks, use turnbuckles instead of deadeyes, dacron sails and running rigging instead of cotton duck and hemp. They have the same grace, however, as those developed on Bremen Long Island nearly a century ago.

The people who sail these boats are unique among yachtsmen. They admit their sloops do not get to windward with the speed of a modern yacht, and they find it hard to explain why they like to sail a living antique. A Friendship sloop has what fishermen call "heft"; she has momentum, power under sail. She slashes through the chop in businesslike fashion. Her motion is easy. She deals with wind and sea confidently, as if she belonged to them, like a duck or a tern.

Her owner likes these qualities, and, out of respect and affection, cares for the sloop himself, rather than delivering her to a boatyard. His work pants are speckled with the colors of her bottom, topsides, and deck. He knows the leads of her halyards and sheets, the patches and darns in her sails, for he put them there himself. He has even nursed her engine through its inevitable indispositions.

The owner also likes the tradition of the Friendship sloop. The boat is most at home among the rocky, forested islands of Maine, for she was built to work there. At anchor in an island harbor, the skipper watches summer fog sift through the trees. He hears a distant fog signal, the ripple along the waterline, the piercing, sweet note of the white-throat in the spruces. Aboard his Friendship sloop, the owner feels he rightfully belongs in that world.

This book chronicles the nearly century-long development of the Friendship sloop from Warren Morse and Robert A. McLain building in oak and pine, to Jarvis Newman building in fiberglass and Harry Quick in Fer-a-lite.™ Writing it has involved many people, more than I can remember – people who spent much time talking with me, remembering the old days and their relatives who built sloops for fishermen. Nettie Winchenbach of Waldoboro, Newell McLain of Rockland, and Roger Morse of Thomaston were among these.

In addition, Captain Ted Spurling of Islesford found the correspondence between Wilbur Morse and Captain Jordan. The late Robin Colcord assembled material on a wide variety of sloops in 1955, all of which he made available to me. Betty Roberts and Caroline Zuber, respectively historian and secretary of the Friendship Sloop Society, provided documents and pictures from their records and the Friendship Museum. J. Malcolm Barter contributed pictures and reminiscences. Al Zink, Kent Murphy, Jim Hamilton, and Harry Quick, who built their own boats, shared their experiences; Dr. Quick was especially generous with his memories of Philip J. Nichols. Paul Cunningham, Ralph Stanley, Farnham Butler, and Jarvis Newman, professional builders of modern boats, contributed much, and David Nutt let me take photographs of the rebuilding of *Depression*. Captain Boyd Guild of *Victory Chimes* told me the story of *Georgie C. Bowden* and filled out E. Pierson Richardson's account of *Susannah*, ex-*Gladys D. Rose*. Bill Peterson, son of the late Murray Peterson, shared some of his father's papers and photographs with me. Dr. Edward Ives of the University of Maine allowed me to use tapes of an interview with Philip Nichols, recorded by the late Kenneth Lynn. Erik Ronnberg, Jr., shared reflections on design.

The staffs of the Blunt White Library at Mystic Seaport, the Cape Ann Historical Society, the Maine Maritime Museum, the Penobscot Marine Museum, the Smithsonian Institution, *National Fisherman*, and *Down East* magazine have also been helpful.

Maynard Bray made available the material on the rebuilding of *Estella A.*, and Don Huston shared his experiences rebuilding *Eagle*. John Gardner was most helpful with material on round-bowed sloops; he also read part of the text for me.

To Carlton Wilder, who painted the picture from which the dust jacket was made, I am very grateful. T. Gray sailed aboard *Eastward* during two of the 1983 races and was a guest aboard Captain Hugh Williams's *Wabasso* for the third race in 1983, thus enabling him to take many of the pictures in this book. Thanks, also, to those who allowed me to use pictures, as indicated by their credit lines.

Gardner Lane flew me over Muscongus Bay to take airplane pictures. Complete Photo, Inc., of Cambridge, Massachusetts, hand-printed my photographs with exceptional care.

I am especially grateful to Roger C. Taylor of the International Marine Publishing Company for getting me started on this project and for helping with material, advice, and encouragement. My wife Mary has also provided support and helpful criticism throughout the project.

Undoubtedly, this book includes some errors of fact and some considerable omissions. Any reader who can correct or expand the text will deeply oblige the author.

Roger F. Duncan
East Boothbay, Maine

Tannis *coming up astern.*
*(T. Gray)*

# *Introduction*

*O**ne may describe a bald eagle*, but when at last you see one, you find that the description, while accurate, is inadequate and unnecessary. From then on, you recognize that majestic bird by the feeling it inspires. So it is with that masterpiece of timber and sail, the Friendship sloop.

The first Friendship sloop I remember was *Eleanor*, owned by Isaac McFarland and anchored in Back Cove off New Harbor in the late 1920s. As a boy, fishing from a punt or sailing a skiff, I had often seen her there, drowsily swinging to her mooring in the narrow cove. I recall in particular one cloudy, summer day, a chill easterly blowing into the harbor. I was trying to beat out, my flat-bottomed skiff bucking and pounding in the sharp chop. Just then, out of Back Cove swept *Eleanor*, now fully awake. Her topsides green and her deck gray, she came fast, heeled to the gray easterly wind under her huge mainsail, her powerful clipper bow trampling the chop. She tacked thunderously right over me, bore off outside the point, and faded in the mist, leaving that deep impression of power and grace that is to me a Friendship sloop.

It was there in the Muscongus Bay that the Friendship sloop was born, crafted to meet fishermen's need for an able, fast, and stable boat from which to haul lobster traps, fish with a handline, set trawls or nets, and carry the catch to market expeditiously in almost any reasonable weather, winter and summer. The family sloop was also needed to carry apples, potatoes, salt fish, or firewood to market and to return with flour, molasses, lumber, and store-bought goods. A man and a boy could carry half a ton of goods to Boothbay or Rockland in a sloop much more easily than they could in a wagon.

In order to understand the needs of the community that developed the Friendship sloop, we must learn something of the life of the Muscongus Bay and its people in the last two decades of the last century and the first decade of this one.

# Fisherman-Farmers of Muscongus Bay

Muscongus Bay lies between the Pemaquid peninsula on the west and the islands forming the lower west side of the St. George River on the east. From Pemaquid Point to Allen Island, the outermost of these, is eight nautical miles. Into the head of the bay flow two rivers: The larger is the Medomak, with Waldoboro at the head of navigation; the smaller, the Meduncook, flows into Friendship Harbor and Morse's Bay. It is seventeen miles from Pemaquid Point to Waldoboro; eleven miles from Pemaquid Point to Friendship.

The islands of the bay lie in ridges running southwesterly, dipping to bars and ledges at low points on the ridges and running off into half-tide rocks and submerged shoals to seaward. Between ridges, the water is deep, soundings of over ten fathoms being common in the upper bay and over twenty fathoms farther out.

There are many harbors among the coves, islands, and ledges, most of them deep and well protected. New Harbor, Round Pond, Bremen, and Friendship are the principal mainland harbors, and there is good shelter at Allen Island, Harbor Island, Cranberry Island, Morse Island, Otter Island, Cow Island, Friendship Long Island, Muscongus Island, Hog Island, Bremen Long Island, and Hungry Island.

Early settlers in the area gathered in small communities near the harbors in the late 1700s. Because land transportation before the advent of the automobile was arduous, involving crossing ridge after ridge with swamps between and fording or ferrying across broad tidal rivers, most transportation was by water.

*Muscongus Bay looking north. Franklin and Harbor Islands in the foreground and Friendship in the center in front of the Camden Hills.*

Under these conditions, living on an island was often more convenient than living on the mainland, for one could be nearer the fishing, and in hard winters the upper part of the bay often froze over so that only New Harbor and the harbors on Harbor, Cranberry, and Allen Islands were open. Ivan Morse, in *Friendship Long Island*, spoke of people walking to Port Clyde over the frozen St. George River as no unusual occurrence.

The people of these Muscongus Bay communities in the last two decades of the last century were mostly fishermen-farmers (or associated tradesmen such as coopers, ship carpenters, riggers, sailmakers, and blacksmiths), living between the industrial communities of Boothbay and Rockland. In the latter half of the nineteenth century, the populations of Friendship and Bremen were each under 1,000, while Boothbay grew to over 3,000. Maine had expanded rapidly in wealth and population since statehood in 1820; but while some of the expansion affected Muscongus Bay, much of it was concentrated to the east and the west.

To the west, Boothbay, with its large, well-protected harbor and easy access by steamer to the rail heads at Portland and Bath, developed rapidly. In the early 1900s, near the peak of prosperity, East Boothbay boasted four yards building both big vessels and smaller fishing boats. Blacksmiths, sparmakers, sailmakers, ship chandlers, and other businessmen supported the shipyards. Four factories made oil and fertilizer from pogies, the local word for menhaden. A fertilizer factory used imported brimstone, phosphate rock, and bones, which were mixed with the dried refuse from the pogy factories.

*Muscongus Bay looking east. Haddock, Ross, Loud's, and Marsh Islands are in the foreground. Friendship is at the left center.*

A large fish packing plant bought fish caught and salted at sea on the Nova Scotia and Newfoundland banks; washed, resalted, and dried them; and shipped the product westward. Fresh mackerel, alewives, and herring were salted and smoked. Cod, hake, haddock, and halibut caught locally were either salted or shipped iced in barrels by steamer to the railroad in Portland. Herring, pogies, alewives, and clams were salted for bait, and after 1893 the cold storage plant froze herring and alewives for bait.

Four sardine factories canned herring from weirs and seines, and two lobster pounds bought lobsters to be held in the pounds, sold locally, or shipped in ice to Boston. Several smacks also bought live lobsters to be carried to Portland or Boston.

The Knickerbocker Ice Company cut tons of ice every winter on Knickerbocker Pond, where three- and four-masted schooners could load from ice houses or directly from the pond, a method impossible on the frozen Kennebec. Also, vessels loaded ice from the West Harbor Pond and from Sawyer's Pond on Southport.

By 1900 the railroad to Portland and Bath and its steamer connection to Boothbay began to draw substantial numbers of summer people, an increasing influence on the region's economy.

With all this activity, service businesses grew to supply the community. Banks, hotels, an opera house, stores of all kinds, four livery stables, schools, and even a gasworks sprang up. Lester Maddocks, one of the town's most enterprising entrepreneurs, agitated for a railroad line to Boothbay, secured a charter and surveyed a route, but was never able to finance the venture.

At the same time, Rockland, with its capacious harbor protected at last by a breakwater in 1888 and a railroad built in 1878, became Muscongus Bay's metropolis on the east. Boat building was big business in Rockland and in nearby Camden and Rockport. The clipper ship *Red Jacket*, built in 1853, epitomized the large, fast, ocean-going wooden vessels built in Rockland and Camden until early in the twentieth century. Carleton, Norwood Co. had a yard in Rockport where they built square-rigged "downeasters," and there were other yards building square-riggers and schooners all the way up the west side of Penobscot Bay. Between 1880 and 1905, Camden's Holly M. Bean built 54 vessels, including 17 three-masted schooners, 20 four-masted schooners, 12 five-masted schooners, and the huge *George W. Wells*, 319 feet long, the first six-masted schooner ever built. And of course, these yards required the supporting trades of blacksmiths, sailmakers, caulkers, coopers, and many others.

Rockland was also the center of an extensive lime burning industry, requiring schooner-loads of cordwood to supply the kilns and the best and tightest vessels in which to ship the finished product. There were also from Rockland and the Penobscot Bay ports active trades in lumber, ice, and granite, and, because of the rail head in Rockland, a large fresh fish and lobster business. Both the railroad and the regular steamer service from Boston brought increasing numbers of summer people, who took island steamers to the picturesque villages eastward as far as Mt. Desert.

Muscongus Bay, between these busy centers, participated to some extent in their activity. A shipyard at Waldoboro built a number of big schooners, among them the *Gov. Ames*, the first five-master. Of course, anyone looking at the Medomak River today may well wonder how such a huge vessel ever floated in such an eel rut. The river has silted in a great deal since those days and the schooner was launched without much of her rigging and towed to Round Pond to be fitted out. Nevertheless, it must have been a near thing. At Round Pond, too, was a small but active granite quarry; another was located on Friendship Long Island. There were brickworks on Friendship Long Island and at Round Pond and New Harbor and grist mills at Goose River and on the Meduncook River. Fish packing plants on Morse Island and at New Harbor operated in much the same way as the one at Boothbay. There was a pogy factory at Moxies Cove and a fertilizer plant at Round Pond. A lobster pound on Friendship Long Island bought and shipped lobsters iced or in smacks, and fishermen took their own lobsters to the factory in Port Clyde or East Boothbay or even to Boston or Portland in smacks, sloops, or schooners with wells in which the lobsters could be transported alive.

Most people in Muscongus Bay communities, however, relied mainly on fish and lobsters for cash income and on farming for subsistence. The islands and shores of Muscongus Bay were well suited to such a life. The deep water running far up the bay meant that marketable fish could be found close to habitable islands. As late as the 1930s, one could catch cod, haddock, and hake between New Harbor and the Sunken Ledges with a handline, trawl, or cod net. Ivan Morse tells of catching a number of large codfish off Crotch Island at the mouth of the Meduncook River in the 1880s. Alewives, herring, smelt, and mackerel schooled in the coves and rivers; clams abounded on the flats. In the 1880s and 1890s, lobsters were so common that when people went for a clambake, they counted on finding enough lobsters under rocks on the shore at low water. The time had gone when a farmer could drive a cart to the shore, fill it with lobsters, and spread them on his field for fertilizer, but mussels were so plentiful that they were used for fertilizer and for hen feed.

The fisherman's life ashore was a busy one. He lived usually in a snug, wood-frame house, often with a granite, brick or field-stone foundation, stoutly framed, clapboarded on the outside and plastered within. In winter the foundation was often insulated with

spruce branches or hay banked half way to the windows. The house was heated with wood, usually cut locally but sometimes brought in small schooners or scows, especially to neighborhoods where little hardwood grew. Spruce and hackmatack were alright for summer cooking, but hardwoods – oak, beech, or birch – were preferred for winter as they "held the heat" better.

Usually, an ell led to a shed or barn where the family kept a cow and a winter supply of hay. More serious farmers often had a horse or a yoke of oxen for heavy hauling. There might also be a shed for sheltering sheep in the winter, a hen house, and a pig sty. Every house had its woodshed and backhouse handy to the kitchen door.

Around the house, land was cleared for garden, pasture, and hayfield. These were fertilized with rockweed, mussels, flats mud, manure, and often refuse from lobster or pogy factories, and they were carefully tended. Sheep were pastured on islands in summer and transported by boat to the mainland for winter.

Roads were little more than paths, and most people walked most of the time. Wagons and sleighs were used for heavy hauling, drawn by a yoke of oxen or a horse. Thus, many roads had three ruts: two for the wheels and one for the horse. In winter, snow was partly plowed off the roads, partly packed down by a wedge of oak timbers hauled by oxen and weighted with a crew who climbed down and shoveled drifts too heavy for the team. In mud time, when the frost was coming out of the ground, the roads developed deep, muddy holes.

In most towns, a store stood near the wharf where freight was landed. This was truly a general store, carrying not only staples like flour, sugar, salt pork, and molasses, but also clothing, fishing gear, rope, paint, axe handles, yard goods, ribbons, pins, dye, and ginger ale. In a shed on the wharf citizens would find a supply of wood and coal for sale.

Usually, a stream was dammed up to make a mill pond and ice pond. Ice was cut there, mostly for local use; little was shipped commercially from Muscongus Bay.

Some towns had a doctor, but home remedies were well known and often effective. An infection might be treated with fat salt pork bound on tightly or by a poultice of corn meal and poppy leaves. Almost any man or woman could splint a broken bone. An aching tooth was "hauled," the victim being given a pan of ashes to spit into and little ceremony. When one man rested his hands on the muzzle of his shotgun and blew three fingers off each hand, his neighbor cleaned the wreckage and the man survived, developing astounding strength in forefinger and thumb. Childbirth attracted little attention. One pregnant woman and her husband, travelling alongshore in a dory, were invited to stop at the settlement on Harbor Island but elected to continue to uninhabited Wreck Island, where there was only a shed on the shore. Here the lady had her baby, and the threesome resumed travel the next day.

Schools were small, one-room buildings heated by a stove and presided over by one teacher who taught as many as six grades simultaneously. The pupils were ranged on benches in ascending order of grades, the front bench reserved for the class reciting. Each grade in turn was called to the front and instructed while the others, still under the eye of the teacher, studied or wrote. Anyone who cared to learn could get a good start in such a school, and almost everyone learned to read, write, and do simple arithmetic.

Some communities supported churches, but many smaller towns got along with only the occasional ministrations of travelling preachers. Morality, however, did not seem to suffer. Thieves appear to have been rare, and, while occasional lurid murders took place, they too were few and far between. In general, community standards seemed sufficient to maintain law and order.

Communication with the world beyond the town was constant and considered easy. Steamers ran regularly from Boston to Portland and Rockland, and, beginning in 1896, the Portland and Rockland Steamboat Company ran from Portland to Boothbay, New Harbor, Round Pond, Friendship, Port Clyde, Tenants Harbor, and Rockland. At the height of the steamer trade, two vessels were employed, *Mineola* and *Monhegan*, one running east while the other ran west. Also, many fishermen sold their catches in Boothbay, Portland, or Boston and bought ice and frozen bait in Boothbay. Schooners from towns to the west came to the fish factories with salt and took away fish. Other schooners loaded granite at Round Pond and Friendship Long Island. The railroad from Bath to Rockland was opened in 1878, but a trip to Waldoboro or Rockland from Friendship was long and left little time for shopping if one was to get home the same day. The railroad brought mail regularly, however, distributing it to post offices on the mainland and even to some on the islands. This was a great convenience, for considerable mail-order business was done with Sears Roebuck and Montgomery Ward, whose "wish books" were eagerly studied. Finally, people rowed and sailed from island to island and "ashore" to the mainland. One of the Morses and his wife moved east to Swans Island and returned occasionally to Muscongus Bay to visit, making the 45-mile trip in a dory.

For fun, people skated on ponds, coasted on hills, visited around stoves in stores or post offices, and gathered at friends' houses to dance and sing. Every community had people who could play the fiddle or the parlor melodeon. The occasional travelling preacher or missionary attracted a social gathering, as did the raising of a building, the hauling or launching of a boat, or the construction of a wharf.

The Muscongus Bay community, then, was active, prosperous, and diverse, its people living close to the sea and the land, working hard, and taking pride in their way of life.

*2*

# *Boats and Gear*

*The fisherman-farmer,* busy as he was ashore, needed a cheap and efficient boat. The simplest and cheapest way to fill this need was with a dory. This flat-bottomed boat with flaring sides and wide, overlapping planks is one of the most seaworthy vessels ever developed and is comparatively easy to build. A good craftsman could build a dory in a day. At least Ivan Morse tells of how Isaiah Osier, a resident of Friendship Long Island, propelled by overwhelming thirst, built a dory, rowed it to Port Clyde, and got gloriously drunk, all in one day. Equipped with a spritsail and sometimes a centerboard, a dory was boat enough in which to row off around the Egg Rocks on a good day and catch 100 pounds of codfish on handline or trawl or haul 30 or 40 lobster traps.

But a dory, while cheap and easy to build, is a heavy boat to row against a head sea and even with a centerboard cannot be described as a smart sailer. The next step is a peapod. This is a double-ended rowboat, sometimes of lapstrake construction, that is, with each plank overlapping the one below it like clapboards on a house. The keel was a wide, heavy board, tapered toward the stem and stern and sometimes pierced for a centerboard trunk in the middle. A peapod, with one pair of raised oarlocks so a man could row standing up, moved through the water much more easily than a dory and sailed well, too. Charlie York at Bailey's Island had one in 1898, when he was 11 years old. "She rowed easy," he recalls. "My father let me have a small spritsail, and when I dropped the centerboard, she would beat to wind'ard like a regular vessel. All of them peapods is good in a seaway."

*A Muscongus Bay sloop in the foreground with a schooner towing a dory.*

*Model of a slightly later Muscongus Bay sloop. (Smithsonian Institution photo no. 2364)*

Dories and peapods were satisfactory boats for hauling traps close inshore and near home, but covering any great distance was slow and tiresome work. The next step was to build a larger boat capable of carrying sail under more difficult conditions with a larger cargo of fish, yet still small enough and handy enough to maneuver among the ledges and be rowed in calm weather. The first solution to this problem was the Muscongus Bay sloop, usually 16 to 26 feet long, sharp and high in the bow, sometimes with a sharp stern but usually a counter. Her mast was stepped far forward so that she could be handled under mainsail alone when hauling traps, and she had a jib on a bowsprit to give her better balance and more speed in light airs. She proved a good answer to Muscongus fishermen's needs.

Often the fisherman could fill the cockpit of his sloop with cod, hake, pollock, or haddock using a handline, a single cotton line about half the diameter of a pencil. A lead weighing three to five pounds was attached about three feet above two hooks baited with herring or clams and held the line more or less vertical against the pull of the tide. Especially in the spring when the fish came into the shoal water to spawn, this was a sufficient rig.

However, with a bigger boat than a peapod or dory, a man could set several tubs of trawl. A trawl is a line 600 feet long with short lines called gangings or gangions every six feet, each with a single hook. Six lines were joined to make a "tub" 3,600 feet long. This line was coiled down in a tub or half a small barrel with the hooks hung in order on the rim of the tub. The hooks were baited, a job taking 40 minutes to an hour per tub, and this time the hooks were laid carefully in order on the coiled line. Two men might set four tubs of trawl. The trawl line was tied to an anchor line about six feet above an anchor or killeck, a rock lashed between the forks of a stick to act as an anchor. Anchor line and trawl were paid out together until the anchor touched bottom. Then the anchor line was buoyed and the trawl paid out as the sloop moved down the wind under easy sail, one man flipping out with a stick each baited hook as it came up. Corks might be attached to the trawl line at intervals to keep it up off the bottom. At the far end, the trawl was bent to another buoy line and anchor and allowed to set for several hours. It would then be under run. That is, one of the men would take the dory that had been towing astern, haul up the trawl line and work along it, taking off the fish, rebaiting the hooks, and passing the line back overboard. While this could be done in gentle weather from a small sloop, a larger boat might well part the trawl line. Usually, trawls were hauled from a dory or peapod towed astern of the sloop. After the trawl had set again for an hour or two, it might be hauled, coiled down again in the tub, and the catch taken to market. In deep water, rough weather, or a heavy tide, hauling a trawl could be hard work, and a loaded dory or peapod could capsize with the weight of the long, sagging line. However, when things went well, a trawl could be a great money maker. Four tubs of trawl brought Charlie York and his partner 1,800 pounds of codfish at one set, and that was not regarded as an exceptionally large catch. For this, each man received $13 on the wharf at Portland, a little less than 1½ cents per pound.

If the fish were to be sold fresh, they were dressed, put in barrels with ice, and shipped from Morse Island or New Harbor in the daily steamer to Portland and thence by rail to Boston, where they would arrive having lost little of their original character.

If the fish were to be salted, they were taken either to the fish factory or to the fisherman's own fish house, beheaded and eviscerated, and the livers dumped in a barrel to soak out the valuable oil. The fish were then put in a butt or hogshead, a big barrel perhaps five feet in diameter, between layers of salt. The fish made their own pickle, that is, the salt pulled the water out of the fish and dissolved. The butt was filled to the top with salt water and salt heaped on the top. Most of the salt came from Italy, Spain, or the West Indies in square-rigged vessels to Boston or Gloucester and was distributed along shore in schooners. It was carried in bulk and shoveled; only in more recent times was it bagged.

After the fish had pickled for a week or so, they were rinsed and laid to dry in the sun, skin side down, on "flakes," wooden frames covered with laths or chicken wire to let the air through. People who salted their own fish preferred to do it in the spring or fall when the flies were not so thick as in summer. At night and on wet days, the fish were piled on the flakes and covered with little boxes with peaked roofs. When the fish were dry, hard, and light brown, they were stored inside and shipped off in schooners going west, many to the West Indies. Thoreau, in Chapter 4 of *Walden*, writes of a train passing the pond by which he lived: "This closed car smells of salt fish, the strong New England and commercial scent, reminding me of the Grand Banks and the fisheries. Who has not seen a salt fish, thoroughly cured for this world, so that nothing can spoil it, and putting the perseverance of the saints to the blush? with which you may sweep or pave the streets, and split your kindlings, and the teamster shelter himself and his lading against sun, wind, and rain behind it – and the trader, as a Concord trader once did, hang it up by his door for a sign when he commences business, until at last his oldest customer cannot tell whether it be animal, vegetable, or mineral, and yet it shall be as pure as a snowflake, and if it be put into a pot and boiled, will come out an excellent dunfish for a Saturday's dinner." W.H. Bishop, writing in *Harpers* magazine in 1880, said of a salt fish, "It was no longer a fish but the mummy of a fish, endowed by salt and dessication with something like immortality."

Slack salted pollock was considered a delicacy. A fisherman of my acquaintance in the early 1930s kept a salt pollock or codfish hung by the tail in his boat shop or fish house and occasionally peeled off a strip with his knife to eat raw. It was said that if one ate the "dream line" out of the middle of a salt fish before going to bed, one's future husband or wife would appear in a dream, offering a cup of water.

After the practice of icing fish at sea was introduced and steamers established regular routes, the market for fresh fish increased dramatically. With the increase in demand came an increase in price, greater pressure on the fishing grounds, and the necessity for coastal fishermen to go farther off shore in harder weather. Thus, a bigger and more rugged sea boat than the Muscongus Bay sloop was needed. In the 1890s, as we shall see in the next chapter, the Friendship sloop evolved to meet that need.

Lobstering was another source of income for Muscongus Bay fishermen. In the early days when lobsters could be collected in quantities among the rockweed, there was little market for them. They were used for bait and for fertilizer and were eaten locally. However, as summer people began to visit the coast and discover the delicacy and as a demand developed in the cities, the lobster trap was invented, smacks built with wells in which lobsters could be transported live, and lobster canneries were built at Port Clyde and East Boothbay. Gradually, lobsters became more scarce and lobstering more profitable.

Lobsters were caught in traps made of spruce or oak bows and covered with laths. The early traps were four feet long with a head at each end and none on the sides. Being so big, they had to be heavily ballasted and were a handful to haul. The traps were baited with whatever could be found. Herring or pogy were preferred, but fish heads were acceptable. The more oily the bait the better, and the lobsters seemed to prefer bait that was a little high. The traps were set along the rocky shores and among the ledges in summer at depths of one to 10 fathoms. With a handy sloop, a man could haul 60 traps in a day, but it was hard work. In the winter, the lobsters moved into deeper water of 10 to 20 fathoms. Muscongus Bay provides numerous places with depths of 20 fathoms quite close to good harbors, but winter lobstering is hard and heavy work. The days are short, the winds heavy, and the seas rough and cold. The North Atlantic is no place for a Muscongus Bay sloop in winter except on the mildest days. As demand for lobsters increased, fishermen stretched the season on both ends into winter weather and went farther off shore. Again, something stouter than a Muscongus Bay sloop was needed.

The fisherman used his boat also for jigging mackerel and squid and only rarely for setting a seine. For this, a larger vessel than a sloop was required, usually a pinky or schooner that could tow a big dory carrying the seine and a smaller one to pick up the purse line. The bigger vessel carried more men, more fish, and made longer voyages off shore. Fine little schooners 50 and 60 feet long had been developed from the old-time pinky and were already widely used. It was the pressure on the inshore fisherman supplying fresh fish and lobsters to the Portland and Boston markets that made the Muscongus Bay sloop almost obsolete and made what came to be called the Friendship sloop a necessity.

Before we leave the fisherman to discuss the design and construction of his new boat, we should consider how he financed that boat on the income from fish and lobsters and boatyard wages.

In 1862 lobsters brought 40 to 50 cents per 100 pounds.

In 1878 a Cape Ann paper reported that 100,000 lobsters were shipped from Friendship to Gloucester at an average price of four cents each. (Charlie York reported that in the 1870s a smack sailed up the Damariscotta River offering three cents apiece for lobsters over three pounds and two for three cents for those under three pounds. Four men filled the smack in two days, catching one lobster that weighed 40 pounds and could be cooked, even in a wash boiler, only by breaking off the claws.

In 1880 a Bristol fisherman might average $110 gross income from one lobstering season extending from April to November. He would set 40 to 50 traps and average per trap one "counter" or market lobster weighing about two pounds and worth to him four or five cents and two smaller ones that could be sold to the canning factory at $1 per 100 pounds or a penny per pound.

In 1887 Bristol area smacks were paying 3.67 cents per pound for market lobsters.

Between 1890 and 1900, hard lobsters were worth 10 cents apiece, and shedders were worth seven cents.

In 1906 on Trap Day, usually about January 1, the first day of the lobster season on Monhegan, lobsters were 25 cents each.

In the case of fish, prices have always fluctuated wildly in response to supply and demand, but a few isolated incidents give us an idea of the level of fish prices. In the early 1900s swordfish was selling at 15 cents per pound on the Boston market with a top price of 25 cents. In addition, the fishermen kept the heads and sold them for bait at a slight profit.

The crew of the schooner *Eva and Mildred*, fishing for four days, made $27.10 each and were away from home a week. This was considered a very profitable trip.

Two men fishing for five days, three of which were too rough to fish, caught 1,800 pounds of codfish and, after spending another day taking the fish to Portland, cleared $13 each, selling the fish at 1.4 cents per pound.

About 1912 pollock were 90 cents per 100 pounds dressed at the fish factory in Boothbay and 75 cents round, that is, just as they came from the water. Smelts were four to five cents per pound.

About 1900 clams brought 25 cents per quart, shucked with the "blacks" removed,

50 cents per bucket to salt for bait, and 25 cents per bushel in the shell at the cannery. Eels were five pounds for a quarter, cleaned.

How, with prices like these, could a fisherman afford a Friendship sloop?

Of course, sloop prices varied widely. In the late 1890s, says Howard Chapelle, a new 25-foot sloop went for about $675, ready to sail except for ballast, which could be picked up on any stony beach.

In 1899 a 28-foot sloop was built for $780. In 1904 a 35-foot sloop brought only $450, and in 1905 another, size not specified, went for $400. Clearly, the size of the boat, the quality of the workmanship and material, and the immediate demand made a big difference in the price; but for comparison, let us assume a price of $600.

To get some idea of what a sloop cost in 1900 in real terms, let us compare the price with what a modern fisherman would have to pay for a first-class lobster boat. If fish was worth 1½ cents per pound, then $600 represented 40,000 pounds of fish. Today a fisherman gets from 35 cents to over $1 per pound for fish. Fifty cents is a fair average. Forty thousands pounds of fish would bring $20,000 – not nearly enough to buy and fit out a boat that would make him competitive today. With a reliable diesel engine and the necessary electronics, winches, and other gear, the modern lobsterman is in for something like $50,000.

In terms of wages, how does a Friendship sloop compare with a modern lobster boat? An expert carpenter in 1900 might expect to get $1.50 per day. The modern boatyard carpenter might get $9 an hour or $72 per day. It would take the man working in 1900 400 days to buy a sloop. Four hundred days' work today would bring in $28,800, still far short of $50,000.

In terms of what he buys in the store, how does the cost of a Friendship sloop compare with the cost of a modern lobster boat? I was fortunate enough to find in the Friendship museum a journal kept by a storekeeper in Friendship in 1891-1893, listing the prices of what he sold. Compare these with supermarket and hardware-store prices today.

Thus, we might conclude that cash costs have increased a matter of 15 times. If we multiply our $600 sloop by 15, we get $9,000, a ridiculously low figure for a modern lobster boat.

Of course, the comparisons are hardly fair for several reasons. First, the modern boatyard worker or fisherman must pay income tax, sales tax, and property tax amounting to perhaps 25% of his income. Secondly, we have figured his income on the basis of an eight-hour working day and a 40-hour week. Many wage earners and most fishermen today work much longer hours, some of the former holding two jobs and some of the latter holding part-time jobs ashore. The employee of the last century worked 10 to 12 hours a day and then went home to tend his farm or garden. He usually was helped by his wife and several children, but today the modern wife may very well help the family along with a paying job and do the housework, too.

The comparison on the basis of store prices is helpful but flawed in that the fisherman-farmer of the last century bought a much smaller proportion of what he ate and wore than does the modern man. Flour, sugar, salt, tea, coffee, molasses, apples, and an occasional can of meat or fruit or box of raisins made up the bulk of the 1890 store purchases. Add to the expenses of the modern man the necessity for a pick-up truck and possibly a car with the necessary fuel, repairs, and insurance, and the high wages of today become a little less impressive and the cost of today's boat even higher.

Similarly, comparing the Friendship sloop of 1900 with the power boat of today is rather like comparing apples and oranges. On the one hand, we have a sloop propelled

| | 1891–3 | 1983 | Fold increase |
|---|---|---|---|
| pork | .12/pound | 2.00/pound | 16.67 |
| flour | .04/pound | .251/pound | 6.25 |
| oatmeal | .07/pound | .99/pound | 14 |
| molasses | .35/gallon | 11.36/gallon | 32.5 |
| tea | .25/pound | 4.30/pound | 17.2 |
| sugar | .05/pound | .378/pound | 7.5 |
| cheese | .12/pound | 3.29/pound | 27.5 |
| kerosene | .12/gallon | 1.55/gallon | 12.9 |
| lard | .10/pound | .61/pound | 6.1 |
| beans | .093/pound | .93/pound | 10 |
| vinegar | .10/gallon | 4.92/gallon | 49.2 |
| firewood | 3.76/cord | 100.00/cord | 27 |
| saw and frame | .85 | 9.39 | 11 |
| axe | 1.00 | 14.95 | 15 |
| broom | .25 | 5.99 | 24 |
| knife | .65 | 16.00 | 24.5 |
| file | .10 | 3.29 | 33 |
| plane | 1.00 | 16.49 | 17 |
| mackerel line | .10 | 5.00 | 50 |
| mackerel jigs | 2 for .05¢ | 3 for 2.89 | 38.5 |
| oars | 1.05 | 25.00 | 24 |

by canvas and white-ash oar; on the other, a modern boat of plastic or aluminum propelled by a powerful and reliable diesel engine and equipped with radar, loran, depth finder, VHF radio, pot hauling winch, and probably another winch for towing otter trawls and shrimp nets.

Thus, although the old-timer had to pay comparatively little money for his boat, he paid heavily in labor, and the money came hard. The modern fisherman pays much more in money. Most must borrow heavily and add interest payments to other costs.

Certainly, the modern fisherman with an engine that can get him home in a hurry in the roughest weather, aided by modern electronic communications and navigational devices, is a great deal safer and more efficient than the fisherman of the 1890s hauling a tub of trawl from a dory off Monhegan in a rising easterly. Yet it may be difficult to determine which, in the long run, is the better life.

# 3

# $T$*he Development of the Design*

$W$*e do not know who built* the first Friendship sloop. Many claim the distinction. It is said that Wilbur Morse, lying in his bunk in a schooner after a hard day fishing on the banks, conceived the design full blown, as Athene sprang from the brow of Zeus. It is more likely that the type evolved from the Muscongus Bay sloop as the need for more rugged boats grew. The experience of local fishermen and the development of the Gloucester fishing schooners and sloop boats developed the Friendship sloop.

Before the market for fresh fish and live lobsters expanded and rapid transportation by coastal steamer and railroad emerged, the Muscongus Bay fisherman could satisfy the demand for fish to salt and lobsters for the canneries and local consumption by fishing from April to November, avoiding the savage winter weather. He needed a shoal-draft handy boat for hauling traps among the ledges; a boat quick to windward, for the fishing grounds lay to windward during the usual summer southerlies; a fairly stiff and able boat, for a gentle air in the morning can breeze up in the afternoon to a 25-knot, smoky sou'wester, and a fierce northwester can burst from a quiet sky. His boat had to carry sail enough to move in the light airs of summer yet be light enough to row in morning and evening calms. The craft that evolved to meet these needs in the 1860s and 1870s was, as we saw in the last chapter, the Muscongus Bay sloop.

This ancestor of the Friendship sloop was lightly timbered and often clinker-built, and usually fitted with a centerboard. In 1891 Abdon Carter built *Sopolio*, a conventional Muscongus Bay sloop, but with a keel. She was so successful that later Muscongus Bay sloops followed suit. The sloop *Ranger*, on exhibit at the Maine Maritime Museum in Bath, and *Lucille*, whose lines appear in this volume, are examples of this type.

*Bow of a late type Muscongus Bay sloop. Note the plumb stem, the wedge-shaped bow with little hollow, and the bowsprit butted between the bitts and mortised over the stemhead without a gammon iron. The chainplates show the mast stepped far forward.*

In these boats, the mast was stepped far forward so they could be handled under mainsail alone, and they carried jibs on their bowsprits over the plumb bow. The gaff mainsail was generous, often extending well over the stern and hoisted on a single halyard of ingenious lead. Although later sloops had shrouds, often there was no standing rigging at all except a forestay, and sometimes the jib was set flying. In such a sloop, a man from Friendship, Cushing, or Bremen Long Island could get to a fishing spot near Eastern Egg Rock, catch several hundred pounds of fish, deliver them to the fish factory on Friendship Island or New Harbor, and be home by dark. He might well have to row in the morning or evening calm, and it made a long day. To shorten it, many families moved off to islands in the summer, and some islands such as Harbor, Otter, Cranberry, and Benner had year-round inhabitants. However, during the heavy winds and short days of winter, little fishing was done.

Salt fish, granite, and farm products such as hay, apples, and potatoes were shipped to Boston from Muscongus Bay in big sloops, pinkys, and schooners manned by local men. Also, many Muscongus Bay men shipped as dory men on these big Boston and Gloucester schooners, and several of them later commanded Gloucester vessels themselves. Therefore, it is scarcely surprising that the radical changes in the design of fishing schooners in the 1880s, 1890s, and early 1900s influenced the design of Muscongus Bay boats.

The accompanying drawings illustrate the similarities between the schooner *Carrie D. Knowles*, from whose lines 30 Gloucester schooners were built, and a Muscongus Bay sloop. Note in the profile drawings that the stem of each vessel is only slightly

**Main halyard lead of the Muscongus Bay sloop.**

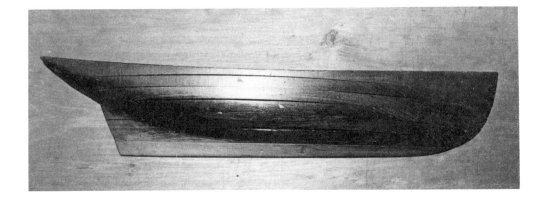

*Builder's model of* Lucille, *a late Muscongus Bay sloop built by Capt. Tom Brackett at New Harbor. The model is in the Maine Maritime Museum at Bath. (Courtesy of the Maine Maritime Museum)*

raked; the keel is long, straight, and almost parallel to the waterline; and the sternpost, although more raked in the sloop, is quite nearly perpendicular to the keel. The schooner was built in 1887 and the sloop in 1889, and, of course, the schooner is a much bigger and more burdensome vessel.

In cross section, notice that in each vessel the turn of the bilge amidships is quite hard, the vessel is comparatively shallow, and there is only the slightest flare in the bow sections. In both cases, too, the after sections have a strong reverse curve, making a rather flat run consistent with the "cod head and mackerel stern" doctrine that had been shipwrights' gospel for centuries. This characteristic is reflected in the only slightly rounded curves of the buttock lines in the profile drawing and in the waterlines.

Also notice that, in both vessels, the waterlines forward, the entrance, is slightly convex, becoming hollow only in the lowest, inner line. The 67-foot schooner and the 22-foot sloop, then, are remarkably similar, granted the difference in size, though the sloop is fitted with a centerboard to help her to windward.

As conditions changed in the latter part of the century in Gloucester and in Muscongus Bay, the design of fishing vessels changed to accommodate them. Boston's demand for fresh fish put a premium on both speed and carrying capacity. Schooners were built longer, leaner, and more heavily canvassed. The draft, however, was not increased in proportion because Gloucester's inner harbor is shoal with a rocky bottom that cannot be dredged, and the outer harbor was not then protected by a breakwater. Furthermore, fishing was extended through the winter, for the demand continued year round. On Georges Bank, where most of the fish were caught, the tides run swiftly over the shoals. In a winter gale, the heavy seas driving in from offshore become higher, shorter, steeper, and more dangerous as they hit the shoal water, especially with the tide running against the wind. The *Carrie D. Knowles*, built in 1887, is an extreme example of the development of the "clipper" fisherman. These long, sharp schooners, running before a quartering sea in a gale with little buoyancy forward due to their sharp bows, had a tendency to charge down the face of a steep wave, bury the bow deeply in the back of the next one, and broach to as the following sea carried the stern around into the trough and rolled them over. A good many fishermen lost their lives in such boats. In 1879, for example, 29 schooners and 249 men disappeared.

In 1882 Joseph W. Collins from Islesboro, Maine, criticized the design of the clipper schooners. An employee of the United States Fish Commission and a former fisherman and skipper of fishing schooners, Collins had fished the Georges Bank in winter and clearly knew what he was talking about. He was supported in the Gloucester papers by "Vidas," probably Dennison J. Lawlor, a designer and builder of yachts and fishing

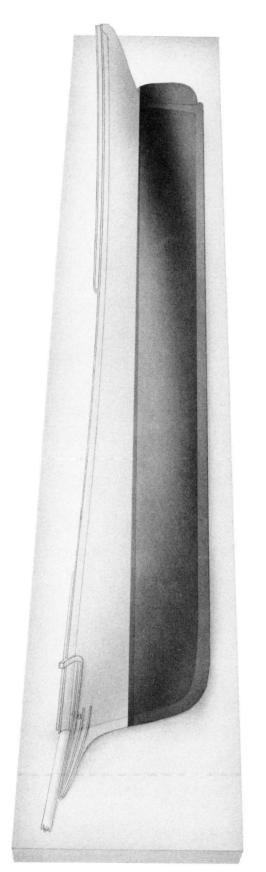

*Carrie Knowles*

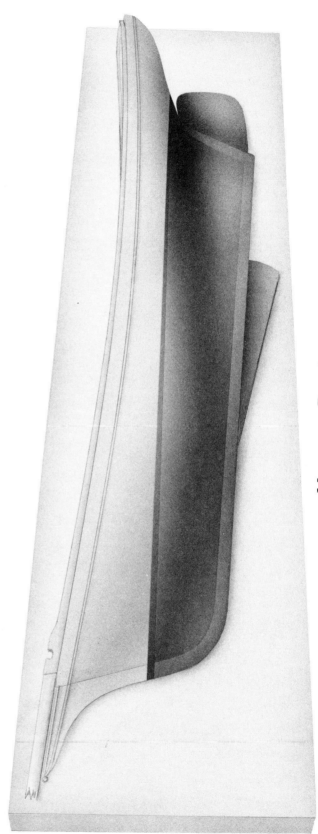

Muscongus Bay sloop

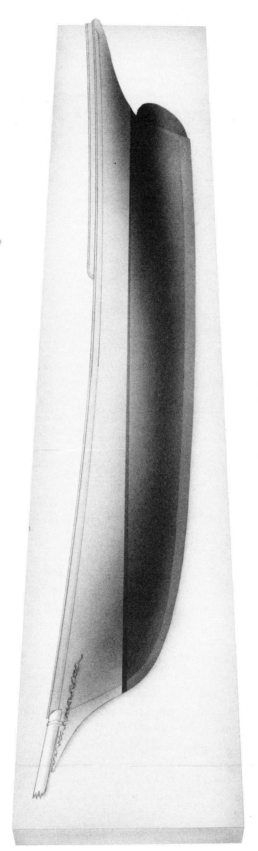

*Senator Lodge*

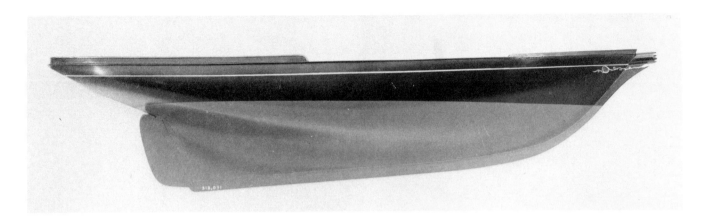

*Half model of* Fredonia.
*(Smithsonian Institution photo
no. 47621L)*

schooners with a yard at Chelsea, Massachusetts. To show what they considered a safer and faster type of vessel, Lawlor and Collins collaborated on the design of *Grampus* in 1885. Like many collaborations, she was not outstandingly successful, but in 1889 Lawlor's *Harry L. Belden* won one of the first fishermen's races and proved the new design fast and able. Both *Grampus* and *Harry Belden* were deeper, with easier curves to their bilges and more drag to their keels than earlier vessels.

Also in 1889 Edward Burgess, already well known as the designer of the America's Cup defenders *Puritan, Mayflower,* and *Volunteer* and of the fast fisherman *Carrie E. Phillips*, designed the schooner *Fredonia*, embodying the ideas of Collins and Lawlor. Used for a season as a yacht by J. Malcolm Forbes, she was then sold into the fishing fleet. She was so successful that she became a symbol of the new type of vessel and was much imitated.

Notice that *Fredonia* is deeper and has easier bilges than either *Howard* or *Carrie D. Knowles*. Her forefoot is more cut away so that her keel slants quite steeply downward from the forefoot aft. This characteristic is called "drag." Both stem and stern are raked considerably, and the waterlines are quite hollow forward, giving her a sharp entrance.

At the same time that Collins, Lawlor, and Burgess were developing a fast and able offshore schooner for the Boston fresh-fish market, George Melville McLain, a Bremen man, was also designing fishing schooners in Gloucester. He had joined the Gloucester fleet as a young man and, in the course of over half a century, commanded 35 different fishing vessels, some of which he designed himself. He designed his first schooner in 1883, and over 100 vessels, counting sisterships, were built from his designs. One of his most successful, *Senator Lodge,* designed in 1890, follows the Fredonia model in general appearance but has slightly more beam, less draft, and harder bilges amidships to make her a steadier platform on which to work and from which to launch dories. The easy bilges, raking stem and stern, considerable drag to the keel, hollow bow, and flattened run are quite characteristic.

Demand for fresh fish and live lobsters increased in Muscongus Bay as in Gloucester. To supply the year-round market, fishermen had to set lobster traps farther offshore in winter as the lobsters migrated to deeper waters. As fish became scarcer in the protected waters of the bay, fishermen had to set their trawls farther offshore, and, like the Gloucester men, they kept fishing through the winter. A light Muscongus Bay sloop simply was not boat enough to endure offshore in winter. The fisherman needed a boat stiff enough to carry sufficient sail in a winter gale to make her way to windward. At the

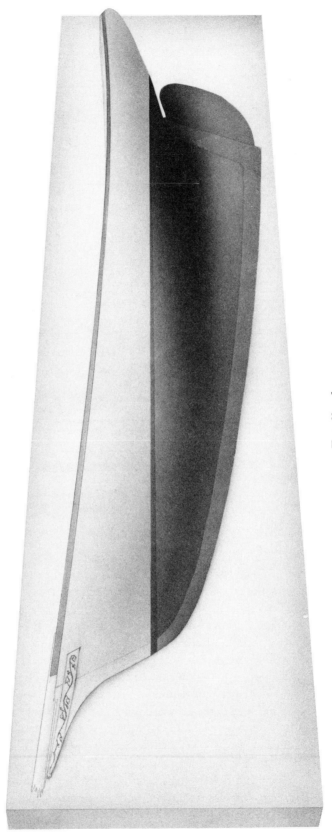

*Estella A.*

*Friendship sloop* Elvia Alice, *a Muscongus Bay sloop, and a peapod. (The Mariners' Museum, Newport News, Virginia)*

same time she had to carry a large cargo of fish, be handy enough for two men to sail, and be fast enough to get to market ahead of the weather when necessary. Much the same characteristics were demanded of the Gloucester schooners. It would have been remarkable indeed if McLain did not share what he had learned from Collins, Lawlor, and Burgess with his relatives at home in Bremen. The way to build a fast and weatherly vessel, whether sloop or schooner, is to give her draft enough and beam enough to hold her on her bottom in heavy weather, sail enough to move her heavy hull in light weather, a hollow bow to cut through the chop, a flat run to let the water slide out from under her, and powerful quarters to give her bearing. Cut away her forefoot and give her keel considerable drag so she will be handy in stays and still run easily before a sea. Such a boat is the Friendship sloop. Compare the lines of *Estella A.*, built by Robert E. McLain in 1904, with those of Mel McLain's *Senator Lodge*. Is it possible that Mel McLain not only talked with Robert about design but actually made *Estella A.*'s half model? Ralph Stanley, current restorer and builder of Friendship sloops, says "the same eyeball" did both.

So, if Wilbur Morse, lying in his bunk, did originate the Friendship design, he surely had ample background. Bradley Beckett in *Friendship Sloop Days 1976*, the annual publication of the Friendship Sloop Society, came up with three men, all claiming to have created the original sloop design. Here is what he wrote:

A short time ago I tried to find the original builder of the Friendship Sloop. Most believe Wilbur Morse of Friendship was the mastermind. Roy Wallace, a boat-builder and grandnephew of Morse, said Wilbur used to lobster in a peapod on Bremen Long Island in the late 1800s. After a while, Wilbur wanted something better. What he came up with was the Friendship Sloop.

Then I talked with Carroll Carter, another boatbuilder. Said he, "I was told 'Waut' Prior built the first one . . . . But as far as a Friendship Sloop goes, there is no *Friendship Sloop*. (That is, the first ones were built on Bremen Long Island.) Of course, a lot of builders moved to Friendship and built over there. There was Wilbur Morse and his brother Charles. Then Al Morse was down in Cushing. There were a lot of others besides."

Next I went to see Newell McLain, another grandnephew of Wilbur Morse and boatbuilder. "The first Friendship Sloop Wilbur Morse built," said Newell. "He borrowed the mold off my grandfather (Rob McLain) to build her out of. But as far as he being the first one – no. Grandfather was the first one!"

A short time after visiting Newell McLain I paid a visit to Carleton Morse on Morse Island off Friendship. Said he, "There were a lot of people who built Friendship Sloops but there was only one person who could have built the original – my father (Warren Morse)!" . . .

So, who built the first Friendship Sloop? Well, who really knows? What can be said is that Wilbur Morse can't be unanimously claimed the original Friendship Sloop builder. There are obviously many interesting versions and a lot of family pride interwoven. But this is what makes history interesting and keeps family traditions alive.

*Bow of* Chance, *built by Wilbur Morse in 1916. Note the hollow waterline and the comparatively slack bilges. (Courtesy of the Maine Maritime Museum)*

Whoever built the first Friendship Sloop, wherever and whenever he built it, he found it a successful design. It had all the characteristics a Muscongus Bay fisherman needed. The high, sharp bow, backed by a heavy hull with lots of heft to it, cut through the sharp chop of a smoky sou'wester and threw the water, for the most part, out and down. The comparatively easy sections amidships blending into the harder wineglass shape aft, made her stable, for in order to heel significantly, she had to submerge her buoyant side. Thus, she provided a steady and comparatively dry working platform with excellent carrying capacity.

Her rig evolved as the hull did, reflecting fishing schooner styles, but was adapted admirably to her use. Her mast stood far forward, about one-fifth of the way aft, so that she could be handled under mainsail and staysail or under reefed mainsail alone. Her mainsail, like that of the Gloucesterman, was enormous. The boom was commonly as long as the boat, and the gaff extended aft to the rudder post. A jib, on a bowsprit one-third as long as the boat and bent downward characteristically, balanced the big mainsail. Often, in the prevailing light airs of summer, she carried main and jib topsails and so was, by modern standards, outrageously over-canvassed but fast in light weather.

She was ballasted with rocks stowed as low in the bilge as possible. Some of the later sloops were ballasted with iron and stood up nobly to their work. Some of the last ones built even carried iron keels outside. The cockpit was deep, wide, and not self-bailing. Slush ice, bait drainings, gurry, and any loose water that came over the coamings could run into the bilge, whence they were pumped out. Her low waist made it easy to lift fish or lobster traps over the side, and her little cuddy forward gave shelter to the crew and some stowage space. The larger sloops were commonly fitted out with two bunks and a small iron stove.

Yet every boat is a compromise, and even the Friendship sloop had her weaknesses. A hollow bow, especially on a short boat, must come out into a hard curve about abreast the rigging if the boat is to have enough beam for stability. This shoulder is evident in the later models, in which the hollow of the bow is accentuated more than it is, for example, in *Estella A.* The shoulder gave the boat buoyancy forward, but when she was well heeled, she drove it down into the water to leeward. There it tended to try to round her up into the wind, thus causing a powerful weather helm that was further increased by the long main boom. Also, the large, open cockpit and heavy ballasting meant that, with a breaking sea or a bad knockdown, she could fill and sink rapidly. But the men who sailed these boats were consummate seamen, and they knew when to be scared. Although vessels did disappear from time to time, accidents were rare.

Even with her weaknesses, the Friendship sloop was a very successful response to the needs of the Maine fisherman — so successful that sloops built in Muscongus Bay were used all up and down the coast. In 1900 22 sloops were under construction on Bremen Long Island alone, and Wilbur Morse is said to have built between 400 and 500 in his time.

Certainly, the beauty of the design had a great deal to do with its popularity. With the high, sharp clipper bow sweeping aft to a neatly tucked-up counter, accented by the long, downward curve of the bowsprit forward and extended by the powerful boom aft, and with the short mast drawn to graceful proportions by a topmast in summer, the sloop sat on the water like a tern, alert and ready, a happy combination of form and function.

Various builders, of course, developed their own models, and each varied his model to accommodate buyers. Also, most of the builders were related or at least knew each other, so that they shared the good points of their designs. Molds were shimmed out a little here or shaved down a little there, and boats were stretched out or "riz up." The few original sloops left today have either changed their shapes through hard use and decay or have been rebuilt, some of them several times. Most now only approximate their original shape and have scarcely a stick or spike of the original. Nevertheless, the fundamental characteristics of clipper bow, hollow entrance, beam of about one-third overall length, deep, easy sections amidships, flat run, considerable drag to the keel, and raking sternpost have been retained to varying degrees by most builders and rebuilders.

In 1900 another change developed in the design of the Gloucester schooners that was reflected in Muscongus Bay just before the gasoline engine made the Friendship sloop obsolete as a fisherman. Thomas H. McManus, disturbed by the loss of so many men off bowsprits of fishing schooners, designed the first schooner without a bowsprit, *Helen B. Thomas*. She was a more or less conventional model, with the bow drawn out to where the end of the bowsprit would have been in order to get the headsails far enough forward to balance the mainsail. Consequently, she had a long, narrow, overhanging bow with a rounded profile, a considerable departure from the fashionable clipper bow of the time. The knockabout gained acceptance slowly, but a number of round-bowed schooners with bowsprits were designed by McManus, Bishop, and Crowninshield beginning in 1898. With Lewis Story's successful knockabout *Shepherd King* in 1904, knockabouts became popular, and after that date, McManus designed several more. It is worth noting that Mel McLain was still designing clipper-bowed schooners of an advanced model in Gloucester and in 1906 did a round-bowed model.

In 1908 Charles Morse built the first round-bowed knockabout Friendship sloop, the 40-foot *Harvey A.*, for a Vinalhaven fisherman who was impressed by the trend in Gloucester. *Harvey A.* retained the hard bilges aft, the flat run, and the traditional Friendship counter, but the round bow swept down to the keel with less forefoot and even more drag than had been customary, and there was less hollow in the bow and the waterlines than in conventional models. *Harvey A.* proved so successful that Charles Morse built several more knockabout sloops between 1910 and 1917. Some of these were converted to yachts by Fred Dion in Salem and proved very successful.

Wilbur Morse also built round-bowed sloops. Among them were *Right Bower* and the *Georgie C. Bowden*, both of which carried bowsprits.

With the coming of the gasoline engine, some sloops were built as auxiliaries, and some of the older sloops were fitted with engines, usually by putting the shaft and wheel off center to the great detriment of sailing qualities. However, by the end of World War I, fishermen were generally using power boats, and few if any sloops were built for fishermen after that time.

Many of the surviving sloops were bought by yachtsmen, downeast people who were not interested in yachting as Newport and Marblehead understood the term. They dressed in working clothes; maintained, rigged, and repaired their sloops themselves; slept on mattresses brought aboard from camps; hauled their own anchors by main strength and ignorance; and navigated by clock and compass. Their cabins were fitted out simply, and very little brass or varnish graced their decks. Many of these summer sailors found the heavy gaffs and huge mainsails difficult to handle, and reefing a mainsail whose boom extended far over the counter they regarded as a mixed pleasure. Consequently, they shortened the mainsail, sometimes by simply cutting it off at the first reef band, and shortened the bowsprit to maintain balance. Thus cut down, the sloop did not sail well in light summer weather, and when an auxiliary engine was added, she was worse. Yachtsmen condemned the Friendship sloop as "dobbie," a "dog," and

**Opposite:** Georgie C. Bowden *as a fisherman. (The Mariners' Museum)* **Below:** Tannis II *with a drastically shortened rig. See the front-ispiece for a picture of her under full sail.*

turned to lighter boats that didn't need as much sail to be fast. Only a few old die-hards, intrigued by the classic beauty of the Friendship sloop or sympathetic with the tradition, kept the type alive.

Few of these boats used as yachts lasted long, for they were sailed only in summer and for nine or 10 months of the year were hauled out and tightly covered. They sweated considerably and were often unventilated. Rot attacked their decks and timbers quickly, so that it became axiomatic on the coast that a man who had a Friendship sloop had a pair of trail boards, a pile of rot, and a damned good pump.

A few of the old sloops survived, and a very few new ones were built before 1960. It was not until the establishment of the Friendship Sloop Society in 1961 that the type attracted wide attention, and yachtsmen came again to realize the values of the traditional design.

# 4

# *H*ow They Built a Friendship Sloop

*A lthough each builder* followed his own methods, most builders in the early days adhered to the same basic process.

The first step was to make a half model of the hull. Several pieces of clear, soft pine, called lifts, exactly ½" or ⅜" thick, were pinned together with wooden pegs and the length of the boat laid off on a scale of ½" or ⅜" to the foot. The beam was to be one-third the length, so as this was to be a half model, one-sixth of the length was laid off as the beam. The shape of the vessel was next sculpted out and finished with the sharpest knife and the finest sandpaper until the model was exactly what builder and owner wanted. When the half model was perfectly smooth and fair so that no humps or hollows were discernible or perceptible to the most delicate touch, the stations were marked out on the back of the model, and on the top, perpendicular to the centerline. There were usually nine stations, dividing the length of the model into 10 equal sections.

In order to enlarge the model to life size on the floor of the mold loft, it was taken apart, the stations marked square across each lift, and the beam of the boat on each lift at the midship section measured with dividers. Each beam measurement was multiplied by 24 if the model was made to a ½" scale. Before laying down the beam measurements on the floor, however, the thickness of the planking was subtracted; for while the model was made to the outside of the planking, the lines had to be laid down on the floor to the inside. When the beam measurements were plotted on the floor, they made a series of points thus:

*A builder's half model showing the lifts. The tape was used by the photographer to emphasize the shape of the boat at several stations. (Courtesy of the Maine Maritime Museum)*

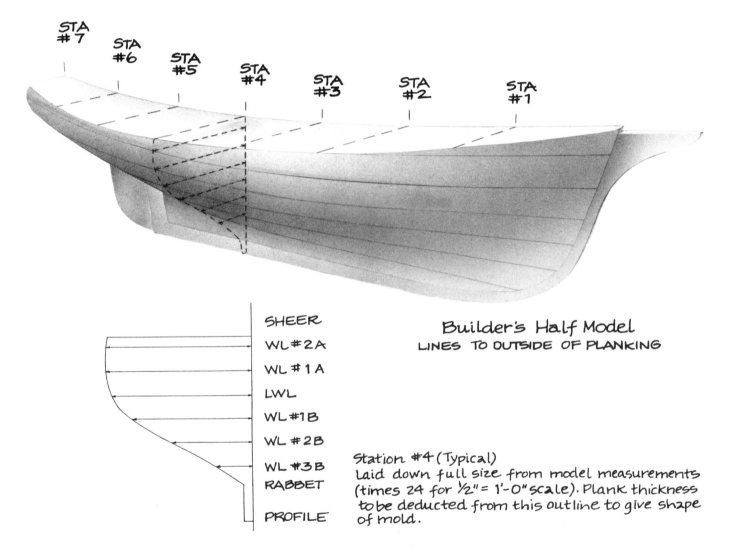

STA #7
STA #6
STA #5
STA #4
STA #3
STA #2
STA #1

SHEER
WL #2A
WL #1A
LWL
WL #1B
WL #2B
WL #3B
RABBET
PROFILE

Builder's Half Model
LINES TO OUTSIDE OF PLANKING

Station #4 (Typical)
Laid down full size from model measurements
(times 24 for ½" = 1'-0" scale). Plank thickness
to be deducted from this outline to give shape
of mold.

Then a thin, straight-grained batten was bent through the points and a line drawn connecting them in a fair curve. This curve was a life-sized representation of the midship section of the new boat to the inside of the plank.

The same process was carried out at each station and marked out on the floor. At the same time, each beam measurement was laid off on the station line that was perpen-

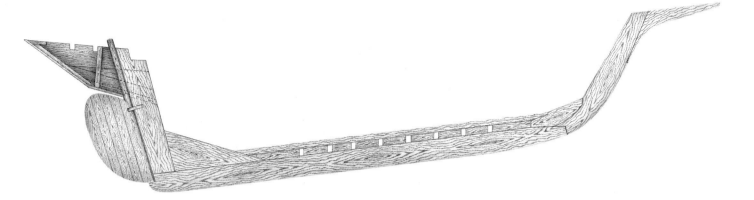

## Friendship sloop construction showing the deadwood

*A modern sloop,* Ansa, *in frame. Note the ear pieces tying together the sternpost, horn timber, and transom. James Hamilton of Andover is the builder. (Courtesy of James Hamilton)*

dicular to the centerline. A batten was laid fore and aft connecting these points in curved waterlines. Any bunches or hollows could be worked out both on the sections and the waterlines to ensure that the process of enlarging the lines of the model to life size had not introduced inaccuracies. A set of lines thus drawn is represented (in small size, of course) by the drawing of the *Estella A.*

From these lines on the floor, patterns were made out of light boards for keel, stem, stern post, and counter. These heavy members formed the backbone of the vessel. They were next to be cut out and were assembled with drifts of galvanized iron rod driven through holes bored just too small for them. The keel was notched to take the heels of the timbers or ribs.

Getting out and setting up the backbone of a big sloop was heavy work and called for exacting craftsmanship. The earliest builders had no power tools but shaped the timbers with broadaxe, adze, and saw so accurately that, when drifted together, the joint was sometimes hard to find.

Instead of a horn timber on top of the stern post, the stern post was carried up nearly

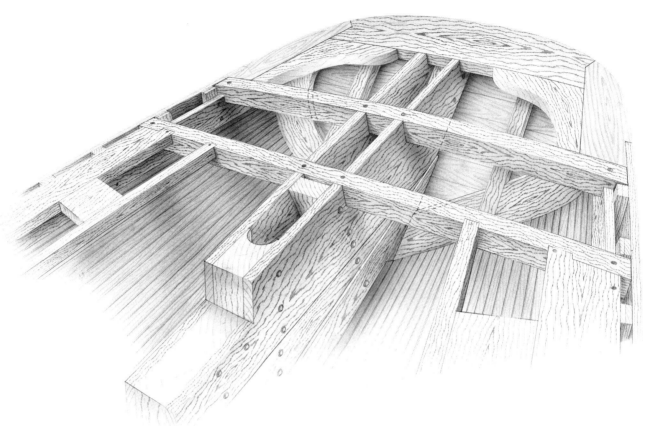

Perspective drawing of the sloop's stern section,
with the deadwood shown

to the deck, and long, fore-and-aft ear pieces were fastened to the sides of it, extending aft to support the counter and providing a slot on the after side of the stern post into which the rudder post fitted. Thus, the rudder could be tipped in, the post pushed up by the top of the stern post, and its heel dropped into a hole in the after end of the keel without having to jack the boat up high enough to fit the rudder head into a straight hole.

With the backbone plumb on blocks, molds made from the cross sections were set up on the keel, also carefully plumb and parallel. Then ribbands were run from bow to stern around the molds so that the latter were held firmly in place. Now the shape of the full-size boat could be seen for the first time.

Next the rabbet was cut. This was a groove in each side of stem, keel, and stern timbers into which the planking was fitted. It had to be cut at the angle the planking would take to the backbone, and this angle was different at every station and every timber. The rabbet was cut out roughly with a chisel, trimmed with an adze, and finished with a plane. It was cut first at each mold, taking the angle at which that mold came to the keel, and then faired off between molds.

Next the timbers were bent in. These were wider than they were thick, like the frames in a canoe, and were usually of red oak, unseasoned so they would bend more easily. Each timber was steamed in a steam box, taken out boiling hot, the butt jammed into the notch in the keel, the timber bent up against the inside of the ribbands and clamped firmly to them. The timbers were put in opposite each other, first one to star-

*Bending in frames on* Depression. *(Courtesy of David Nutt)*

board and then one to port, in order to keep the hull symmetrical. With all the timbers in, the planking was started, usually with the bottom or garboard plank. This and the next few planks often had to be steamed, because while vertical at stem and stern, they were nearly horizontal amidships. Early builders usually planked with white pine, which then was obtainable in wide, clear planks, but in the larger vessels they sometimes used oak. Later, cedar was popular.

In planking a boat, a thin batten was first tacked to the molds at the point where the top of the plank was to come. This batten had to be further from the plank below it amidships than it was at the bow because the distance from rail to keel rabbet becomes longer as one goes aft. Then another thin board was tacked in where the plank was to be, leaving spaces between the plank below and the batten above. This board was crossed at about one-foot intervals by lines perpendicular to the axis of the plank. Then, with a compass at a constant setting, arcs were cut across the lines with the point of the compass on the board. The board was then laid down on a plank, and, with the compass still at the same setting, arcs were cut across the extensions of the perpendiculars marked onto the plank. These points were connected in a fair curve, and the plank was then sawed out to the curve. One edge was beveled to make a caulking seam. This process of taking a plank's shape off the boat by drawing it on a light board is called spiling.

Ribbands were taken off to make room for each plank. The plank was then fitted into the stem rabbet, bent over the timbers, and clamped firmly. At the turn of the bilge the plank was hollowed on the inside to fit the timber. If the plank did not reach the full length of the boat, it was sawed off where it came on the middle of a timber. It was then fastened to the timber, and another plank, the continuation of the first, butted up to it. Some builders did not favor butting planks on timbers, instead butting them between

*Planking* Depression. *Note the twist that the plank must take. (Courtesy of David Nutt)*

timbers, backing up the joint with a butt block almost as long as the space between timbers and wider than the plank. Thus, the butt block caught the planks above and below the joint. The top edge of the butt block was beveled on the outboard side so that any water that might accumulate above it could drain off. Each plank was fastened not only to the timbers but also to the butt block with five nails. The butt block held two butting plank ends and so took 10 nails.

Fastenings were generally galvanized nails. These were iron, not steel, and they were hot dipped. The galvanizing clung hard to the iron and seldom rusted. The fastenings were counter bored, driven through the timbers, and headed over on the inside by one man holding a bucking iron against the nail while another drove it home. Sometimes, however, the nails were simply driven into the timbers and did not come through. The head of the nail was covered with white-lead putty, and seldom did a boat show weeps of rust until many years had passed.

When the boat had been planked up to the deck, temporary braces were put in to hold the sides of the boat out where they belonged, and the molds were removed. Floor timbers were put in if the boat was to have them. The McLains used about half a dozen floor timbers in a boat, sometimes as many as one for every other frame. The Morse boats, as Newell McLain said, "wasn't overburdened with them," and some had none at all. In some cases, certainly in *Estella A.*, *Dictator,* and *Gladiator,* grown floor timbers were used, pieces cut out of a hackmatack tree where the roots spread from the trunk in such a way that the grain of the wood ran right around from side to side. These floor timbers were drifted down into the keel and the planking nailed to them, thus tying the two sides of the boat together at the keel. In the best boats, a mast step spanned several floor timbers, but usually the mast just set into a mortise atop the keel. Any fresh water that leaked through the partners ran down the mast, gathered in the step, and promoted rot in the keel.

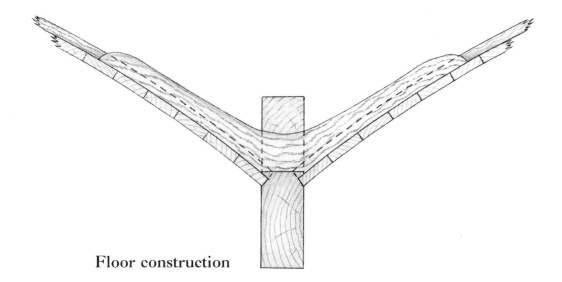

Floor construction

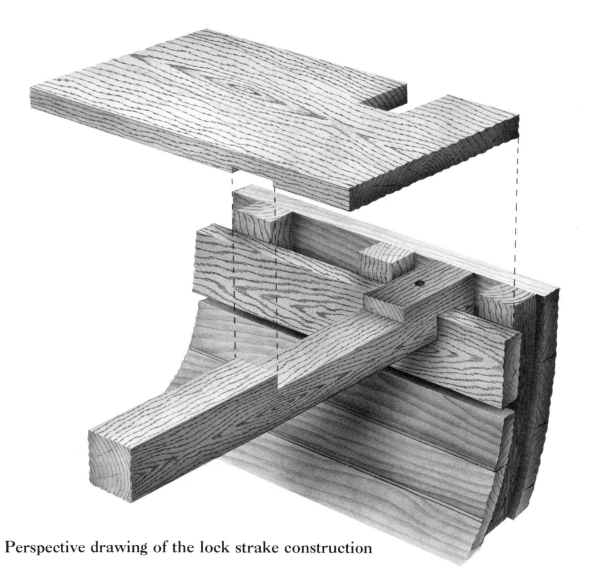

Perspective drawing of the lock strake construction

**Above:** *Bow of* Gladiator *from inside. The stem, breast hook, and lock streaks show clearly. (Courtesy of William Zuber)* **Below:** *Deck framing in* Depression. *The square hole is for the bit. The clamp shows under the deck plank. She does not have a lock streak. (Courtesy of David Nutt)*

From bow to stern along the rail on each side just below the deck, a heavy timber, a deck clamp, was sprung in and drifted or bolted through the tops of the timbers. On this were laid the deck beams, spanning the hull from side to side. They were specially reinforced at the partners where the mast came through the deck. Then a lock streak was put in. This was a heavy plank, perhaps 2" thick and 10" wide, laid against the side of the boat on top of the deck beams, which were halved to let it lie flush with the tops of the beams. The lock streak had to be made in several pieces to take the curve of the sheer and of the side of the boat. It was usually drifted through the tops of the timbers but apparently in rare cases was notched to take the tops of the timbers and laid flush against the top plank. In this case it would be nailed not only to the deck beams, but also to the planking, a procedure that strengthened and stiffened the boat tremendously.

Next the hull was caulked and sheathed up inside. Usually, ½" cedar or pine was used for sheathing, and an air streak or gap was left below the clamp for ventilation. The sheathing was sprung to fit the curve of the boat, and it stiffened her further. So did the caulking, usually cotton, that drove one plank hard against its neighbors and imparted strength to the whole structure.

The sides of the house and the coaming were sprung in, taking an elliptical shape at the forward and after ends. The cockpit platform was installed, leaving the boards loose for access to the bilge and permitting any water that came aboard to drain into the bilge and be pumped out. What with pot warps, handlines, spray, and rain, the boat could take on considerable water in a day.

The spars were cut from local spruce trees, squared up and tapered with a broadaxe, made eight-sided, rounded off with adze and plane, and finally treated with linseed oil. It was the custom to paint the masthead and the ends of the boom and gaff white. The bowsprit was butted against double bitts on the foredeck. The bitts were drifted or bolted to the keel. A simple gammon iron held the bowsprit to the stem, or a mortise in the bowsprit dropped over a tenon cut in the stem head, and the bobstay held it so.

Sails were of cotton duck, single-bighted and sewn up by the ladies on treadle sewing machines. Boats were usually painted white on the topsides and trim, white lead and linseed oil being considered champion preservatives. Decks were often a dark buff, the color produced by combining locally mined yellow ocher with seal or pogy oil and skimmed milk.

The mast was stepped with a gin pole or shears.

If a topmast was carried, it was stepped on trestle trees forward of the lower mast and supported by one shroud on each side running over a short crosstree to a chainplate aft of the main rigging. The topmast stay sprung the topmast well forward, the sign of a well-set-up rig.

The bowsprit was round or octagonal and bowed down at the end by the pull of a taut bobstay in order to keep the jibstay tight. This often sprung the mast forward, which seemed to do no harm. Whisker shrouds took the sideways strain and also served as footropes.

Shrouds, usually two on a side, were formed of one wire seized around the mast above the crosstree and led to chainplates a little aft of the mast. Often they were set up with deadeyes, but sometimes the lanyard was led through a pear-shaped iron attached to the chainplate.

The boom jaws were straight but made the same way, usually fully three feet long and bolted through the spar. Both spars were oiled except for their white ends. Both boom and gaff bore on pillow blocks between the jaws.

The gaff was held to the mast with jaws and a parrel line, the jaws often being made of naturally grown crooks of hardwood so they would be horizontal when the gaff was peaked up.

The staysail boom was sometimes rigged on a pivot just aft of the forestay.

The forestay was shackled to a strap around the mast over the trestle trees and crosstrees or simply to an eye in a band around the mast. The lower end led through a slot in the bowsprit and was set up to a stem iron at the waterline. This arrangement avoided a turnbuckle or lanyard at the foot of the staysail.

The jibstay was spliced on its lower end into a spider iron on the end of the bowsprit. Its upper end was secured as was the forestay, except that if a topmast was carried, the upper end of the jibstay was led to a bail around the topmast.

A topping lift ran from the masthead, sometimes supported by an iron crane, to a block near the end of the boom. A line from the boom led through this block, back to a cheek block on the boom, and thence forward. The mainsail was usually controlled by

*Launching day. (Friendship Museum and Ed Coffin)*

lazyjacks when lowered. The bigger vessels, which carried dories on deck, had two dory tackles, one from the mast above the crosstrees and the other from the end of the gaff.

The peak halyard, especially in larger boats, was made fast to the becket of a single block shackled to the eye of a band on the mast. It was led through a block on the gaff, often rigged on a bridle, back through the becket block, down to another block on the gaff, again on a bridle, aloft to a block lower on the mast, and then to the deck. The halyard was belayed to a cleat on the mast under the round support for the boom. The throat halyard had a double block aloft and a single block with a becket to which the halyard was spliced at the forward end of the gaff.

Headsail halyards were commonly spliced into a becket on a single block hung below the stay, led through a single block on the head of the sail, aloft again through the becket block, and thence to the deck. To control the headsails and avoid having to work on the bowsprit in rough weather, downhauls were usually rigged. These were light lines leading from the head of the sail down through several of the hanks to a block close to the foot of the stay and thence inboard. A downhaul smothers a jib quickly and keeps it from slatting up the stay. It is a device much neglected on modern vessels.

Topsails appear to have been set from the deck on a jackstay, for I find no pictures of topsails set on hoops with clewline, buntline, and downhaul, as the coasters and big fishermen rigged them.

The mainsheet usually had a double block and a single block, or two double blocks. The lower block ran on a traveller. The staysail sheet sometimes had a traveller but was sometimes rigged with an athwartships part through a block on the club so it would be self-tending. The jib had pendants with bullet blocks. Each sheet ran from the deck through the block and back through a fairlead on deck. The headsail sheets were led aft and belayed either on the outside of the coaming or led through holes in the coaming to cleats inside.

The mainsail was laced to boom and gaff and lashed to oak or ash hoops riveted around the mast. The staysail usually was laced to a boom. In winter topmasts were sent down, and often a smaller mainsail was used.

The cuddy was nicely finished out with two bunks, a locker, and a stove for cooking and for warmth in winter. It is said that one man would steer until his mate, standing in the hatchway next to the stove, saw his nose or ears begin to turn white with frostbite. Then they would switch.

Most sloops steered with a tiller that was fitted with a metal tongue underneath that could be dropped into a comb to hold the tiller at any angle.

Ballast in the early sloops was all inside and usually consisted of beach stones. Newell McLain used to go down to Hart Island bar with a 15-foot dory and a shovel and dig up all the ballast he wanted. Some of the later sloops were built with iron ballast outside and iron inside. These boats, of course, were stiffer than those ballasted with rocks.

Equipped with anchors, rodes, a dory, and fishing gear, the sloop was now ready to go to work.

This, then, was how many Friendships were built. We must bear in mind, however, that the basic process of building a sloop was probably as variable as the builders themselves. As mentioned at the beginning of this chapter, different builders worked differently, and a great deal was undoubtedly done by rule of thumb, by eye, or by established patterns. The lovely curve of a Friendship sloop's counter, for instance, is so difficult to loft, the patterns so difficult to take off and to follow, that each builder probably had a form to follow and never bothered to loft the shape.

Also, as Newell McLain said, the men of Bremen Long Island worked on their sloops six days a week and on the seventh visited each others' shops to see how their neighbors were getting on. Certainly, models, methods, and patterns were shared.

# 5

## *Early Builders*

*Bremen Long Island* lies on the west side of the Medomak River, protected from the sea and surrounded by deep water. It is well wooded and indented on the south and west sides by pleasant coves and rocky beaches. The island is quiet today, deserted in winter, its few old houses and newer cottages occupied in summer by vacationers, its road grassy and overhung with trees. Eighty years ago, however, the island was a busy community with two schools and an active fishing and boat-building population. Here, during the 1880s, 1890s, and 1900s, lived Morses, Carters, Collamores, Priors, and McLains.

Robert A. McLain, "Grandpa Rob," lived on a hill over a cove on the west side of the island. He married Mary Morse, a sister of the famous Wilbur A. Morse, later of Friendship, and had four sons: Robert E., Eugene, Almond, and Alexander – all boat builders. Their practice was to build a boat in the winter, take her fishing in the spring when the codfish came into the shoal water to spawn, lobster and set trawls offshore in the summer and fall, then sell the boat and build another in the winter.

The boats they built were at first Muscongus Bay sloops, although there were many variations. Some were little more than big rowboats with a mast that could be lifted out. Robert A. McLain is credited by his grandson Newell with building the first sloop with a permanent mast:

Fishermen used to have little 14- or 16-foot centerboard boats. They'd sail out to the traps, take the mast out, and row around the traps. Well, Gramp Rob said he didn't see why he couldn't sail up to a trap, haul it, trim the jibboom, keep her off the rocks, and set the trap again. Well, "Waut" Prior said it couldn't be done. So

*South end of Bremen Long Island, Robert and Eugene McLain lived at the head of the field in the center and had their boat shops on the white rocks at its foot.*

they argued over it for years till after a while Gramp Rob said, "Damned if I don't try it." And he built one he couldn't take the mast out of about 18 or 20 feet in length. So he built the first Friendship sloop and was the first ever to haul a trap under sail in Maine waters.

Still, the sloops were small, shoal-draft, comparatively lightly built centerboard boats.

According to Newell McLain, it wasn't until the early 1890s that deeper, heavier sloops were built on the island, probably in response to the development of heavy, year-round demand for fresh fish and lobsters on the Boston market and the influence of George Melville McLain of Gloucester. When asked whether he remembered Mel McLain, Newell did not recognize the name but said, "There was one that designed big fishermen there. Used to go in 'em too." In view of the similarities described in Chapter 3 between the Friendship sloops and the Gloucester schooners, the presence of such a man, whether or not he was Mel McLain, seems suggestive if not significant.

Records of who built which boat in what years are scanty and often depend on people's recollections stretching back over half a century. We know, however, that Robert A. McLain and his son Almond built *Lottie Mae* in 1900. She was renamed *Truant* and ended her days in a cradle beside Route 1 in Searsport, an eye-catcher for the Penobscot Marine Museum.

In 1902 McLain and son built a 32-foot sloop that, around 1950, was named *Ranger*.

Estella A. *about 1955.*

In 1951, under the ownership of Wesley C. Casson, the boat was renamed *Friendship*. Casson replaced the deck, then covered with tar paper; reframed and refastened the boat; and reported her in good shape. She still had most of her original planking. Her mainsail had been cut down to 410 square feet, and an iron keel and an engine had been added; yet she sailed well.

Another son, Robert E. McLain, built his first sloop in 1884. She was probably a centerboard boat. He built *Dictator* in 1904. After a long fishing career, she was bought by Alan M. Chesney at Sylvester's Cove on Deer Isle. She was surveyed by Captain Walter E. Scott of Deer Isle in 1951 and found in excellent shape. In 1954 Chesney celebrated *Dictator*'s 50th birthday with appropriate ceremony and continued to use her for many years thereafter. Finally, she succumbed to old age and, in decrepit condition, was purchased by Jarvis Newman of Southwest Harbor, rebuilt, and used as a plug to make a mold for a new generation of fiberglass sloops. Rebuilt, *Dictator* still sails, trim and sharp, under new Hood sails.

Robert E. McLain also built *Estella A.* in 1904 and launched her on New Year's Day for Jack Ames of Matinicus, who named her after his year-old daughter Julia Estella Ames. When the sloop was built, she was the last word in offshore lobster boats. She was 34'9" long, beam 11'9", and drew 5'6". Built of red oak and white pine, she was ballasted inside with iron and carried a two-cylinder, nine-horsepower Knox engine that drove through a chain drive a horizontal shaft with a winch head for hauling traps. *Estella A.* was used consistently at Matinicus for hauling traps, handlining, trawling, and seining until 1930, when she was sold to Lieutenant Commander Duncan I. Selfridge in Jamestown, Rhode Island. He took out the iron, added a lead shoe, converted her to marconi rig, built a doghouse on her, and used her as a yacht until his death. In 1957 Mrs. Selfridge gave *Estella A.* to the Mystic Marine Museum. The museum returned her to her original rig, strengthened her with sister frames, and kept her afloat in the Mystic River as an exhibit. By 1967 she had deteriorated so badly that she would no longer float. After two years ashore, planks were actually falling off. She was taken by trailer to Thomaston, where she was rebuilt by Newbert and Wallace under the supervision of Maynard Bray of the museum and restored to as near her original condition as possible. New cotton sails were made by Nathaniel S. Wilson of East Boothbay, and the boat now floats at Mystic in sailing condition, a living exhibit of a working Friendship sloop.

Robert E. McLain had a strong reputation as a builder. It is said that he used grown floor timbers of hackmatack; *Dictator* and *Estella A.*, at least, were so constructed. McLain used to take the pattern for a boat out in the woods, hold it up against one tree

Estella A. *restored to very much her original rig. (Photo by Kenneth Mahler, Mystic Seaport)*

after another until he found one with a suitable bend, cut it down, and take home the piece. However, while this was probably true for some of McLain's work, most of the lumber for sloops built after 1900 came from the saw mill at Bristol Mills and was floated out to the island across two dories. During the first decade of the 1900s, Robert E. McLain built at least five sloops for Deer Isle fishermen at Stonington and Green's Landing as well as others for local people, and he also went fishing in the spring and lobstering in the summer.

In 1914 the shed in which *Estella A.*, *Dictator*, and numerous other sloops were built blew down, and Robert moved to Thomaston with his son Newell. In a shop on Thatcher Street they built mostly power vessels except for *Antoine Roux*, a ketch with a Friendship hull. She burned only shortly after in a fire that destroyed much of Ellsworth. In the 1930s Newell built *Electron II*, a gaff-rigged yawl designed by Ralph Winslow much after the style of the later, round-bowed Friendship sloops. Commander Ralph Holmes was her owner.

Sailcloth for the McLain sloops was "bighted" on old-fashioned treadle-operated sewing machines. The cloth came 36" wide, but if used that wide, it would sag between seams, giving the sail a corrugated appearance. To avoid this and to strengthen the sail, a 1" bight or fold was taken lengthwise in the middle of the cloth and sewn down on each side. Then the cloths were laid out on the grass, sewn together, the shape of the sail cut out with the proper curves on the edges. Cringles, reef points, grommets, and reinforcements at the corners were sewn in by hand, and head, foot, and luff were usually roped.

The trail boards under the bow were the builder's signature on a work of art. The McLains usually used a morning-glory vine, gilded or gold leafed, with red cherries. Later, they sometimes used maple leaves with acorns. The Morses, building in Friendship, favored the olive branch.

Eugene McLain, born in 1863, another son of Robert A. McLain and Mary Morse, built a number of sloops on Bremen Long Island in a shed beside that of his brother and lived in a house on the hill behind it. The house still stands to the south of the old road. He built his first boat, *Martha E.*, in 1883 and in successive years built *Lettie Belle*, *Champion*, *Mary C.*, *Jennie Hooper*, *Rough Rider*, *Paul Revere*, *Uncle Sam*, *Myrtle E.*, *Ralph A.*, and *Mystic Bell*. His last was a schooner named after the same lady as his first, *Martha E. McLain*. On January 11, 1911, he and Waut Prior were sailing in her off Otter Island in a heavy breeze. Eugene went forward to attend to something on the foredeck, perhaps slipped on a patch of ice, and went overboard. Prior hauled the dory alongside, left the schooner to take care of herself, and rowed after Eugene. He hauled him into the dory, but too late: Even brief immersion in 40-degree water can be fatal. Eventually, the Coast Guard from Burnt Island caught up with the schooner.

Eugene launched his boats, as most did, by hauling them down the stony beach at low water and letting the tide float them. Only Robert had a set of launching ways. Sometimes they set the boats up in a cradle, but usually they let them lie over. With no spars and no ballast, they floated easily. If the river was frozen, it is said that boats were hauled out on the ice and left to launch themselves when the ice melted, although this seems more likely to have occurred in Friendship than in Bremen. Once rigged, the boats were taken to Hart Island bar, where, as described earlier, they could be given quickly all the ballast they needed.

One of Eugene McLain's boats, *Uncle Sam*, got ashore, was abandoned by her crew, pounded over a ledge, and was recovered on the other side, perfectly sound. Eugene, like his father and brothers, built solid craft.

Jolly Buccaneer, *ex*-Sky Pilot, *ex*-Myrtle E., *during an early Friendship Sloop Society regatta.*

Another of Eugene's boats, *Myrtle E.*, built in 1909, was sold after a year of fishing to Nehemiah Boynton of Five Islands in the Sheepscot River. She was decked over, given a nice cabin, ballasted with lead, and used as a yacht for many years under the name of *Sky Pilot*. In December 1949 she sank in the passage behind MacMahan's Island at her winter mooring due to a neglected intake valve. She was raised by Frank L. Sample, Jr., of Boothbay Harbor, partly rebuilt, ballasted with 9,000 two-pound axe heads, and sold to Richard Swanson of Rockport, Massachusetts. He renamed her *Jolly Buccaneer*, and she became a regular competitor in Friendship Sloop Society races, winning second place in Class A in 1962. In 1967 she was sold to Bill Johnson and taken to Florida. Finally, *Jolly Buccaneer* sank in the Dania Waterway and was ordered removed in 1973 as an obstruction to navigation. When she was lifted by a crane, she fell apart. A piece of her is preserved in the Friendship Museum.

Almond McLain, another brother, built boats with his father and later by himself. Among those built with his father were *Mamie E. McLain*, *Cake Walk*, *Maude Grandeur*, and the previously mentioned *Lottie Mae*. Almond's brother Alexander, known as "Bug," built *Gladiator* in 1902.

*Gladiator* fished out of Maine harbors without an engine until 1911. Then such a big one was installed that her documentation became invalid because her net tonnage (volume of usable space) was reduced. She continued fishing, however, through World War I, after which she was sold to a Chesapeake Bay yachtsman. He had her replanked with cypress, and she sailed the Chesapeake until 1967 when Bill Zuber and Stuart Hancock of New Jersey bought her. In 1973, after several summer cruises from New Jersey to Maine and back, the Zubers moved to Maine permanently, and *Gladiator* moved with them. Bill Zuber is now doing a major reconstruction job on her at his home in Friendship.

The records reveal nothing of the later boats built by Alexander McLain, but he did build one every winter for a number of years.

Also living on Bremen Long Island were other boat-building families. Starting at the southern end and working up the west side, Newell McLain remembers Ed Carter, Wash and Norris Carter, George Carter, Charles Carter, Billy Collamore, Vin Collamore in the cove still known locally as Vin's Cove, Eugene McLain, "Grandpa Rob" (Robert A. McLain), Robert E. McLain, Alexander "Bug" McLain, Steve Prior, Waut Prior, and Bill Prior. The Morses lived on the north end of the island.

Doubtless there were others at work on sloops. We know, for instance, that Abdon Carter built *Florida,* a 25-foot sloop of classic model, on the island about 1914. After fishing for several years, she was used as a yacht by Willard Thorpe, and renamed *Pemaquid,* and sold to Andrew Hepburn about 1925. He had a naval architect, Charles B. MacGregor, take off her lines. Thorpe had a copy of MacGregor's lines; from them his son John built *Ellie T.* in 1960 and Stuart Ford built *Content* at Bailey's Island in 1961. The lines were printed in Howard I. Chapelle's *American Small Sailing Craft* in 1951. Since at that time they were almost the only lines of a Friendship sloop easily available, the model was popular with builders both amateur and professional. One of the latter was James Rockefeller. His *Old Baldy* was smoothed up after several years of service and used by Jarvis Newman to make a plug for a generation of Pemaquids.

On Morse Island just east of Friendship lived Warren Morse, a distant relative of the Morses on Bremen Long Island. He went to the Pacific in 1866 as second mate of the

**Left:** Gladiator, *built by Alexander McLain.* **Right:** Pemaquid, *ex-*Florida, *built by Abdon Carter.*

*The same vessel afloat with a dory astern. She is obviously far more of a boat than is a Muscongus Bay sloop.*

mission brig *Morning Star* and returned in 1869 as first mate. He built a 40-foot-square building and a wharf for his business of curing and shipping salt fish. The lower two floors were given to the fish business, but the top floor, where there was more height under the pitch of the roof, was a boat shop. Here, declared his son Carlton, Warren Morse built the first Friendship sloop. The accompanying photographs, taken in 1874, of a Warren Morse boat certainly show some Friendship sloop characteristics, even without the elegant clipper bow. Morse built several quite large sloops, the biggest being 45 feet long. Her stern extended out the end of the building, and Warren had to build a staging to work around her after end.

Launching a boat from Morse's third-floor shop was difficult, but each boat was lowered to the ground, turned 90 degrees, and slid in alongside the wharf.

Warren Morse died in 1905, and the family left the island for a year. When they returned, they found that someone had broken in and stolen most of the half models and the molds from which Warren's boats had been built. They left the backbone of a Muscongus Bay sloop, pierced for a centerboard, and at least one half model, which is still in the family.

The fish house is gone and only the ruins of Warren's wharf are left. His house still stands, but no one lives on the island in the winter.

Of course, the most productive of all Friendship sloop builders and the man who made the model popular all along the coast was Wilbur A. Morse, born on the north end of Bremen Long Island in 1853. In his own words, Wilbur outlined the story of his early years:

> The fall of 1874 we were living in the chamber of Father's house on Bremen Long Island. I wanted a boat. I rowed to the mainland and walked to Jefferson, about halfway up on the west side of Damariscotta Pond, about 21 miles. Bought lumber of Erskin & Wilkin. Rode back on the lumber. I built a 19-foot boat in Father's shop. Went lobster fishing. Started about March 10, 1875. Quit lobstering about May 15th, sold boat to Randel Simmons and went seining with Elbridge Wotton.
>
> Winter of 1875-76, built a 22-foot boat. Went lobstering until May 20th; went trawling until Sept., then went herring fishing at Wood Island and Gloucester.

While I was fishing, my family moved to Hungry Island (Bremen). The following winter I did not build any boat.

Then I sold my boat to Joseph Cushman and built a workshop on the east side of Hungry Island and built a boat. In May sold the boat and sold the workshop to Father. Built a boat in the summer in Father's shop. Sold that boat and went fall fishing, then built a workshop on the west side of Hungry Island and built two boats that winter. I bought of Martin Collamore a farm on Bremen Long Island. Moved the shop down there and built several boats. Was there three years, sold to Alfred and Charles Carter and moved to Friendship in 1882.

I built boats winters and went fishing part of the time the first two years. After that I hired Brother Jonah and Charles. Charles worked for me three years, and Jonah kept right on. The other men that worked were Charles Wallace, Levett Wincapaw, Damon Benner and some others that did not work year around.

Built mostly sloops. The *Hilda Emma* was a schooner. The *Hattie Lawry* was a well-smack. Built new shop at Friendship Harbor in 1900. In 1900, only built 13 sloops that year. 1901, 1902, 1903, built on the average of a little better than one in two weeks, all rigged complete. After that, built several power boats and a beam trawler, also built sloops up to about 1915.

*Down East*, July 1981

Wilbur Morse defined a Friendship sloop as "a sloop built in Friendship by Wilbur Morse." That is, he used the term "Friendship sloop" as a proprietary trademark. But just as Ford builds many different models of Ford cars, so Wilbur Morse built many different sizes and designs of sloops. It is quite likely that the boat he built in 1874 was more like what we would call a Muscongus Bay sloop than what we would call a Friendship sloop. As late as 1894, he was still building sloops with centerboards, and certainly the round-bowed sloops that he built in his later days were, by his definition, Friendship sloops, although their design, particularly in their forward sections, was quite different from the clipper-bowed sloops he had built earlier.

*A portrait of Wilbur A. Morse, which hangs in the Friendship Museum.*

Wilbur Morse's move to Friendship in 1882 took him not to the harbor at Friendship but to an inland location near Goose River where there was a saw mill. In 1900 he moved to the waterfront in Friendship harbor, just east of where the wharves are now. Here, he really swung into action. With his brother Jonah as shop foreman, Wilbur pressed the business forward at every opportunity and soon was selling sloops east to Mt. Desert and Deer Isle and west to Massachusetts.

It is difficult to find much authentic information about Wilbur Morse's methods of construction. Apparently, his approach varied according to the wishes and pocketbook of the owner. For an inexpensive boat, one could expect frames toe-nailed to the keel, few if any floor timbers, iron fastenings, pine or spruce planking, few if any knees at the partners where the mast goes through the deck, and rock ballast. A boat of 28 feet would cost about $400. She would be good looking, fast, and handy, and she would have the Morse trademarks, olive leaves on her trail boards and the name "W. Morse" carved below them. She would not, however, stand up to hard use over the years as well as a more expensive boat. If price were less significant, a man might expect frames boxed into the keel, cedar planking, galvanized fastenings, and either an iron keel or iron ballast inside. The model could be varied or even a new model made by request. *Genie W.*, a 23-foot sloop built in 1896, and *Nellie F. Parsons*, a 37-footer built the next year, were two of Wilbur's most popular models. The half model for the *Parsons* was used by Winfield Lash as the basis for *Mary Anne, Downeaster, Dirigo*, and *Rights of Man*, all built at Hatchet Cove, Friendship, between 1958 and 1965. This half model is now on display at the Maine Maritime Museum in Bath.

Wilbur and Jonah Morse ran their shop on a production-line basis with sometimes as many as five or even six sloops under construction at once. Wilbur was interested in efficiency. No talking; it wasted time. It is said that he employed a boy to search the shop daily for bent nails and throw them overboard in order to prevent carpenters from straightening them. Their time was worth more than the nail. Wages varied from 75 cents to $1 a day at first and later climbed to $2 a day; the hours varied from 12 a day in summer to 10 in winter. Ivan Morse told how Wilbur once employed a rather simple young man to saw scrap wood to feed the stove and the steam box.

"All of it?" asked the boy.

"All of it," said Wilbur.

Shortly after, one of the carpenters asked Wilbur if he had intended the boy to saw up a new oak wheelbarrow frame that had been left near the pile.

"Damn it!" exclaimed Wilbur, "the only man in the shop who does exactly what I tell him to!"

The Morse brothers early installed a steam engine to provide power for a band saw and a planer. It was the custom at that time to work 10 hours a day for $2, but the short winter days gave only nine hours of daylight. Wilbur proposed a nine-hour day with a 10 percent reduction in pay. The crew objected strenuously but agreed to finish the boats for which Wilbur had contracted at the reduced rate. Shortly thereafter, when the band saw and planer were working to capacity and the steam engine was doing its best, a piston blew up through the roof and made another hole coming down. A gasoline engine running a generator replaced the steam engine, providing electric lights and more power for power tools, and the 10-hour day became standard year round.

When the Morse yard built a boat, it was complete. Spars, rigging, sails, and later, if the owner ordered them, an engine and an iron keel were included. The boat was delivered ready to sail. At the height of production, the yard turned out a boat every two weeks, although three a month was more common.

The following correspondence between Wilbur Morse and Captain A.H. Jordan of Islesford gives an idea of the way the Morse yard did business. Captain Jordan was a successful fisherman out of Cranberry Island off Mt. Desert and in his later years sailed parties in *Wanderer*.

Parts of these letters are illegible. I have put in parenthesis the words I had to guess at and have indicated omissions with ellipses. I have transcribed the letters line by line, as Mr. Morse appears to have occasionally used the end of a line as a punctuation device.

Friendship Maine 26, 93
Mr Jordan
Dear Sir yours of
17th is at hand and in reply
will say Charles Morse
built one of the boats
at Swans Island and
i built the other this spring
. . . . . . since
. . . 1892 we are building
one every month
have got two orders ahead
now and . . . . .
can build you
one this fall
    Respectfully
      yours
        Wilbur A Morse

Friendship Oct 18 1893
Mr Jordan Dear Sir
yours Received
in regard to the price
of boats All riged
first class every way
24 ft $275 26 $300 28 $375
that is the prices that
we have been haveing
keel or senterbord
as to the iron i have
not built any with
iron on the keel dont
know what it would
cost would put the
iron on for what the
iron would cost that
is would not charge
anything for the work only
you pay for the iron
    Respectfully
      yours
      Wilbur A Morse

Friendship Dec 20 1893
Mr Jordan Dear Sir
Yours Received, got the
Model all rite
I sent to Portland
to see how much
the iron would cost
and they neglected
to see to it and i
have just rote to
two different foundreys
expect to hear from them
soon, i see that you
want the keel longer
and les overhang i will
make that change if you
like you can send me
$50.00 if it is convenant
if you have the iron the
keel will be thicker
please send me how
thick you want it
    Respectfully yours
      Wilbur A. Morse
PS i have rote to find out how much
the iron will weigh per cub
ft
  will build as near
what you want as i can
understand and i think
i understand just what
you want

Emma, *built for Alden Jordan in 1894, the first boat Wilbur Morse built with an iron keel. Note the plumb stem. (Courtesy of Capt. Ted Spurling)*

Friendship Jan 16 1894
Mr Jordan Dear Sir
yours Received With
fifty dollars, Could
you Wait longer
than the first of april
for her my brother
that helped launch the
boat when your brother
was hear will help
me rite along but the
other one is liabel
to leave any day
and i did not know it
untill now and i have
engaged work
enough for all three
of us and i dont know
what to do we are
building a boat now
that i could have laid
by if i had known it
two weeks before I have
made arrangements to
build your boat the
same as you want
now if he should leave
could you wait untill
the first of June if
i cant get another man
if i find that i cant
get her redy for you
by the time that
i agreed to and you
dont want to wait i

shall have to send your
money back to you
i shall make every efort
to do as agread but
if i find that i cant
which shall i do send
the money back or will
you wait i have built
between sixty and seventy
boats and this is the
first time that i
have failed to do as
agread if i fail to
have her redy the first
of april and i will have
her redy if posebel
i dont want you
to think that i am
trying to take the
advantage of you
I am riting the plain
facts
think it over and let
me hear from you
as soon as posibel
I may see my way
clear all rite in a
few days but if not
which shall i do send
the money back or will
you wait
be sure and rite as
soon as you can
        Respectfully yours
        Wilbur A. Morse

Friendship Feb 12 1894
Mr Jordan Dear Sir
have got the casting
cast it is to the deapot
it weighs 1072 lbs
shall put it on with
six 5/8 bolts galvenised with
nuts on the inside
shall bed it in lead
to keep it from rusting
the Keel shall put on
(hard) woodburry duck for Sails
shall commence (them) this week
if i remember aright you
want one jib
She will be redy for you
by the first of april
or before
        Wilbur A. Morse

Leawry Maine April 9
Mr Jordan Dear Sir
send me the masshre
of the outrigers and will
send them to you with the
chainplates and shrouds
without any charge
i find you rote to me
about them but i got
the two boats mixed
up i allways (calculate)
to do as i agree but
i mad a mistake and
am willing to rectyfy
it. what time did
you get home please
rite as soon as convinant
how do you like your boat
if there is any
others there that
want boats rite
direct to
Leawry Maine
i will get mail just
the same directed to
Friendship but it
will be a little handyer
directed to Leawry
    Respectfully yours
      Wilbur A Morse

Friendship, Me., Apr 27, 1898
Capt Jordan Dear Sir
We Have got your boat
sealed. Platform in bulkhead in
stearn seat in the lock streaks
in forward pardners in
she is Partley Planed up
and over Half Calked
we shall work on the
Cud to morrow will
try and Have a Private place
in locker as we talked
about (I've) rote to you twice
Have not got any answer
as yet Please answer at once
you can look for a good job
    Very Respectfully yours

you have got something
like this marked round the
mast what is it for
    Please explain

Friendship Me., May 3 1898
Capt Jordan Dear Sir
Please send me name and Hale
for boat she is all smooth out
side the washbord is on
sails i expect are Partley made
Have had the boat (turned?)
    Very Respectfully yours
      Wilbur A Morse

Presumably, Jordan was pleased with his 26-foot sloop *Emma*, for three years later he wrote to Wilbur about building him another. Morse replied:

Friendship, Me. Nov 22 1897
Captain Jordan Dear Sir
yours of the 15th at Hand
and contents noted
in reply would (say) would be
pleased to build you another boat
and will meat you in rockland
any day that will be most Convinant
to you
as to prices i Can get the iron
Keel less than i got the other one for
you
I have just built a 28 ft boat for
one of my neighbors without
shro ds for $375 am building a 30 ft
one now for a winter Harbor Partey
for 450 with shrouds an chainplates
you name the day you will meat
me in rockland and i know we can . . . .
(the rest of the letter is missing)

Friendship, Me. Feb 21 1898
Mr Jordan Dear Sir
i Put your Model together
the first of last week
but i Have ben about
sick ever since but am
better now will
Make model this week
    Very Respectfully yours
      Wilbur A Morse

Friendship, Me. Apr 22 1898
Capt Jordan Dear Sir
We finished Planking
your boat today
    Will rite in a few
days again
Very Respectfully
    yours
      Wilbur A Morse

This letter was written by Captain Jordan to his wife.

Lawry May 12 1898
    My dear Wife
My boat, Mr. Morse thinks
will be ready next Tuesday
if it is good wether. I
hope it will be good
wether so I can get her
home. Will and Ev
were here yesterday it blowed
to hard for them to go
over to bristol
    from your Husband
        A.H. Jordan Jr.

*Capt. Alden Jordan at the wheel of* Wanderer. *(Courtesy of Capt. Ted Spurling)*

There follows an application for number to the United States Custom Service in Waldoboro for the sloop *Wanderer* dated May 14, also a receipt from Wilbur Morse for $493.52, the balance due for *Wanderer*.

It is significant that in 1893 Wilbur Morse wrote that he was still building centerboard boats, presumably Muscongus Bay sloops for summer and inshore use. Hence, these boats did not become obsolete when the Friendship sloop was developed. Also, notice that Jordan's *Emma* was the first with outside ballast.

Wilbur's second brother who was leaving him could have been Albion, for Charles had evidently left several years before. The rate of production at the shop at Lawry, where each boat had to be transported to the water, was one a month, and this with only three men working.

The prices quoted are probably about as low as Wilbur could manage. Notice that Jordan paid $493.52 for the balance on *Wanderer*, and there was probably at least a $50 deposit, as there had been with *Emma*. An iron keel, wire rigging, chainplates, and other extras may have raised the base price considerably. Still, even in those days, this was a very reasonable price for a sloop.

The mention of a model in the letter of February 1, 1898, suggests that although many Morse boats were built off the same molds with only a little shaving off here and shimming out there, Wilbur would build a boat to a model to suit the owner. He was evidently making a new half model from which to loft Jordan's boat.

As marine engines came into wider use, the Morse brothers at first installed them in sloops and later built power boats and finally big draggers, building only an occasional sloop as a yacht. An example of the latter is *White Eagle*, a 28-foot sloop built in 1916 for a yachtsman down east. She is of shoaler draft and far more hollow in both her waterline and bow sections than earlier boats were. Her cabin and cockpit are finished a little more elegantly than those of her earlier sisters, and her trail boards, which may have been replaced, do not have the olive branch scroll and Morse signature. However, details of construction, especially the elliptical coaming, and her papers define her as a Wilbur Morse sloop.

Jonah Morse, Wilbur's younger brother, started working for Wilbur at the age of 19 and soon became his foreman. While Wilbur was a good boat carpenter, he was even better as a salesman and promoter. Jonah was a superb craftsman and an excellent

*Wilbur Morse's shop.*

leader. He was the one largely responsible for the smooth, efficient operation of the yard and for its being, on the whole, a pleasant place to work. Jonah, according to his stepdaughter, the late Carrie McFarland, made the yard his life. He used to bring home the trail boards for each new sloop and carve the traditional olive branch design himself, after which his children did the final sanding. At first, only Wilbur's initial appeared on the trail boards, but when Jonah became a partner, his were added.

Jonah did not spare himself. If it breezed up in the night, he was the one who went to the shore to be sure all was well. It was Jonah who at launchings insisted on knocking out the last wedge, a job at which a man could be hurt if everything didn't go just right.

In 1924 the partnership was dissolved, and Jonah moved to Damariscotta where he set up a yard building wooden fishing vessels, mostly draggers, as there was no longer a demand for sloops.

Another brother, Sylvester, moved down to Swans Island and opened a fish business. So far as we know, he was not a boat builder.

Albion Morse, Wilbur's older brother, owned a small yard at Pleasant Point in Cushing. An interview with his son Ferdinand appears in the 1964 edition of the Friendship Sloop Society's annual booklet:

One of the first questions to Ferdinand Morse of Cushing was, "How many sloops did your father build?" This brought a wrinkle to Ferd's brow, for he didn't know the answer. Finally he ventured, "The best I could tell you, it must have been close to a hundred. There were at least six at one time right here in the harbor at Pleasant Point."

At this point in our conversation, Ferd disappeared for a moment and returned with a beautiful half model from which Albion had built many of his sloops. "I have a fully rigged sailing model of this same sloop," he said. With little or no urging, Ferd brought out the sailing model too and told us the story connected with it.

When Ferd was young, his father, Albion Morse, had built him this beautiful sailing model, built to scale, following the half model plan. "We used to take it out to Dick's Cove and sail it," he said, "and I was known as a pretty good rower but I never could catch her 'til she fetched up on the opposite shore."

One day she sailed away from Ferd, and a stranger intercepted it and hauled it out of the water. Ferd thought sure the fellow was going to steal it, and his heart went into his mouth. Come to find out, he was interested in buying a Friendship sloop

that would sail like that model. To make a long story short, a deal was made and Albion built the stranger a sloop. This experience was not unique and four other orders for sloops resulted from having someone see the way that model would sail. One went to Stonington, one to Vinalhaven, one to Walter Davis on Monhegan, and one to Frank Towle from Port Clyde.

Albion built boats all his life, and after sloops were no longer in demand as lobster boats, he switched to building smaller craft and continued 'til his death in 1929 when he was 78 years old. He used the same trailboard design as his brother Wilbur was using in Friendship with only his first name making any distinction . . . . Ferd worked with his father until Albion's death, and then Ferd continued constructing boats in a Thomaston yard until his retirement.

*Ferd Morse with the sailing model from which his father Albion built several sloops.*

Of course, as mentioned earlier, there were other builders around Muscongus Bay besides the Morses and the residents of Bremen Long Island. Clifford Winchenbach was perhaps typical. He built his first sloop in 1883, a 26-foot centerboarder, and continued to build one each winter until 1915. These were built in the loft over his store at Eugley's Corner in West Waldoboro, lowered to the ground, and hauled by seven or eight yoke of oxen to the creek at Dutch Neck. His boat building was done when he was not tending store or fulfilling his obligations to the town as selectman and assessor. His sloops were popular in New England, and one was bought by New Zealanders and sailed home.

Paul Lehrman built the 30-foot sloop *Siren*, later owned as a yacht by George K. Briggs. She came from Marblehead to South Bristol under triple-reefed mainsail and reefed jumbo on the edge of the hurricane of 1927, in which the famous schooner *Columbia* and crew were lost off Sable Island. Fred Winchapaw (sic) built *Lizzie M.* for Fred Greenlaw in 1904 and *Julia A.* for Frank Rossiter in 1905. The latter cost $400 including an engine. Edward A. McFarland and Tom Brackett built sloops at one time or another at New Harbor, and there must have been others. We can regard those we have mentioned as typical of a great many other Maine men all up and down the coast who spent a winter "getting up a boat" either for themselves or others. The omission of their names results more from incomplete records and spotty memory than from unfavorable judgment of their work.

Occasionally, a sloop of an unknown builder survives. In 1984 *Depression* was being rebuilt by David Nutt on Southport Island. There is no record of her builder or of her early life — some say she came from Boothbay, others say Matinicus in 1899 — but judging from her construction, she was built by no Morse, McLain, Carter, Prior, or Winchenbach. Yet she must have served her purpose for years. She was abandoned, rescued, and sold in the early 1930s to Myron Hahn on Bremen Long Island for $15. During World War II, she was partly rebuilt and in 1972 gained a new counter. Just before his death in 1974, Hahn gave the boat to Mel Burns, who had cared for her for years. Burns's grandson raced her in the 1974 Friendship Sloop regatta, then sold her to Larry Harris of New Orleans, who sold her to Lloyd Olson of Edgecomb. Olson is having her rebuilt completely, her stem being the only monument to her original builder.

When Wilbur Morse moved to Lawry in 1882, he was joined by brothers Charles and Jonah. Charles left in 1887 to set up shop near Hatchet Cove. He was probably more of a loner than Wilbur, probably built boats one at a time with a small crew and did much of the actual work himself. His son worked with him, and in 1911 they moved to Thomaston, where they established a yard well known later for construction of fine yachts and fishing vessels under the name of C.A. Morse and Son.

Depression *being rebuilt in 1984. The stem is the only original part remaining. (Courtesy of David Nutt)*

Charles Morse was probably the first to build a round-bowed sloop. In 1908 Frank Rossiter of Vinalhaven came to him, impressed with the round-bowed knockabout schooners being built for the Gloucester fishing fleet. Today's cruise schooner *Adventure*, sailing from Camden, is a good example of the type, although she was not built until 1927. Rossiter wanted a sloop about 35 feet long for dory trawling, a sloop with no bowsprit. Accordingly, Charles Morse made a model with less overhang than the Gloucester schooners and with fuller sections forward than the Friendship sloops he had been building. He said she ought to be 38 feet long from the model, so Rossiter agreed to pay $25 more for the extra three feet. Set up, she grew to 40 feet. She carried a ton of iron on her keel, had hard pine floors, a Knox engine, copper tanks, a Shipmate stove, two anchors and rodes, spreaders so she could carry a topmast, and a removable bowsprit for summer sailing. She was finished out in cypress below, her name and hail picked out in gold leaf. She cost $1,100.

The sloop proved a successful fishing vessel — fast, able, and handy. However, with the advent of full-powered fishermen, she was no longer competitive. At the same time, about 1920, Fred Dion, who had a yard at Salem, was buying all the big, round-bowed fishing vessels he could find for conversion into yachts. He bought *Harvey A.*, rerigged her as a schooner with a marconi mainsail, gaff foresail, and bowsprit, and sold her. She was renamed *Maryleigh* and sailed the coast under that name until 1952, when she was badly damaged in a hurricane and was too far gone to repair. Her owner, Captain Eben Whitcomb of Ellsworth, had her lines taken off, built a new boat to the same lines, and gave her the same name. The new *Maryleigh*, in the shape of the old *Harvey A.*, has made many offshore passages and still sails the coast. The writer sailed her on three cruises and found her handy and able.

Less is known about another Charles Morse sloop, *Get There*, a 43-footer built in 1907 for Edward Rossiter. She is said to have been round-bowed. If so, she had a bowsprit, for Frank Rossiter described *Harvey A.* as the first round-bowed sloop without a bowsprit. Charles Morse also built *On Time*, a 36-foot sloop that may have had a round bow.

In 1914 Charles Morse built *Pennesewassee*, another 40-foot, round-bowed sloop without a bowsprit. She too had a successful career as a fisherman and in 1924 was bought by Fred Dion, converted to a schooner, and raced successfully in Massachusetts Bay. She won the Jeffrey's Ledge race in 1928. She sailed under the names *Golden Rose, Vega,* and *Tinker III.* As late as 1959, she was sailing the Maine coast, owned by W. Blanchard Ford of Scituate, Massachusetts.

*Lowell Boys,* another sloop of the same size and type, followed a similar course. She too was purchased by Fred Dion and rerigged as a staysail schooner in 1925. She was renamed *Yankee* and later *Rescue.* In 1930 she was owned by Arthur Bull of Marblehead and in 1940 by Evans Dick, Jr., of Manchester. She was reputed to be the fastest sloop that ever sailed the Maine coast. In that connection, it is interesting to note that she was the only one that carried a bowsprit when Fred Dion bought her. Perhaps her better balance accounted for her edge in speed.

The last and most colorful of the round-bowed sloops was *Lizzie M.,* built in 1917 for Tom Martelock of Rockland and named for his mother. Tom used *Lizzie M.* hard. A later owner, George K. Briggs, reported:

> . . . *Lizzie M.* had the reputation of being the ablest sloop on the Maine coast. She gained her fame by coming into Rockland one winter night with a northeaster with snow in the making. Tommy Martelock could not get his price for his fish locally and 'lowed he would take her to Portland. He was advised he would never make it, but said, "To hell with you anyway." He drove all night through snow squalls to Portland and got his price in the morning. This story has been told to me by no less than four fishermen, who came aboard for a gam any place between Port Clyde and Camden. Each teller of the same tale insisted that *he* was one of the two men with Tommy Martelock that night.

After Martelock drowned while fishing from a dory in about 1925, Fred Dion bought *Lizzie M.,* extended her cuddy to make a cabin, and sold her to Bill Hall, changing neither her name nor her rig. Hall sold her to Briggs in 1929. Briggs sailed her in many Massachusetts Bay races, including close Jeffrey's Ledge contests with *Pennessewassee* in 1932 and 1936. *Lizzie M.* won her class in the Boston Lightship race in 1929, beating *Malay,* a schooner who had won her class in the race to Bermuda. Briggs never changed his boat's rig or cut down her mainsail, although when he bought her, she had already been fitted with a bowsprit and jib by either Dion or Hall. Briggs said of her:

> With a 32-foot boom and a 22-foot gaff, she had something like 975 square feet in her mainsail alone. She was an exceptionally smart sailer, fast to windward in a blow, and with an unusual ability to keep moving through a chop in light airs.
> *Lizzie M.* would lay to under mainsail alone. She would heave to like a duck with a backed jib. She was easy to reef down. I carried my second reef gasket rove in the leech of my sail and down through a cheek block on the boom. Under two reefs and the jumbo she balanced beautifully and could carry through any summer westerly. In short, she was a vessel.

Just the same, Briggs found some fault with *Lizzie M.*'s construction. He wrote:

> . . . it is axiomatic that a sportsman will drive a boat harder than a professional in commercial use — more money and less sense. Capt. Rossiter mentions the low cost of construction. These boats in all certainty were "country built." I drove the mast all but out through the bottom of *Lizzie* only to find that she had no proper mast step — it was let into the keel — and no floor timbers! Nothing but the garboard fastenings and the pressure of the water holding her together. Fred Dion fixed her up on that, installing mast step and floor timbers together with a tie rod to the mast partners to offset the upward thrust at the chainplates. That held her

together for another twenty years, although I have it that Mr. Cook, her owner in 1962, saw daylight through the topsides in the way of the chainplates in a breeze in Vineyard Sound which probably cost him money. So even with low prices, you got only what you paid for.

Briggs sold *Lizzie M.* in 1941. In 1962 she was owned by Lester Cook of the National Gallery of Art and sailed out of Annapolis, Maryland. In 1965 she was reported to have been lying for two years at the head of a marine railway in Eastport, Maryland, across Spa Creek from Annapolis, without mast or bowsprit and in an advanced state of decay. Then she was bought, bolted together, and moved to Margate, Maryland, where she

Lizzie M. *as a yacht. As a fisherman she carried no bowsprit. (Courtesy William Peterson)*

was to have been smoothed up and used as a plug to build fiberglass Lizzies. Apparently, however, the scheme never came off and she probably fell apart somewhere on the banks of the Chesapeake.

In his search for big sloops to convert into yachts, Dion was unable to purchase another Charles Morse boat, *Crustacean*, that reportedly was sailing out of Newburyport, Massachusetts, in the 1930s. Nothing further has come to light regarding that boat.

Wilbur Morse also built round-bowed sloops, commonly called Cape Ann or Gloucester model sloops in the last days of fishing under sail. Two of them were the previously mentioned *Right Bower* and *Georgie C. Bowden*. *Right Bower* was a 47-foot sloop built for Edward Rossiter in 1915 for about $1,400. She fished out of Camden for years and then was converted to a party boat and sailed out of Atlantic City, New Jersey. In 1959 she was owned by Frank Smith, and her name was changed to *Finette*. Some time later, she came into the possession of Thomas K. Baldwin. He found her too far gone to repair and dismantled her in about 1968.

*Georgie C. Bowden* had a colorful life. She was a 48-foot, round-bowed sloop with a bowsprit, built in Friendship in 1912 by Wilbur Morse for Captain Ernest Darling of Cundy's Harbor. She was named for a young lady friend of Darling's youth, Georgia C. Bowden. He used *Georgie* for dory trawling and night seining, carrying five dories on deck and swinging them over the side on purchases from the end of the gaff and the mast above the crosstrees. In March 1939 Captain Boyd Guild bought her and, with his friend Clarence Hale, took her down east to his home in Sargentville in April. At that time she had a big, slow-turning, four-cylinder Lathrop engine. Guild used her for fishing for two years and sailed parties on the side. Early one May morning in 1941, a neighbor, Rollie Gray, ran up to Guild's house, hollering that *Georgie* was afire. Guild and Clarence Hale ran for the shore and were soon joined by Horace Wardwell and others carrying the entire stock of buckets from Horace's general store. Every available man turned out. Ignoring the two drums of gasoline on deck, they boarded her and fought the fire. It had such a start that the paint on the masthead was badly blistered and burned. Fortunately, though, the fire was in the forecastle. Her sheathing and the bulkheads of the fish hold next aft were saturated with salt water and therefore burned slowly. But the fire worked aft toward the engine room and soon burned a hole through the topsides close to the waterline in spite of all they could do. Finally, Guild determined to scuttle her and took a hatchet into the engine room aft of the fish hold. He raised the hatchet to smash a seacock but at the last minute couldn't bring himself to do it. He said he would stay and fight the fire. Clarence said he would, too, and so did the others. They went at it again and finally managed to put out the last smouldering ember. She had started to sink when a hole had burned through her hull, so they stuffed the breach with clothes and anything they could find, including Clarence's coat. At last, they got the pump running and got her up where she was safe until a temporary patch could be made.

*Georgie Bowden* was in hard shape. Her forward half was gutted, there was a hole in her topsides, and her mast was partly burned through below the deck. Nonetheless, Guild patched her up and ran her under power from Sargentville to Thomaston. It was rough going between White Head and Mosquito Island, and the skipper feared for the mast. If it went, it would pry the deck out of her, creating a terrible mess with the wire headstays holding the mast. It held, however, and the captain brought the boat safely alongside the Dunn & Elliott Wharf just below the bridge. It had been decided that she would be rebuilt by Newbert and Wallace at their yard above the bridge. Accord-

Left: Georgie C. Bowden *just after the fire. (Courtesy Capt. Boyd Guild)* Right: Georgie C. Bowden *after rebuilding. (Courtesy Capt. Boyd Guild)*

ingly, the yard replaced all frames from well below the waterline to the deck, all the deck framing and deck, and much of the planking, using oak and yellow pine. In his rebuilt boat, Guild sailed parties out of Rockland exclusively for the Samoset Hotel in the summer and fished in the spring and fall. Captain Guild is to this day a superb seaman. I saw him beat the 48-foot *Bowden* into narrow New Harbor, a feat I was proud to accomplish in a 28-foot sloop. He is now owner and skipper of the three-masted schooner *Victory Chimes,* which he handles as neatly as a sloop.

During World War II, the *Bowden* was taken over by the Coast Guard for coastal patrol work, her skipper, also in the Coast Guard, assigned to a much larger vessel.

In 1945, when he got out of the service, Guild bought *Georgie* back from the government and immediately started to refit her. He sailed parties out of Boothbay Harbor in 1945 and sold her in the fall of that year to Donald Macomber of Boston, a member of the Cruising Club of America. Macomber and his wife, then in their 70s, took her to Florida and the West Indies for the winter and, upon return, sold her to Richard Y. Chadwick of Portland. He enjoyed her for several years, installed a diesel engine, and sold her to Hardy.

In the hurricane of 1954, *Georgie* was moored off the Portland Yacht Club, went adrift, and was lying well up on the shore when I passed a week later. She was floated, however, and taken to a yard on the Royal River just below the Route 1 bridge. Extensive litigation between her owner and an insurance company ensued. Guild offered to buy her back but was refused until the insurance matter was settled.

Meanwhile, she occupied space at the yard, running up a storage bill and deteriorating further. At length, she was sold to a religious group, which planned to sail her to the Pacific and use her in missionary work; but her years on the bank had been too much for her. She had degenerated beyond the point from which the group's limited resources could bring her back. She was stripped and burned where she lay, to the distress of her many friends.

Round-bowed sloops like *Georgie Bowden* were quite different from the earlier clipper-bowed Friendships. The forward sections of the latter were wedge-shaped, tending a little toward the concave. In Wilbur Morse's later boats like *White Eagle,* they were decidedly concave both in sections and in waterlines. In *Lizzie M.*, which might be taken as typical, the forward sections are all convex, and the waterlines are straight wedges, rounding into gentle convex curves. Also the round bow swept down into the keel in an easy curve, giving the later boat less forefoot and making her a little quicker in stays. These changes appear largely to have eliminated the shoulder that gave clipper-bowed sloops such a heavy weather helm and stopped them dead when heeled into a steep chop.

The midship sections were similar, but the after sections in the later boats had an easier turn to the bilge and not quite so flat a run.

With no bowsprit and less forefoot, it was necessary to move the mast a considerable distance farther aft than it had been in the clipper-bowed boats. This meant that the boom had to be shortened a little to enable a man to reach the clew earring in reefing. Even so, the knockabout sloops appeared to have had still a considerable weather helm. *Lowell Boys,* which, the reader will remember, had a short bowsprit, was considered the fastest sloop on the coast of Maine; and when Dion converted *Harvey A., Pennessewassee,* and *Lizzie M.* to yachts, he added bowsprits and improved their sailing qualities.

The distinguished naval architect John G. Alden of Boston was impressed with these round-bowed Friendships and sent two of his men, Frank Swain and Charles MacGregor, to Dion's yard in Salem to measure them up before *Malabar I* was built. The connection between these sloops, Charles Morse, and *Malabar I* is briefly described in a quotation from *The Sportsman* written by John Alden and quoted by Richard Henderson in his biography of Alden.*

What then is the Malabar type? Why and how was it developed? Let us first look at the true fisherman as exemplified in the Gloucesterman, which I have always admired and with a few of which I had something to do years ago. Simple in section, all her ballast inside, short ended, low sided for ease of handling dories, beamy to gain capacity, fast and able but never quite at her best until loaded, easy to build and therefore cheap — we find many qualities here desirable for the yachtsman.

Let us also look at the *Lloyd W. Berry* – now on the Pacific Coast as *Zingara* – a sixty-foot schooner designed or rather modeled by Charles A. Morse of Friendship sloop fame, and built by C.A. Morse and Son at Thomaston, Maine . . . . She is a slightly modified fisherman and a fairly successful yacht.*

Everyone interested in boats has a dream ship of some kind, vague though he may be as to just what it should be. It was in just such a position that I found myself at the close of the War [World War II]. To complicate matters, my pocketbook was decidedly low. Nevertheless, I started on a hunt to acquire that dream ship.

Recalling the ease with which the *Lloyd W. Berry* handled and how well she sailed, my mind became fixed on the schooner rig and I wandered Down East to Morse's yard hoping to find some small fisherman that could be converted at small cost. My greeting was anything but encouraging. As Mr. Morse put it, he was "too busy to talk." He further volunteered the information that it would probably be cheaper to build than fix up an old boat. Disappointed by further endeavors to interest him, I gave up and walked off. I was half way up the hill when I was hailed to

---

* *The* Lloyd W. Berry *was influenced not only by the Gloucesterman but also by the round-bowed Friendship sloops that Morse modeled and built. She made a celebrated double crossing of the Atlantic in 1921 and 1922, weathering a severe winter gale on the notorious Bay of Biscay. At one point her all-amateur crew was forced to chop away her bulwarks with axes to clear her decks of ice.*

*(The footnote is Henderson's. Reprinted by permission of the publisher from:* John G. Alden and His Yacht Designs *by Robert W. Carrick and Richard Henderson, copyright 1983 by International Marine Publishing Company, 21 Elm Street, Camden, Maine04843.)*

"come back here." I returned and Mr. Morse took me into his inner office to "thrash it out." The result was that I ordered a schooner from him, the 41½-foot-overall *Malabar I.* This had been far from my intentions, but, being the result, I hastened back to my office to draw the plans.

The idea of the round-bowed sloop was developed in smaller boats, too. In the December 1924 issue of *Yachting* appeared this statement after a paragraph in praise of the Friendship sloop:

Today there are very few of them available, and with this fact in mind, John G. Alden has designed the little twenty-nine footer shown in the accompanying plan. She retains all the best features of the Friendship sloop, but has been refined to better meet the requirements of the yachtsman.

There follows a plan of the Malabar Junior.

That same winter J. Arthur Stevens of Goudy & Stevens had designed for my father Robert F. Duncan the 28-foot, round-bowed knockabout sloop *Dorothy* on much the same lines. She was, however, rounder amidships, less flat in the run, and had a little hollow in the waterline forward. She had a heavy weather helm and was sluggish in light air, so several years later John Alden designed a double head rig that proved quite successful. Goudy and Stevens went on to build three more such sloops, the first and last of which were *Scylla* and *Half Hitch. Scylla* had a marconi mainsail, and both had bowsprits. They were finer amidships than *Dorothy*, but all were successful and reflected a definite if distant Friendship tradition. The naval architect Ralph Winslow followed the same course in a number of stout, round-bowed vessels, one of which, *Electron II*, was mentioned earlier.

*Sloop* Dorothy, *designed by J. Arthur Stevens in 1925. She shows the influence of the round-bowed Friendship sloop.*

Thus, it is not too extravagant to claim that the round-bowed Friendship sloop developed by Charles and Wilbur Morse was the final achievement of the small New England fishing vessel. It owes a debt to the clipper-bowed Friendship, to the Gloucester schooners, and far back to the Muscongus Bay sloops. Its image is reflected in the Malabar sloops and schooners that led all cruising and ocean-racing yachts until the advent of yachts like Olin Stephens's *Dorade*, *Stormy Weather*, and *Mustang*, and the subsequent development of fast, light-displacement ocean-racers.

6

*Later Builders 1920-1960*

W*ith the advent of* reasonably dependable gasoline engines in the second decade of the twentieth century, Friendship sloops became practically obsolete, both as fishing vessels and as yachts. Fishermen turned to motorboats, which developed into the fast, handsome, able lobster boats used today; and yachts became lighter and faster, losing resemblance to the old fishing sloops in hull design or rig.

A number of the old sloops still floated, however, and were used as yachts by people who cared little to race but enjoyed cruising or day sailing in the boats in which they had grown up. Some liked a dry, stiff, handy boat, even if she had a big mainsail and was slow to windward by modern standards. Others liked the commercial tradition. Still others liked what they had always been used to, and many, no doubt, liked the low prices at which some of the old sloops were available. The people interested in Friendship sloops, for whatever reason, were so few, however, that few Friendships were built between 1920 and 1960. The records of the Friendship Sloop Society, while admittedly incomplete, show only 25 of the 221 sloops on their roster as having been built in this period. Except for boats built by amateur builders for personal use or the occasional boat built professionally for a client who wanted a "character boat," the boats of this era were built by only four builders: W. Scott Carter in Friendship, Warren Prescott Gannett in Scituate, Massachusetts, Philip J. Nichols in Round Pond, and Winfield and Douglas Lash at Hatchet Cove, Friendship.

Flying Jib. *(T. Gray)*

Winfield Scott Carter was born on Bremen Long Island in 1892. With his father George he rowed daily to Hatchet Cove to work in Charles Morse's shop, which was just up over the shore and still stands. After Charles moved his business to Thomaston in 1911, Scott worked for Wilbur Morse. In *Friendship Long Island,* Ivan Morse told of an incident in Wilbur's shop:

> They were working on some kind of a good big dragger in there at one time. Scott Carter was working there . . . . And who made out the plank I don't know, but I guess he wasn't exactly an expert, because they had some seams there that would have stood a little fitting somewhere. Well, Scott was caulking and he came to this big old seam and, of course, they raised the devil in there. He grabbed up a cotton glove. He was working that in for all he was worth and he got it all in there but one finger. Wilbur come along and I guess they heard something right then and there. I don't know whether he hauled it out, but if he could have got it out, I guess he did.

In 1926 Scott Carter bought land from the town of Friendship at the head of Hatchet Cove and set up shop. When Wilbur Morse retired in 1927, he gave Scott many of his patterns, tools, and models and, even more valuable, the benefit of his experience. This teaching may have been what influenced Scott to build a number of sloops as yachts in the 1930s.

The first Scott Carter sloop appears to have been *Jib,* about which nothing is known but the name. He built *Flying Jib* in 1936 from a model that he "obtained possession of," probably from Wilbur Morse, and modified slightly for use as a yacht. She was 29'10" long and drew 5'6" – rather deep for a Friendship, especially as she carried no outside ballast, only two tons of sashweights inside. In 1955 she had been owned for some time by A.J. Derbyshire of Detroit, Michigan, and named *Monique.* In 1964 she entered the Friendship Sloop Society with the new name of *Flying Jib* under the ownership of Elbert Powell of Arlington, Massachusetts, who kept her at Friendship. In 1968 *Flying Jib* was purchased by Newton Hinckley of Wayland, Massachusetts, but her home port remained Friendship. Hinckley painted her a strong, dark red and raced her with great enthusiasm.

In 1937 Carter built a 38-foot sloop for Stanton Garfield of Concord, Massachusetts.

She was very hollow-bowed, with her mast far forward, and sailed under the name of *Lively Lady*. In 1942 she was bought by the Reverend James Holland Beal and renamed *Monkey Wench*. The parson rigged her with a topmast and a big reaching jib. He sailed her until 1955 and sold her to John Savage, who renamed her *Tannis II*. She appeared for the first Friendship Sloop Society regatta in 1961, owned by John Niering. With no topsail and her mainsail much cut down, *Tannis* did not distinguish herself in the race. In 1969 she was sold to John Cronin of Sturbridge, Massachusetts. He restored her mainsail to its original size and set a topsail and jib topsail, too. Manned by a crew large in numbers and, at first, physically diminutive in size, *Tannis* was a formidable opponent. To get to leeward of that tower of sail was to lose a quarter mile on the fleet. Captain Cronin sailed her aggressively and despite her large handicap – see page 92 in the next chapter for a description of this system – she was usually well up in the fleet. See her booming down on the finish line in a brisk southerly, every sail wung out and drawing, her crew clustered on the end of her bowsprit, and a huge white bone in her teeth!

In 1938 Carter built a 38-foot sloop, *Eleazar*, named for the founder of Dartmouth College. Harry Schellhorn sold her in 1966 to Carl Arra, who sold her in 1970 to Harry Marden, who changed her name to *Gold Ivy*. In 1971 she went to Captain David Smith of Marshfield, Massachusetts.

In 1941 *Amity*, a 47-foot sloop, was built in the Carter yard. In 1980 she was owned by Benjamin Plotkin of Norwalk, Connecticut.

Mary Anne *and* Tannis *under full sail. (Boutilier Photos)*

Mandalay. *(Courtesy of James Rockefeller and Capt. Robin Colcord)*

Another Carter boat, *Sea Gull*, her date and size unknown to the author, was owned in 1980 by Mike Dolan of Hollywood, Florida.

Not strictly a Friendship sloop was a 40-foot Friendship hull with ketch rig, designed by Wilbur Morse and built by Carter for a man who intended to sail her around the world. James S. Rockefeller, a later owner, wrote of Wilbur Morse's design process:

> Apparently he did the rigging by eye, scorning the drawing board and such things as technical centers of effort, etc. He had the two masts put in her; then he walked off to a distance and squinted hard at her for a time. The mizzen to his eye looked too high. He sent a man up and had him saw off a foot. He squinted again. It still looked too high to him. "Saw off another foot," he said; and that is how her sail plan was born.

The circumnavigator got as far as the Caribbean, where he found such an attractive spot ashore that he sold the boat and settled down. Under her second owner, a Florida man, she weathered two hurricanes. She was then sold to two men from Chicago who kept her in Florida and Caribbean waters until James Rockefeller found her in an Annapolis yard in 1950.

He too had ambitions to circumnavigate. She was in rather hard shape by this time and had been fitted with a raised deck and high bulwarks forward, quite evident in the picture. Rockefeller had her repaired, reduced her sail plan, fitted her with twin spinnakers for tradewind runs, named her *Mandalay*, and set off around Hatteras in November 1951. The rest of her story, leading to her wreck in the New Hebrides, is told in Chapter 10.

Not registered as a Carter boat but heavily influenced by him and built in his yard was *Sarah E. II*. Her story was told in the December 1939 issue of *Yachting*. Robert McKean, a summer resident of Jefferson, determined to build a Friendship sloop in his barn. He decided on a Friendship because he had sailed many kinds of boats and had found the 25-foot Robert McLain sloop *Sarah E.* to be able, fast, and comfortable. "When I find something I like and know is good, such as a breed of dog or even a brand of cheese, I stick to it," McKean declared.

Carefully he took off the lines of *Sarah E.*, had a naval architect fair them up, and lofted them in his barn. He persuaded John Winchapaw of Friendship, a dory builder who had worked on sloops, to help him. John suggested that, instead of building in a barn, miles from salt water and with limited tools, he should talk with Scott Carter about building the boat next to his shop at Hatchet Cove. Scott was willing, at the cost of whatever tools, materials, labor, and advice McKean needed, to let him set her up outdoors next to his shop. Scott's cousin Sid and his father George, the "Old Man," were of great help, and the job went forward. This was in 1938. Keel, stem, sternpost, and frames were cut at a local mill from a 30-foot oak log, two feet thick. Most of the shaping was done with adze and plane, although the yard's power tools were used for the heavy work. The rabbets were cut before the molds were set, the angles presumably taken from the lofting, and the keel was notched to take the ends of the timbers. She was then set up, molds put in place, and battened out. The timbers were 1¼" x 2" oak, cooked in the steam box for three hours, and all bent in on one day with the help of the yard crew. Scott said they had done "quite a little lot" that day.

The after three pairs of frames, which have the tightest bends, were sawed down the

Sarah E. *(Courtesy of Eldon Homesey)*

1¼" dimension to keep them from breaking. Floor timbers of 1¼" oak were drifted to the keel at every other frame, and an extra heavy one drifted to the sternpost as well. Planking was ⅞" pine, coming from the mill with live edges, bark on. The garboard, which the Old Man had picked before it was off the truck, was 15 feet long and 16 inches wide, clear all the way. She was fastened with 1¾" boat nails that apparently did not come through the frames. They started with the garboard, planked up to the curve of the bilge, then put on an oak sheer strake, and planked down. The last plank to go in the remaining space is called the shutter plank. Although no liquor was available for shutter grease, the nearest liquor store being in Rockland and Friendship being a dry town, the shutter was finally worked into place "with the greatest difficulty" using "soft stuff."

Molds were removed, planking planed first across the grain with a very sharp plane to make the hull perfectly fair and then planed fore and aft and sanded smooth. Then she was caulked.

Deck framing, of 3" x 3" oak, was mortised into the sheer clamp, and then a lock streak of 1¾" x 8" oak was let into the top of the deck beams, fastened to them, and drifted through sheer plank and timber heads with ⅝" galvanized drifts. A breast hook in the bow of 1¾" oak was also mortised into the deck beams and tied the whole structure tightly together. House sides were 1" oak planks, 16 inches wide, steamed for four hours, bent into elliptical form at the forward end, and continued around the coaming aft. She was decked and left for the winter.

The next year, she was finished out inside, ballasted with iron, and rigged, complete with topmast and gaff topsail. That summer, McKean's son sailed her to New York for a shakedown. The total cost for the project, including lumber, labor from Carter's yard, use of some tools and yard space, engine, ballast, sails, and equipment was $1,400 — a reasonable price indeed for a sound, plain boat.

In 1945 *Sarah E. II* was purchased by Mr. and Mrs. John P. Riesman, who renamed her *Peggoty*. They lived aboard her that winter in Mamaroneck, New York, and sold her in 1952. In 1963 she was owned by John Kollett in Johnston, Rhode Island, under the name of *Yankee Trader* (not the same *Yankee Trader* built by Albion Morse in 1919). In 1970 she was sold to Eric Osborn, an Englishman and steward of the Bristol Yacht Club in Bristol, Rhode Island. He renamed her *Red Coat* and in 1975 sold her to Eldon and Elizabeth Homesey of Wilmington, Delaware. In 1979 they restored her to her original appearance with new main and jib topsails and "started to reap the numerous compliments pretty sloop owners receive. Especially under full sail were the Chesapeake Bay 'Tupperware' sailors impressed." Mr. Homesey reports that *Sarah E.*, for she now carries her original name, needs retimbering. Well protected and ventilated, she awaits surgery in his yard.

During World War II, Scott Carter opened a yard in Waldoboro, where he built four 60-foot tugs. After the war, he returned to Hatchet Cove. He was building *Nellie G.*, a ferry for Casco Bay, when he died in 1946. The *Maine Coast Fisherman* said of him, "Carter-built boats . . . became famous from Castine, Maine, to Montauk Point, Long Island. For fine workmanship, grace and design, and rugged durability, his boats and vessels earned him the highest reputation among fishermen and yachtsmen throughout New England. In building boats, Mr. Carter put durability and strength ahead of profit and often repeated his maxim: that he would build all boats as though his own son were taking them to sea."

Charles Sylvester and Scott's nephew Winfield Lash took over the yard, finished *Nellie G.*, and built two more boats. In 1948 Sylvester sold out, and Douglas Lash joined Winfield in the Lash Brothers yard.

*Winfield Lash with the half model of* Nellie F. Parsons, *made by Wilbur Morse and used for a number of his sloops.* Mary Anne, Downeaster, Dirigo, *and* Rights of Man *were built from this model, now at the Maine Maritime Museum. (Boutilier Photos)*

A few years later, John Dallett of Friendship was trying to sell a schooner. The offers he got he felt were too low. He declared that he would burn her before he would sell her cheap. And he did. He burned her, first removing everything salvageable. Then he went to Winnie Lash for a fast, able, easily handled sloop, smaller than his schooner. Winnie brought out the half model of the 37-foot *Nellie F. Parsons,* one of Wilbur Morse's most popular models. They agreed she could be scaled down to 31 feet, raised up a little to provide cruising accommodations, and fitted out with much of the gear from the schooner. Winnie launched her in 1958; she was named *Mary Anne.* She proved to be a smart sailer and was the first of four sloops built after 1961 from much the same model, the other three being *Downeaster, Dirigo,* and *Rights of Man. Mary Anne,* still with her original name and rig, is now owned by Joe Griffin of Damariscotta. He bought her in 1969 and under his command, she took part in the re-enactment of the Arnold expedition to Quebec in 1975.

Warren Prescott Gannett, born in 1876, was a plumber by trade, but liked building boats. He started with skiffs and developed an able boat that towed well and rowed easily. It was a handsome boat, too, and so distinctive that it could be recognized easily from a distance. Gannett also built Friendship sloops, for he was much taken by the grace of the design. First he built a little schooner, *Mary Jane,* in 1935 and then went on to build the Friendship sloops *Dorothy G., Beatrice, Polly, Rookie, Surprise, Jane, Martha D., Retriever, Bounty, Volunteer, Sinbad,* and *Pal O' Mine,* the last in 1947. All of these sloops were about 25 feet long, for that was the length of the Gannett shop. They were light, neat little sloops, quite fine forward. One of them, built in 1938, was owned by John Adams of Marblehead in 1961 and was then named *L'aigle D'or.* In 1965 she was renamed *Old Friendly* and was owned by Jack Hensley of East Boothbay. In 1967

Shulamite. *(Boutilier Photos)*

Donald Hall of Amherst, Massachusetts, owned her. In 1973 she was sold to James and Pauline Doolittle, and in 1983 they still registered her with the Friendship Sloop Society under the name of *Shulamite*, sailing out of Five Islands, Maine. For more comfortable cruising, a higher deckhouse has been added to her original cabin.

*Retriever*, built in 1942, is owned by John and Clarice Rice of Hingham, Massachusetts, and has several times come east to the regatta in Friendship.

*Bounty*, a 22-footer built in 1932, was owned by George McFadden from 1961 to 1968, was sold to Roy Gumpert, and in 1973 to Richard Bailey of Peekskill, New York.

*Volunteer* was owned in 1980 by Brian Neri of Buffalo, New York.

*Pal O' Mine*, a 27-foot sloop, was one of Gannett's last and biggest, built in 1947. She is owned by James Lane of Winchester, Massachusetts.

Warren Gannett worked alone, built from half models, and invented his own ways to do things when necessary. He worked out a way to determine the displacement of a boat by burying a model up to the waterline in a box of sand. He liked to cruise alone in boats he built and often went off for weekends in Massachusetts Bay, but for some reason, he would never leave on a Friday. He often sailed at 12:01 a.m. on Saturday. He never started building a boat on Friday either. He would notch a board with his knife on Thursday so she would be started before Friday. In addition to building boats, he was an omnivorous reader and a grafter of apple trees. In short, Warren Prescott Gannett, named after two Revolutionary War heroes, was an independent Renaissance man who did what he wanted to do and did it very well, for several of his sloops still sail.

Philip J. Nichols was born in 1894. He was one of the leading students at Bristol, Maine, High School. The principal, who was related to someone in the Baldwin Locomotive Co., arranged for Phil to take an engineering course with that company. Later, Nichols worked for Baldwin in Philadelphia and then for General Electric in Schenectady. About 1928 he came home to work as a designer and engineer for Hyde Windlass Company in Bath. In 1932 he bought an old stable on the shore at Round Pond and rebuilt it as a boat shop. He bought an old and badly decayed Friendship sloop on Loud's Island for $10, filled her with empty barrels, and towed her home. He took off her lines, then sold a sloop his brother had owned with him for $500. With the money, the lines of the two sloops, and a model from Charles Carter, Nichols set up a 33-foot sloop. Despite difficulty getting lumber, but with the help of his brother-in-law and a hired man, he finished her in 1935 and named her *Result*. He kept her for three years, cruising down east as the spirit moved him, and sold her in 1938. In 1955 she was owned by Harold W. Birk in Niantic, Connecticut, and in 1980 she was owned by the Sea Scout ship in Westerly, Rhode Island, and named *Temptress*.

Soon after Nichols sold *Result*, he started a 28-foot sloop, which he named *Pressure*. She was launched in 1942. In 1961 she was owned by Richard Falkeneau and named *Suchel*. Richard Usen of Manchester, Massachusetts, sold her in 1965 to George Putz, who named her *Cyrano*. He sold her in 1967 to Thomas Montgomery, who passed her on the next year to Arthur Krouse. In 1973 she was sold to Sinclair Kenney of Edgewood, Rhode Island, and is now named *Smuggler*.

When *Pressure* was sold, Nichols laid down another sloop, a 33-footer. She came on slowly, for he was working for Hyde as an engineer and draftsman until his retirement in 1961, and he had other projects under way at the same time. One of them he called Philip's Folly. It was a new type of steam valve for a locomotive. The Maine Central Railroad was much interested in it and offered to buy it for a handsome price. Nichols preferred to retain ownership and let the railroad use it on a royalty basis. The railroad accepted the deal; three years later, they changed to diesel locomotives.

Smuggler, *ex-*Cyrano, *ex-*
Pressure. *(Don E. Gammon)*

Nichols's new sloop was finished in 1964. He named her *Surprise.* She was a big, handsome sloop, high and fine forward, with a mainsail big enough to move her. The sail was cut in the old-time way, with the cloths running parallel to the leach, and was cotton duck, not dacron. In fact, all Nichols's boats were very much in the tradition of the old fishing sloops. They were built on lines that he drew up from the old Morse sloops and the Charles Carter model. They were built of pine and oak and fastened with galvanized nails driven through the timbers and headed over. Bolts and drifts were of galvanized iron. Ballast was all inside, usually painted iron sash weights, although some beach rocks were used. The platforms were not watertight but were loose boards set low in the old way, to provide depth in the cockpit. As Nichols said, "If I poke a hole in her, I want to get down in there and stuff it up." Although *Result* had three engines *seriatim* while Nichols owned her, *Surprise* had none.

Nichols sold *Surprise* in 1972 to Bill Payne, who kept her on Monhegan Island and used her to carry firewood from Boothbay to the island in summer. She still had no engine. In 1978 Robert Phaneuf of Chelmsford, Massachusetts, owned her and still does. It is believed that he put an engine in her.

Before Phil Nichols sold *Surprise,* he started a 28-foot sloop. When asked what he was up to, he said, "Building a boat." Those who knew him well said he built boats because he liked to build boats and so always had one going. This little sloop was named *Secret.* When asked why, Phil replied: "They asked me what the name was, and

*Philip J. Nichols aboard* Surprise. *(Courtesy of J. Malcolm Barter)*

I said it was a secret, and when I came down next morning, the damned gremlins had painted it right on the stern."

Phil was reluctant to sell *Secret*, despite one young lady's constant urging. Before *Secret* was decked, she wanted to buy her, and Phil kept putting her off. Wait till she's launched, wait till she's rigged, wait till . . . . When asked why he didn't sell the boat when he had such an eager buyer, he answered, "I'd be foolish to sell her. Then I'd lose my boat and my girlfriend too."

Before *Secret* was sold, she was used to make a TV movie for children, *On A Summer's Day*, a movie that would have benefitted had Phil been turned loose to play the part of the old fisherman.

Nichols sold *Secret* in 1975 to Melvin Cohen of Port Clyde. In 1978 she was owned by John Stiles, Robin Mackel, and Douglas and Gail Faust. Since 1981 she has been owned by Robert and Elizabeth Monk of Chelmsford, Massachusetts.

Lynn Franklin did an oral history interview with Phil Nichols. Nichols told of a bad fall: He was hauling his skiff up the stony shore when the painter parted and he went down hard on his back among the rocks. "I laid there a while to see if I was dead, because if I was, 't w'ant no use to get up."

He was far from dead, however. He had more than enough vigor to draw up plans for Robert Gardner's *Red Jacket* and to help Harry Quick get started on his Fer-a-Lite™ sloop. He died in March 1979, at the age of 84, leaving happy memories behind him.

Surprise.
*(Irving Nevells Photographs)*

**Above:** *Philip J. Nichols at the bow of* Secret. *(James Rockefeller)* **Below:** Gypsy. *(T. Gray)*

During the years from 1920 to 1969, several builders, amateur and professional, built or rebuilt single sloops either for themselves or for someone afflicted with that peculiar, contagious, and incurable malady that drives him to want a Friendship sloop. A list follows of the boats for which we have records, and a few of the better-known ones are described:

| Friendship Sloop Society Number | Name | Length | Builder | Year | Owner (1984) |
| --- | --- | --- | --- | --- | --- |
| 109 | *Petrel* | 31 | G. Cooper | 1933 | Michael Brown, Dorchester, Mass. |
| 188 | *Maude* | 32 | N. Savage | 1937 | M/M G. R. Axelson, Newburyport, Mass. (1980) |
| 43 | *Gypsy* | 23 | Judson Crouse | 1939 | Bob and Jane Lash, Orland, Maine (1980) |
| 48 | *Channel Fever* | 33 | F.A. Provener | 1939 | Jim Nesbit, Ft. Myers, Fla. |
| 80 | *Headway* | 35 | Buck & Adams | 1941 | Christopher Head, Stow, Mass. |
| 15 | *Vida Mia* | | E.L. Stevens | 1942 | George Loos, Cape May, N.J. |
| 14 | *Vigor* ex- *Sadie M.* | 30 | W. Morse in Thomaston | 1946 | Robt. K. Emerson, Hancock Pt., Maine |
| 21 | *Wilbur Morse* | 30 | Carlton Simmons | 1947 | Karl Heiser and Thomas Olson, Cundy's Harbor, Maine |
| 73 | *West Indian* | | Pamet Harbor | 1951 | Richard Faredy, Naples, Fla. |
| 63 | *Kochab* | 28 | Speers | 1953 | |
| 79 | *Nimbus* | 32 | A. Chenault | 1954 | Fred Savigart, New Orleans, La. (1980) |
| 6 | *Eastward* | 32 | James Chadwick | 1956 | Roger and Mary Duncan, East Boothbay, Maine |
| 78 | *Emmie B.* | 37 | Reginald Wilcox | 1958 | Burned |

*Gypsy*, a little 23-foot sloop, appears annually at the Friendship Sloop Society regatta, skippered by Bob Lash and crewed by a merry and larger-than-adequate crew. Bob wrote: "I had been crawling the boatyards for years, looking for a boat that would fit my budget and yet suit my fancy, but the two were worlds apart." In 1963 he scored, finding *Gypsy* in a boathouse in Orcutt's Harbor. She is not exactly your classic Morse or McLain model, but is close enough to be admitted in Class C, a "near replica," by the Society. Bob painted her, launched her, sailed her, and in the following July, while pushing her to make it to the regatta, he and his wife Jane found themselves bailing to stay afloat. *Gypsy* had started a seam as a result of seven broken timbers. The rebuilding job included 42 new timbers, new deck, deck beams and partners, new ceiling, and two new garboards. Bob added, "While all this was going on, a strange phenomenon was taking place. People had started 'giving' me things." Thus, her mast is the boom of an old schooner. On the tack of her recut mainsail is the name of a bigger boat. Her wheel is another gift, and its gearbox steered a truck before it went to sea. Her two-cycle engine was the gift of a friend who moored nearby, and its coil came from Bob's father-in-law's junk box, where it had been lying since 1911. Trail boards were carved and donated by another friend. *Gypsy*, Bob said, is appropriately named: "A thing of hand-me-downs and patches as well as a low-budget wanderer."

*Gypsy* was nearly trampled to death one windy day when the Gloucester schooner *Adventure* dragged down on her, but quick hands dropped her mooring in time to save her, and the little resistance she was able to put up may have helped the schooner.

On another windy day, this time at the regatta, Bob said he was going to change her

Channel Fever *picking up her handicap buoy.*

**Above:** Vida Mia. **Below left:** Sadie M. *under Harrison Prindle as she was built without trail boards.* **Below right:** Wilbur Morse *and* Vida Mia.

name to *Tuna*, Chicken of the Sea, but she stood up nobly to her work that day and scudded home to Friendship before the blustery southerly among the leaders of her class.

*Channel Fever*, a big, round-bowed sloop, is rated in Class C, but is more or less in the Friendship tradition. She was sailed for several years by Gorden Winslow with the help of a retired admiral and Jim Stevens, one of the Stevenses of Goudy & Stevens, the East Boothbay yard. Captain Winslow was a hard man to beat, especially after he fitted *Channel Fever* with a club topsail. Winslow sold her to Jim Nesbit of Fort Myers, Florida. She is now in Rockport, Maine, looking for someone to work on her.

*Vida Mia* was owned for many years by Captain Ted Brown of Kittery and was named for his wife. Brown brought *Vida Mia* to Friendship every year until 1976 and has been to the regatta almost every year since on one boat or another. In 1976 David King, a near neighbor of Ted's, bought *Vida Mia* and brought her down to Friendship with the same name on her stern. She is now owned by George Loos of Cape May, New Jersey. *Vida Mia*, like many sloops built in the 1930s and 1940s, is not strictly in the Friendship tradition, but she has a clipper bow and a gaff rig and so is welcome in Class C. Ted flew the Commodore's square blue flag on *Vida Mia* in 1973 and 1974.

*Vigor*, formerly *Sadie M.*, was built by Wilbur Morse, not the renowned Wilbur A. Morse but his grandnephew, grandson of his brother and partner Jonah. Wilbur laid down *Sadie M.* in 1940 and built her alongside a succession of draggers at the Morse Boatbuilding Co., in Thomaston. He worked on her as he could find time and materials and did not launch her until 1946. He did not fit her with the customary trail boards and billet head, but otherwise she is a Friendship sloop all over. Eventually, she was sold to Harrison Prindle of Castine and was sailed by him in the first Friendship Sloop Society regatta in 1961. Prindle sailed her until 1969, when she was sold to Robert K. Emerson of Hancock Point, Maine. Emerson fitted her with trail boards and the classic clipper bow. In 1984 he still owned her.

In 1946 Carlton Simmons, postmaster at Friendship and a nephew of Wilbur A. Morse, built a 30-foot sloop off the traditional model for Robert Armstrong of Winchester, Massachusetts, and Friendship. He named his new boat *Wilbur A. Morse*, after the 93-year-old gentleman whose model was used for the sloop. She is 9'6" in beam, and draws 4½ feet, classic Friendship dimensions, and, like most Friendships, her ballast is all inside. Instead of the traditional lock streak, however, she has a clamp and shelf under the deck, as do most modern boats. She has a generous complement of floor timbers, and she carries an engine on center. Her cockpit is not self-bailing, or was not when she was built, but the deck extends some distance inside the coaming. She is generously but simply rigged with a mainsail of 500 square feet, a short mast well forward, and small jib and staysail. She carries no spreaders, just two shrouds on each side. Her forestay runs through the bowsprit and is set up on the stem. She is as strong, as simple, and as handsome as any her namesake built, and when he saw her sailing, he commented that she was a fine boat indeed, but needed more ballast.

In 1949, after a summer of party boating out of Perkins Cove near Ogunquit, Armstrong's son John and Frank Perkins took her down the inland waterway to Florida and across to the Bahamas, sailing parties out of Miami and returning to Maine the following spring. In 1950 Philip Hussey of Kennebunkport bought her and kept her in Cape Porpoise. He used her for day sailing and an annual cruise to the eastward. A little regretfully, he installed a wheel and had a dacron mainsail made for her in 1955, feeling they were a little out of character, but . . . . William H. Taylor wrote a good article about her in the December 1946 issue of *Yachting*.

Eastward.

In 1961 *Wilbur A. Morse* sailed in the first regatta under C. Wilfred Brann of Gardiner and Friendship. In 1975 she was owned by Karl Heiser of Cundy's Harbor, and in 1981 Thomas Olson became a co-owner. *Wilbur A. Morse* is a handsome vessel and, with her big mainsail, looks as if she should be fast, but too often at the regattas in Friendship her sail has not been well set, and she has not done herself justice. In 1984 she was again for sale as her owners were leaving the state of Maine.

*Nimbus* is a backyard boat, built far from her natural habitat by A.T. Chenault III of New Orleans. He wrote: "I wanted a good cruising boat that would not pound, one that would sail on her bottom, a keel boat, and one that would not sink by the stern if more than six people sat in the cockpit at one time." Extensive research convinced him that a Friendship sloop was what he wanted, but in 1951 he could find no plans. Having owned a Crosby cat, he wrote to William F. Crosby asking for information on Friendship sloops and received the answer, "Friendship sloops were built in Friendship, Maine, from no plans. None have been built in more than 40 years. The plan is as out of date as the dodo and cannot compare with modern designs. Sorry, no plans available."

But then Chenault came upon William H. Taylor's article about *Wilbur A. Morse* in the December 1946 *Yachting*. He obtained her plans from Carlton Simmons, and in November 1952 set up a sloop in Madisonville, Louisiana. Her stem, rudder post, and horn timbers are mahogany, frames mulberry, and keel pine. She is planked with mahogany and fastened with copper rivets. Her mast is pine, and other spars are spruce. She is ballasted with three tons of iron inside. Chenault built her in two years of weekends with the help of Louis LeFrere, an experienced builder, and Mrs. Chenault. *Nimbus* was launched in February 1954 and showed herself a very capable sea boat, keeping her rail dry in 20- to 25-knot winds in open water. In 1969 she was registered with the Friendship Sloop Society by Fred Sevigart of New Orleans; in 1984 he still owned her.

*Eastward* is a 32-foot sloop designed by Murray G. Peterson of South Bristol, Maine, in 1954 for the author. We had three young sons we wanted to get on the water. We had all summer free but needed to bring in some income, so we decided to sail parties out of Boothbay Harbor, using our sons as crew. We wanted a Friendship sloop because the same characteristics that made her a good fishing boat made her a good party boat. She is stiff, dry, and roomy, as well as handy and good looking. Peterson designed exactly what we wanted, and she was built in Pemaquid Beach by James Chadwick, working pretty much alone. Her timbers are gray oak, and her lower four planks are oak. The rest of her planking is Philippine mahogany, and her deck is pine. She was launched in May 1956 and delivered "bare hull" in June. We had prepared her rigging in advance, so we rigged her, bent on her sails made by Clarence Hale in Sargentville, and sailed her to Boothbay, where we spent a month fitting out. Since then we have extended the house to accommodate four people cruising and added a topmast with gaff topsail and jib topsail. *Eastward* won the Lash Brothers trophy in the 1961 regatta and was first to finish and first overall in that race. She has done very well since.

*Eastward* has served not only as a party boat, but also as a base for research for *A Cruising Guide To The New England Coast*, and is recognized from Newport, Rhode Island, to Saint John, New Brunswick. Her more detailed history is recounted in a book, *Eastward*.

Finally, we must chronicle the short, sad history of *Emmie B.* She was built and owned by Reginald Wilcox, son of a Newfoundland fisherman, himself a fisherman and for ten years mate on Captain Bob Bartlett's arctic exploration schooner *Effie M. Morrissey*. In 1947 Wilcox became mate of Commander David Nutt's research schooner *Blue Dolphin*, in which he made more arctic voyages. He was a real deep-water seaman.

*Emmie B.'s keel in the woods. (Courtesy of Capt. Robin Colcord)* **Following pages:** *Emmie B. framed up. (Courtesy of Capt. Robin Colcord)* Emmie B. *partly planked.* Emmie B. *ready to launch. She was built from the* Nellie F. Parsons *model, an early Morse boat. Note the very slight hollow in the waterline.*

After having owned a Friendship sloop named *Little Andre* and sold her in 1947, he determined to build one of his own. He talked at length with Carlton Simmons and Winfield Lash and so impressed them with his seriousness and ability that he left with a set of plans drawn by Lash, probably based on Wilbur Morse's model of the *Nellie F. Parsons*.

In 1951, at home in Newington, Connecticut, Wilcox set up *Emmie B*. She was timbered with Connecticut white oak. Her keel was 31 feet long, 29 inches wide, and five inches thick and was cut out entirely with a hand saw. It took 48 working hours. She was planked and decked with yellow pine. After she was finished in 1958, Wilcox moved to Boothbay and brought her with him. She was flush decked with only a skylight, a companionway, and a wheel box for deck structures, and she had quite a high rail – perhaps six inches or more. She was somewhat underrigged for a Friendship sloop, as her skipper planned to go to sea in her. She first appeared as a member of the Friendship Sloop Society fleet in 1969 and sailed in several regattas. But in 1974, while lying at her mooring off Brewer's Boat Yard in Southport, Maine, she caught fire from a short circuit and was towed ashore in order not to imperil other boats. She was a total loss. Her owner died soon after.

Thus, we come to the fall of 1960 and the significant race of the Boston Power Squadron. What few original Friendship sloops were still afloat in 1960 had either been substantially rebuilt or were in dire need of such attention. They and the few that had been built since 1920 were all yachts, and most of them had had their rigs shortened to make them "easy to handle." Thus cut down, they were heavy, slow, and logy. In the yachting community they were admired for their graceful design but laughed at for their stodgy ways. Their owners, however, appear to have been inordinately proud of them and of the Friendship tradition. When Captain Robin Colcord wrote to all the Friendship sloop owners he could locate in 1955, he received enthusiastic replies, many of which have proved useful in the preparation of this book. In 1961, when Bernard W. MacKenzie, Earl Banner, John Gould, and a number of Friendship residents started the Friendship Sloop Society, response was quick, eager, and unexpectedly large. The Friendship sloop tradition had neither decayed nor died; it was merely dormant.

Emmie B. *under way. (All the* Emmie B. *photos above by courtesy of Capt. Robin Colcord)*

7

## *T*he Friendship Sloop Society

*O*n September 17, 1960, the Boston Power Squadron organized a race for auxiliaries called colloquially a "bang-and-go-back" race. The idea was to develop an
automatic handicap in terms of distance, rather than time. When the first boat reached
a "scoring mark," a gun was to be fired, and all boats could then head for the next mark.
Sixteen boats started: four racing sloops; two yawls; a schooner; and a Friendship
sloop, *Voyager*, owned by Bernard MacKenzie of Scituate, Massachusetts. She was a
Charles Morse boat built in 1906 and largely rebuilt in 1946. *Voyager* was 15th at the
start, ninth at the first mark, eighth at the next. When the gun sounded for all vessels to
up helm and run for the finish line, *Voyager* swung off her 450 square feet of mainsail
before an 18-knot easterly and began to show what she could do. The breeze increased
as the fleet ran in among the islands of Boston Harbor, *Voyager* leading. Astern came the
racing fleet, lugging their spinnakers, rolling down heavily in the puffs. *Voyager* fled
down the wind, running for home, and crossed the finish line first.

Due to vagaries of the handicapping system, *Alcyone* won the race, but MacKenzie
was awarded third place and, far more important to him, he had crossed the line first,
ahead of all the five-figure modern yachts, in a Friendship sloop.

He was justly proud of *Voyager*'s achievement, so proud that he conceived the idea of
a race for Friendship sloops to be held in Friendship the following summer. He wrote
first to Carlton Simmons, Friendship's postmaster and nephew of Wilbur Morse,
because he thought he had corresponded with Carlton previously about Charles Morse

and *Voyager*'s background; but he had Carlton confused with Harvey Simmons, from whom he had had a most informative letter in 1952. The confusion was a happy one, for Carlton at once responded, calling in Herold Jones, a semiretired professor and head of the Village Improvement Association. Next MacKenzie went to Earl Banner, a sports writer for the *Boston Globe* who had written an account of the race. Banner was enthusiastic about a race at Friendship and suggested that they talk with John Gould, editor of the Lisbon Falls paper and contributor to the *Christian Science Monitor*. A meeting was arranged in late February 1961 at Herold Jones's home. Invited were MacKenzie and his friend Gleason, John Gould, Carlton Simmons, and Herold Jones. The matter of a race was discussed and considerable objection raised on the ground that the town of Friendship did not have the facilities to accommodate the crowds that might be attracted. However, MacKenzie had already given a story to the *Maine Coast Fisherman*'s March issue announcing the race. It was a *fait accompli*, and all hands turned to to make the affair a success.

It was suggested that a Friendship Sloop Society be formed to sponsor the race, henceforth to be called a regatta. The Society was incorporated on April 23, 1961, with MacKenzie as president; state Representative Ralph Winchenpaw, vice-president; Carlton Simmons, treasurer; and Herold Jones, secretary. Trustees consisted of the elected officers of the Society and the selectmen of Friendship: Bernard Brow, Charles Sylvester, and Frank Foster. A Town Committee was appointed, including Betty Roberts, wife of Al Roberts, one of Friendship's principal lobster buyers.

But MacKenzie had not waited for formal incorporation. He had approached the governor of Maine, John Reed, through Reed's friend Philip Hussey, then owner of *Wilbur A. Morse*. He had sent releases to the Associated Press, *Yachting*, the *New York Times*, the *Boston Globe*, the *Quincy Patriot-Ledger*, and even a paper in New Jersey. After the incorporation, he followed up with *Down East* magazine and continued to supply all of these publications and the *Maine Coast Fisherman* with frequent news flashes. He had also written a number of sloop owners whom he knew or who had risen to the surface in response to the newspaper and magazine coverage. Before the Society was formed, even before anyone in Friendship had agreed to have a race, he had signed up eight sloop owners to enter the contest, six of whom actually came.

Governor Reed proclaimed July 22 as Friendship Day and agreed to be present to award the Governor's Cup, donated by the Department of Economic Development.

The Friendship Town Meeting voted to appropriate the money usually given to the Maine Publicity Bureau to the support of the regatta. Stationery, applications, and membership cards were printed, and members began to join in satisfying numbers.

As the date of the race approached, more entries came in. Besides the Governor's Cup for the first sloop built before 1920, the Lash Brothers Boatyard donated a trophy for the winning replica sloop. Cyrus Hamlin, a distinguished naval architect and consultant to the Cruising Club of America on handicapping, designed a simplified handicapping system for Friendship sloops, based on distance rather than time, whereby each boat would sail away from the course a distance proportional to its handicap and there pick up a buoy set for it. Thus, the first boat to finish was the winner. However, when the day came, the handicap buoys all sank, so Cy Hamlin refigured the handicaps on the conventional seconds-per-mile basis while the race was in progress.

George Morrill of Burnham & Morrill in Portland offered his motor-sailer as a committee boat, equipped with a brass cannon from the War of 1812. Leon E. Nickerson, ex-commodore of the Edgewood Yacht Club, agreed to be chairman of the race committee. The Friendship Day Committee set up an information booth, planned a printed program, had trophies engraved, alerted the Coast Guard to patrol the course with power-squadron boats from Boothbay and Rockland, secured press boats, and made dinner arrangements, most of this through the efforts of Herold Jones, Betty Roberts, and the Town Committee.

As July 22 came closer, MacKenzie organized a Friendship fleet to sail from Massachusetts, and sloops from Maine harbors headed toward Friendship.

About this time, a significant event occurred in Boothbay. *Eastward* had been sailing parties out of the Boothbay region since 1956. A summer resident, Winthrop Bancroft, became interested in Friendship sloops, inspected *Mary Anne* in Friendship in July 1961, and was much impressed. He asked where he could sail a Friendship sloop and was referred to the writer. Accordingly, he chartered *Eastward* for half a day and, with the writer and his son, tried her out. He found her to be just what he wanted but thought that *Mary Anne* was faster. Indeed, at first, he declared that *Mary Anne* would win the coming race at Friendship easily.

In the course of our sail, we crossed Linekin Bay and noticed a beautiful, varnished sloop casting off from Paul Luke's yard. Bancroft recognized her as a Sparkman & Stevens designed yacht that he had seen launched the day before and spoke of her as undoubtedly one of the fastest boats afloat. We passed to leeward of her on opposite courses, tacked, and sailed right by her to windward. Of course, we were on a reach, our best point of sailing. The new boat set no genoa jib, and her sails and rigging had not been stretched out; she was not at her best. Nevertheless, Bancroft at once switched his bets to *Eastward* and, as soon as he got ashore, called upon Murray Peterson, *Eastward*'s designer, for a replica of *Eastward*. J. Ervin Jones built this boat in the winter of 1961-1962, and Bancroft named her *Elicia III*. So began the revival of the Friendship sloop.

The day of the race was clear and warm with a pleasant southerly breeze. On the beat down to Black Island, the fleet sorted itself out. As they passed north of Hall's Island on a reach across toward Thompson Island, three replicas, *Eastward*, John Dallett's *Mary Anne*, and John Thorpe's *Ellie T.*, were ahead and within a biscuit-toss of each other. The two reaches and the ensuing run up the west side of Friendship Long Island separated them, and they finished in that order, *Eastward* the winner by 20 minutes. As she crossed the line, the 1812 cannon fired a magnificent charge of black powder, emitting not only a loud report and a cloud of smoke, but also a flaming wad of oakum that landed in *Eastward*'s cockpit. *Eastward* was awarded the Lash Brothers trophy; and MacKenzie's *Voyager*, the fourth boat and the first sloop built before 1920 to finish, won the Governor's Cup.

At the banquet that evening, Wilbert Snow of Spruce Head, a 77-year-old poet, read by the light of a shaky candle a long and colorful poem that he had written about a Fourth of July fisherman's race. John Gould served as master of ceremonies. Governor Reed presented the awards, and the first annual regatta was over – a great success. (See the Appendix for the detailed racing record.)

MacKenzie continued writing letters indefatigably, gaining coverage for the regatta in Rockland, Portland, and Boston papers as well as in *Down East* and various yachting publications. He then planned a meeting of the Society at the Boston Yacht Club in Marblehead for November 25. Bill Haskell of *Golden Eagle* made the arrangements.

No one took attendance, but the minutes state that the dining room was "filled to capacity." After a brief movie and Carlton Simmons's financial report, it was resolved to hold a three-day regatta in 1962. It was proposed that a course be laid out to bring the

**Opposite page:** Voyager. *(Carlton Simmons)* **Opposite below:** *Start of the first regatta of the Friendship Sloop Society in 1961.* Mary Anne *is leading with* Eastward *close astern and to windward. The finish of the first race.* Eastward *first across the line and the winner on corrected time.*

*Al and Betty Roberts receive a token of the Society's appreciation. John Gould on the left; Bill Danforth and Bob Lash on the right.*

contestants through Morse's Bay and Garrison Island passage to finish in the harbor. It was also proposed that the start be made with all boats anchored on the line, sails furled and crew below. These schemes were tried and found too complicated.

The only other matter of lasting interest was the election of Betty Roberts as secretary. She had served on the Town Committee and had assumed much of the committee's responsibility. As secretary, she became the force that held the Society together for many years. She has been quick to make friends, thoughtful, sympathetic, and very accommodating. She has also been efficient and energetic, quick to answer letters, respond to requests, and take care of the innumerable details that arise day after day, year after year. The Society's annual booklet was dedicated to her in 1976 with this citation.

> She is Friendship's sweetheart, and although honored only by the term "secretary," she is everything to the Friendship Sloop Society from custodian of cannon ammunition to *garde-malade* in sickness and cheer-leader in health. The Society will never have, and neither will Fort Knox, enough money to recompense her for her unstinting faithfulness to Friendship Sloopers. Smiling, she answers the good letters, and smiling she does the drudgery of replying to odd correspondence that she should (probably) file in the cuddy. As secretary, only she can do a good part of this booklet. She arranges, manages, and supervises all meetings, and her notes at the speakers' table are explicit, competent, adequate, ample, and correct. ("What's next?" . . . "Ask Betty.")
>
> She buys the trophies, calls the newspapers with race results and other stories, tells inquiring tourists about motels, arranges accommodations for reporters and photographers, finds waitresses for the skippers' banquet, takes orders for the beer

run, finds berths for would-be crew members, feeds transient sloopers, remembers everybody, loves everybody, and finds time to do many other things.

Locally, she fritters her idle time in good deeds – visiting shut-ins and elderly on schedule, bringing goodies and brightening each corner. She is a registered ambulance attendant and drops all else if the 'phone rings and a run to the hospital comes up. She paints better than most, does needlework, and she could teach Oscar how to cook. Each morning she telephones about half the homes in Friendship to be sure all is well, and if all is not well – "What can I do?"

Unfortunately, Betty is "from away." Born in Lexington, Massachusetts, her training in Physical Education brought her to Friendship (with Al) as an attendant at Oceanward Camp. They bought a home here, and bought the Wallace lobster wharf. Thank God, they'll never leave.

For so many things, and for being you, we thank you, Betty Roberts, we love you – and with no strings attached we dedicate this Sloop Days booklet and the Bicentennial Regatta to you. To the Friendship Sloop Society, Queen Elizabeth is here.

Through the years, Betty has received many other expressions of the Society's appreciation.

In 1977 she resigned as secretary but continues, whether she intended to or not, as fountain of all wisdom on Friendship sloops and recently as historian of the Society.

One of the problems that early beset the Society was that of defining a Friendship sloop. "A sloop built in Friendship by Wilbur Morse," was scarcely adequate, as it included centerboard boats and excluded all the boats he and others had built on Bremen Long Island as well as boats built by other builders elsewhere. The Society's best effort has proved not only historically inaccurate but useless as a means of classifying a particular boat as a Friendship sloop. Thus far, however, no one has done better.

The Society has defined a Friendship sloop as "one built from the models* of the Morse family, originating at Friendship, Maine. The hull must possess the original Morse lines, comprising the distinctive bilges, deep sloping keel running full length, hollow garboards, sharp clipper bow, and overhanging stern with elliptical transom. The approved rig must be a gaff main with the customary working jib or jib and staysail. Although the original scale plans may be reduced somewhat, the following specifications are applicable:

1. The mast is located one-fifth of the waterline length abaft the stem.
2. Beam is one-third the waterline length.
3. Length of mast should equal the length overall plus half the draft.
4. Length of boom is equal to length overall.
5. Bowsprit overhang is equal to one-third the length of the boom.

The installation of an auxiliary engine and modification of the cockpit, cabin house, and interior to suit cruising accommodations are acceptable. Wheel or tiller is optional."

This definition is more of a description than a definition. It excludes all sloops other than those built by Morse, McLain, Simmons, or Carter or from models other than theirs. Also, the reader will see at once that none of the sloops built since 1960 can meet the test. An authentication committee of three, Winfield Lash, Cyrus Hamlin, and Murray Peterson, with Howard Chapelle as final authority, discussed the point, debated length-beam ratios to the second decimal place, and developed technical requirements to which no one was likely to build. They were superseded by a group of owners who judged boats "by eye," inexpertly and probably unfairly.

* *Sloops built by Carter, McLain, or Simmons are accepted as having originated from Morse models.*

The fact must be admitted that accurate physical definition of the Friendship sloop is impossible. A romantic paragraph the author wrote for *Enduring Friendships* may be the best that can be done:

> A Friendship sloop is a gaff-rigged sloop with a fisherman look about her. A Friendship sloop is a beautiful fusion of form and function. A Friendship sloop is a state of mind composed of independence, tradition, resourcefulness, and a fortuitous combination of geography and language in the name of Friendship.

Sarah Mead, *built by Newbert & Wallace for Dr. Henry White. (Carlton Simmons)*

During the winter of 1961 and the spring of 1962, the Society noted increased interest in Friendship sloops, however they were defined. At least seven new sloops were under construction: *Hieronymus* by Ralph Stanley in Southwest Harbor; *Patience* by Malcolm Brewer in Camden; *Sarah Mead* by Newbert and Wallace in Thomaston; *Elicia III* by J. Ervin Jones in East Boothbay; *Friendship* by Fred Dion in Salem; and *Content* by Stuart Ford at Bailey's Island.

Murray Peterson had for many years been interested in adapting commercial designs for yachts. He had been working with John Alden when Alden developed the Malabar schooners from round-bowed fishermen. Later, Peterson designed a successful series of schooners based on Maine coasters. As noted earlier, he designed *Eastward*, *Elicia III*, and later *Ollie M.* in the Friendship sloop tradition. In 1961 he adapted the design of the Rockport sloop to a pretty yacht, *Heritage*, built by Elmer Collemer in Camden for Bill

*Content, built by Stuart Ford at Bailey's Island.*

Downeaster *and* Mary Anne,
*both built by Lash Brothers.*

and Barbara Hadlock of South Freeport. While too full forward to be classed as a replica of a Friendship sloop, *Heritage*'s clipper bow and gaff topsail rig easily qualified her in Class C, a near replica. She has been a prominent member of the Friendship fleet since 1962.

In addition, there were doubtless more Friendships started in barns, garages, and side yards by eager amateur builders working nights and weekends, scrounging fittings and inventing what they could not buy. The seven boats listed above took from two to five years to finish and joined the fleet as they were launched during the 1960s.

By 1971 the Society's roster had grown to 123 sloops with 16 more listed as nonmembers. The regatta had grown from 14 starters in 1961 to 41 in 1970. There were no races in 1971 because of three days of fog. Not counting sloops launched in 1971, the Society's first 10 years saw at least 32 new wooden sloops launched and at least 10 fiberglass sloops built. This does not include some boats of whose exact dates we are uncertain and includes only those registered with the Society; the great Friendship revival doubtless includes many more.

Of the wooden boats, Lash Brothers Boatyard built three, *Downeaster* for Randolph Major, *Dirigo* for Ernest Sprowl, and *Rights of Man* for Philip Cronin. The yard also built *Voyager II* for Bernard MacKenzie and *Amicitia* for Colpoys, but because MacKenzie did not want to follow the lines developed for *Mary Anne* and the other three from the

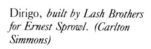

Dirigo, *built by Lash Brothers for Ernest Sprowl. (Carlton Simmons)*

Rights of Man.

Amicitia, *built by Lash Brothers for Dr. Francis Colpoys. (Boutilier Photos)*

Morse model of *Nellie F. Parsons*, Winfield Lash refuses to call them Friendship sloops. The Society, taking a more liberal view, included them in Class B. *Downeaster, Dirigo,* and *Rights of Man* were all built to the same model except that the last has an iron keel instead of lead. She is perhaps a little more tender, a characteristic accentuated by a jib topsail of impressive proportions. All four, including *Mary Anne*, are simply and strongly built in the Morse tradition and have always done well racing. *Dirigo* was shipped to New York and launched at the 1964 World's Fair. On one occasion, she won the Maine Retired Skippers' Race at Castine.

*Nancy* was also built in Friendship, another of Carlton Simmons's contributions to the revival.

McKie Roth, building in a shop in Edgecomb on the Sheepscot River, produced *Galatea, Eagle,* and *Avoir. Margaret Motte* was built by Roger Morse, grandson of Charles Morse, in Thomaston.

Jim Rockefeller, in a yard near the top of Bald Mountain, built *Old Baldy, Windward,* and *Puffin*. He also rebuilt *Sazerac*.

*Sazerac*, a 33-foot sloop built in 1913 by Wilbur Morse, has a rather unusual cocked-up stern, recognizable from afar. In 1945 Clinton D. Merrill of Falmouth, Maine, bought her from a family named Lilliput, who had purchased her for $250 "as is," after she had lain hauled up in Portland for several years. The Lilliputs, just married, spent $3,500 fixing her up and, with a professional captain, took her to the Great Lakes via the Hudson River.

Clinton Merrill had her rebuilt in 1947, replanking her with 1½" hard pine, each plank running the full length of the vessel with no butts, and he extended the cabin house. Under his ownership, she was a familiar sight on the Maine coast until 1954, when she was driven ashore near the Portland Yacht Club in the same hurricane that wrecked *Georgie C. Bowden* in the same place.

Robert Dillenbeck bought her as she lay in a muddy cove behind a ledge, repaired her, dug a trench at low water, and floated her out at high water, pretty much on her side. He had her recaulked and replaced several planks and her rudder.

Above left: Eagle, *built by McKie Roth in Edgecomb for Dr. Groetzinger. (Boutilier Photos)* Above right: Spirit, *ex-*Symbolon, *ex-*Margaret Motte, *built by Roger Morse in Thomaston. (T. Gray)* Below: Old Baldy, *built by James Rockefeller to the lines of* Pemaquid *and later used to make the mold for Jarvis Newman's 25-foot fiberglass sloops.*

*Sazerac in 1983, reefed down.*
*(T. Gray)*

At various times she has been named *Cheryl Lynne* and *Ranger*. When she was ashore after the hurricane in 1954, she was named *Sazerac* and has carried that name ever since.

In 1965 the boat was registered in the Friendship Sloop Society under the ownership of Clinton Merrill, who evidently had bought her back. The next year, she was owned by George B. Morrill of Portland. He raced her each year in the annual regatta, and in 1969 and 1970 she was the flagship of the Friendship fleet. During the winter of 1966-1967, he had her largely rebuilt by Rockefeller's Bald Mountain Boat Works.

In 1972 she was owned by Newton Hinckley of Sudbury and the next year by Roland Barth of Alna and a syndicate of his friends. Since then, she has sailed in almost every regatta, one of the most distinguished of the "original" class.

Many of the other sloops were built by individuals and can be found in the Society's roster at the end of this volume.

The fiberglass sloops and the amateur builders deserve chapters to themselves as do those who tackled the even more difficult task of rebuilding old sloops.

While the Society, and especially its founder, Bernard MacKenzie, deserve great credit for this renaissance, mention should be made of Joe Richards, a marine artist who acquired an ancient Wilbur Morse sloop, *Princess*, in Flushing, Long Island, in 1938. She was in sad shape, but Richards rebuilt her and sailed her to Florida and back. Then he wrote about his experience in the book *Princess*, published in 1956. Joe Richards, to judge from his book, is a sentimental man, one who falls in love with a boat and buys her without going aboard. Yet he is enough of a practical realist to rebuild her. He invested *Princess* with a personality and with her overcame perils of the sea, the shore, and the canals between. There is no record of how many people read *Princess* and now own Friendship sloops, but surely, they are many.

When the Society was founded, Richards heard of it and offered to trade one of his paintings for the expense of trucking *Princess* from Florida to Friendship. However, the negotiations collapsed, and while *Princess* is listed as No. 195 on the Society's roster, she has never returned to Friendship.

Mention should be made too of John Biddle, who made a 16mm. sound movie from *Eastward* in the 1962 race and showed it widely around the country. The film showed the Friendship sloop at its best.

Carlton Simmons also deserves considerable credit for the revival of the Friendship sloop. Not only did he build *Wilbur A. Morse,* as described in an earlier chapter, but also he developed a number of sets of Friendship sloop lines from Wilbur Morse models and shared them with interested people, at least two of whom, Chenault in Louisiana and Wilcox in Connecticut, actually built Friendship sloops. He also planned seriously to build two more sloops side by side in 1961-1962 at the suggestion of Bernard MacKenzie, but the plan fell through, and he built only one, *Nancy.* He served as treasurer of the Society and took numerous pictures of sloops, many of which were published in newspapers, magazines, and the Society's books and annual booklets.

From 1962 through 1970, regular regattas have been held at Friendship on Thursday, Friday, and Saturday of the last full weekend in July; and although fog occasionally forced the cancellation of a race, at least one or two races were sailed every year. In 1962 and 1963, at least one race each year was run around Morse Island and finished with a beat up the harbor. After several near collisions and the crushing of a moored skiff between two sloops, that course was abandoned. In 1962 the sloops started from anchor, an exciting experiment leading to a few minor collisions and some frantic anchor pulling and sail setting. Aboard *Eastward,* a well-oiled snap shackle at the head of the topsail unhooked with the sail part way up. An eager young deck hand scrambled up halyards and mast hoops, snapped the shackle on, and moused it. As the topsail was mast-headed, the snap shackle on the sheet let go and ran out to the cheek block at the end of the gaff. The same deck hand, still standing on the gaff jaws, shouted down to the skipper at the wheel, "Shall I go out and get it?"

"No," answered the skipper.

But already the boy was out on the gaff, clinging to the spar and the peak halyard. He grabbed the shackle and was in with it.

"It was alright," he said afterwards. "I was over the water all the time."

The Society faced many problems brought up by the regatta. Sloops built before 1921, whether or not ever rebuilt, were Class A. Replicas, wooden boats built close to traditional lines, were Class B. Class C consisted of gaff-headed sloops more or less in the Friendship tradition, and in 1969 Class D was established for any sloop in the Friendship tradition not built of wood. All distinctions except that of Class A have now been dropped.

A considerable controversy arose in the Society over the use of racing sails. It was early decided in the interests of preserving tradition and of preventing expensive excesses that only working sails should be used. This clearly outlawed spinnakers. However, it soon appeared that old-timers in summer used gaff topsails and jib topsails. These, then, were accepted and included in the handicap measurement. Then arose the question of how big a jib could be carried. Clearly, genoa jibs were not working sails. How far aft could a working jib come? It was at length decided that no sail could be sheeted outside the after shroud. But this outlawed jib topsails. So after extensive discussion, it was agreed that no jib could overlap the mast. This simplified the measurement procedure, for now it is not necessary to measure each jib, merely to measure the area of the fore triangle.

The handicapping system established penalty points, a means of preventing any one sloop from winning consistently. Any sloop that won a race had a five-percent added penalty, compounded. At first rather successful, *Eastward* accumulated such a handicap that it was said only half in jest that her crew must land on Hog Island bar and dig a hod of clams in order to continue the race. Penalty points have since been eliminated.

The matter of racing rules came before various committees, formal and informal. The intention was to sail by North American Yacht Racing Union rules. Many of the skippers had never seen these rules, which fill a booklet big enough to choke a shark. Some, indeed, apparently did not know the difference between port tack and starboard, and rules concerning barging the starting line, overlap at buoys, amd luffing rights were to them uncharted waters. Race committee chairman Bill Danforth at first patiently and then impatiently explained the difference between port and starboard tacks year after year, but even today some skippers in any crossing situation simply bellow "starboard!" and hold their course.

Even so, there are few protests and surprisingly few collisions, perhaps because the sight of a 10-ton sloop under a cloud of sail bearing down on your beloved living antique engenders a generous spirit that yields the right of way. Bill Danforth in *White Falcon*, anchored to establish one end of the starting line, found himself a sitting duck when a dozen sloops, ignorant of the barging rule, swept bowsprits over his cockpit. He set a buoy 30 yards off his stern for a starting mark and threatened disqualification for any sloop passing between it and *White Falcon*. That did not teach anyone the barging rule, however, and there was often close work around the buoy. On the whole, though, the races were conducted by all hands with good spirit and a feeling of camaraderie. This was especially evident whenever the fleet lay becalmed, and both beer and conversation passed freely between boats.

*Start of a race off Friendship. The committee boat is clearly in peril. (Irving Nevells Photographs)*

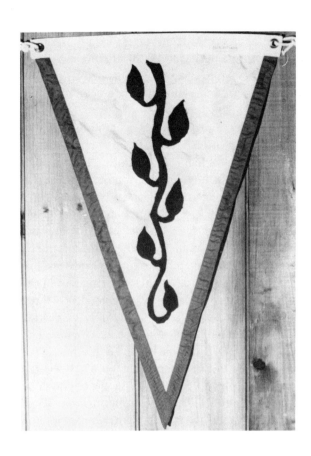

*Club burgee.*

One innovation was the establishment of a regatta off Marblehead, Massachusetts, in the late summer. This was started in 1963 with Bill Haskell of *Golden Eagle* in charge and the Boston Yacht Club managing the race and holding a party afterwards for contestants and friends. Nine sloops participated. Bill Haskell and Don Huston continued in charge until 1968, when Lincoln Ridgway took over and ran the event with the help of the Corinthian Yacht Club until his death in 1980. David Graham then took over. This annual race is much enjoyed by Massachusetts owners who find it a long way down east to Friendship and by many Massachusetts yachtsmen who seldom see two gaff-rigged boats at the same time.

With several fiberglass sloops built in 1969 by Bruno and Stillman and by Jarvis Newman, the question arose of the relative speeds of these boats and wooden boats. It was decided with the aid of Cy Hamlin, fiberglass builders, and boat owners of all classes to establish a Class D for any boat not built of wood, to give Class D separate awards, but to have all classes start together. After several years, it was hoped that experience would have shown the relative merits of the two materials. This arrangement proved satisfactory for a time. However, a quick look at the racing results suggests that rig is more important than hull material, and that the computer inside the hat of the skipper is probably the most important single factor involved. Except for special awards, Class D has now been dropped and the boats have raced against each other since 1982.

Early in the Society's existence, a burgee was designed and distributed among members. It is a white pennant with a red border on which in black is the traditional olive leaf design used on the trail boards of Morse boats.

Not all the Society's attention, however, was taken up with activity afloat. In 1963 the Town of Friendship, mostly through the efforts of Al Roberts, set up a museum to preserve records and artifacts of the town's maritime heritage. To this the Society voted $500 and continues annually to support it. The museum was established in the old brick schoolhouse, and the first curator was Carrie McFarland, who had been to school in the building and was the granddaughter of Jonah Morse.

In 1966 the Society set up a scholarship fund to be supported by voluntary contributions and any other fundraising method the Society could devise. The income was to be divided in two parts, half for an endowment fund and half for distribution to deserving Friendship residents seeking to carry their educations beyond high school. Interest was to be applied to the endowment fund until such time as that fund was large enough to produce significant interest to add to distribution. Bill Pendleton assumed the chairmanship of this fund. The names of other members of the committee were not publicized, but one was a member of the School Committee; another was Al Roberts. The 1966 annual meeting voted $200 to get the fund started and another $200 in 1967. In 1968 the fund was named the Beatrice Pendleton Memorial Scholarship in honor of the chairman's wife, who had died suddenly. In that year, awards were made to three students. The committee had begun actively canvassing for contributions, suggesting that each skipper contribute 10 percent of his annual outfitting cost. Large blue and white badges, suitable for hat or jacket and legible from one sloop to another, were given to recognize contributions. Ice was supplied free to sloop owners on Al Roberts's wharf in return for a contribution. The young people of Friendship who waited on table at the awards banquet contributed their tip money. Seilers, a catering firm of which Newton Hinckley, owner of *Flying Jib,* was a member, provided the dinner for the awards banquet at no cost to the Society, all ticket money going to the Scholarship Fund.

John Gould, true to character, came up with the most colorful device yet. He persuaded Jerry Froiano of Portland to donate to the Society an old-fashioned whistling peanut roaster that Jerry's father had bought secondhand in 1905. Then John persuaded his cousin Ralph, who owned a machine shop, to put the roaster in first-class operating condition. After a successful test run, John bought 100 pounds of raw peanuts and, during Sloop Days 1970, went into operation. In subsequent years, the peanuts have been donated by a Portland grocery firm and the peanut cart supervised by Friendship girls. At the awards banquet each year, the gross income, about $200 in small change, jingles into the treasury. Not to be outdone by John, Dorothy Gould set up a gift shop, solicited donations of salable items, some of them beautifully handmade, and sold them to the crowds who gathered to watch the sloops. By the fall of 1971, the fund had an endowment of nearly $6,000 and was annually helping several students finance their higher education.

During the winter of 1961-1962, Herold Jones edited a paperbound book, *Ships That Came Home,* containing many of Carlton Simmons's photographs, brief articles about early builders, and pictures and descriptions of sloops then members of the Society. Over 500 copies were sold within the year.

The Society published a second book, *It's a Friendship,* in 1965. This volume was put together largely by Herold Jones, first secretary of the Society and one of the strong moving forces behind it in its earliest days. It reflects his scholarly approach to the project. After an introduction by Howard I. Chapelle comes a detailed account of the Society's formation and the preparations for the first regatta, an article by John Gould giving a woodsman's view of the regatta, an article on handicapping by Cy Hamlin, excellent pictures and brief biographies of many of the sloops registered with the Society, and, most valuable of all, accounts of early builders written when some of them or their near relations were available for interviews with recollections still sharp. It was printed by Seth Low Press, bound in hard covers, and sold for $4.95. The first 2,000 copies were numbered; the next 1,000 were not. All were quickly sold. *It's a Friendship* is now, as it deserves to be, a collector's item. Professor Jones continued to help the Society in a variety of ways, from mopping out the rest rooms on Friendship Day to writing a fantasy based solidly on fact for *Enduring Friendships,* the Society's third book. The 1977 annual booklet of the Society bids him an affectionate farewell.

*Enduring Friendships* was engineered mainly by Al Roberts, lobster buyer and owner of the wharf that served as headquarters for the Society's activity on Friendship Days. Before he undertook *Enduring Friendships,* Roberts had done several annual booklets. He persuaded Howard I. Chapelle to write a foreword; Bill Thon, a well-known artist and sloop owner, to contribute sketches; and a galaxy consisting of Herold Jones, John Gould, J. Malcolm Barter, Edward Coffin, Cyrus Hamlin, James Rockefeller, and the present writer to contribute articles. He wrote one himself and found Carlton Simmons and others ready with photographs. The result was an accurate and readable book, illustrated with excellent photographs and again fortified with sloop biographies and plans. The book was published by International Marine Publishing Company of Camden and sold for $11.95. It is long out of print and is a rare bird today.

Annually, the Society publishes a booklet containing the program for Friendship Days and articles of historical or nostalgic interest. This is financed by advertising from local businesses. For years, Al Roberts undertook the formidable annual task, succeeded by John Gould, then by Bruce Morang, John de Sousa, and Caroline Zuber. Recently, the mantle has fallen upon this writer.

From 1971 until 1984, there have been few fundamental changes in the Society. The roster has grown to 221 sloops with 24 more known but unregistered. Of the total list, several sloops have been lost or have deteriorated beyond salvage, accounts of which are given in the Appendix. Class C has been eliminated, its members included in Class B. Class A, the "originals," is smaller and is now composed entirely of rebuilt sloops, some recently rebuilt so completely as to contain scarcely a spike or stick of the original. In most cases, the original had deteriorated before rebuilding to the point at which she was badly deformed, so the rebuilder had to restore what he believed to be her original lines. Nevertheless, although such a boat is practically new, she is still an original, races in Class A for the Eda Lawry Cup, and may fly a long, blue pennant from her peak. The Society so voted in 1982 with the intent of preserving the idea if not the fabric of the original Friendship sloops.

From 1971 to 1983, 45 new wooden Friendship sloops were built. Ralph Stanley built three, Nick Roth built one, and Harvey Gamage built one. All the rest were done by amateur builders. Bruno and Stillman built 10 fiberglass sloops, and Jarvis Newman supplied 28 fiberglass hulls, some of which were finished out by the owners. These, of course, represent only sloops registered with the Society, but even so, it is a phenomenal increase, especially considering that a Friendship sloop is not easy to build.

To illustrate and commemorate the building and sailing of Friendship sloops, Lowell Wentworth spent a number of years compiling an excellent movie and television tape of Ralph Stanley building *Endeavor,* of Jarvis Newman building a fiberglass Dictator, and of several skippers sailing their boats and talking about them. The film was completed in 1982 and shown both at the races and at the annual meeting. It is an outstanding production, both as a document and as a work of cinematographic art.

Annual races continued with the number of starters rising to 49 in 1973 and falling off to 29 in 1983. The reasons for the decline are many and not clearly defined. The exciting atmosphere of enthusiasm that sparked the early days has waned somewhat as the event has become standardized. Also, many sailors from the west found it less exciting to take almost their whole vacation voyaging to Maine and back. Adverse economic conditions of the 1980s and the rapidly escalating expense of keeping and fitting out a boat discouraged some. A feeling also grew, as a result of a very few unfortunate incidents, that the town of Friendship welcomed the visitors with something less than its original enthusiasm.

Accordingly, in 1984 it was planned to try an entirely different program. The Maine Maritime Museum in Bath invited the Society to visit its exhibits at the Percy & Small shipyard, where workers are rebuilding the steam tug *Seguin*, the arctic exploration schooner *Bowdoin,* and the Muscongus Bay sloop *Ranger*. The museum was also developing an exhibit of Maine inshore fishing and lobstering, in which Friendship sloop people were naturally interested. Following two days at Percy & Small's, which included a lobster bake and a concert, the fleet moved to Boothbay Harbor as guests of the yacht club there for three days of racing among the islands off Boothbay. The town, a busy tourist center, affords all the facilities that Friendship lacks: moorings, restaurants, motels, marine supplies, grocery stores near the shore, excursion boats for watching races, and entertainment facilities ashore. Nevertheless, many nostalgic sloop owners missed visiting Friendship and Muscongus Bay where the type originated, where there were many friends ashore, where Elbert Pratt fired a welcoming cannon from his front porch, and where the big Friendship Sloop Society burgee flew from the memorial flagpole.

As early as 1974, there was formal opposition to continuing the use of Handicap Alley, that is, handicapping by distance rather than time. While picking up a buoy is in the workboat tradition, it had been abandoned in favor of rounding a buoy. The setting of 40 buoys, the difficulty of keeping them on station, the perils involved in rounding buoys set close together, the crowding at marks, and the effects of varying wind conditions were adduced against the alley.

Nostalgia and inertia as well as the simplicity of calling the first boat across the finish line the winner were the arguments of the pro forces. The debate continued until 1983, when two races were run with the sloops starting in accordance with their time allowances. Thus, the first across the finish line was still the winner. In 1984, since it was impossible to lay out Handicap Alley in busy Boothbay Harbor, a time-based handicap system had to be used in all three races.

Other changes have also come to the Society. Bill Danforth, honorary member and chairman of the race committee, resigned in 1981. He had been a member of that committee since the first race in 1961 and had been chairman of it since 1963. He conducted each regatta with professional precision and in the spirit of the occasion. He was succeeded by Bruce Morang, for many years a member of *Chrissy*'s crew, and editor of the annual booklet for several years.

Carlton Simmons turned the treasurer's job over to Ernst Wiegleb, who has performed with devotion and accuracy. The 1983 annual meeting voted that the Beatrice Pendleton Scholarship Fund be set up as a separate trust; the fund now has an endowment of over $30,000. Since the death of Bill Pendleton, the fund has been renamed the Pendleton Trust. It continues to benefit Friendship students annually.

On Betty Roberts's resignation, Constance Pratt became secretary, succeeded in turn by Caroline Zuber. The burden of this job has increased steadily as a growing

*Close work in Handicap Alley.*
*(T. Gray)*

membership requires more paper work, more projects, and more meetings. In 1984 the job was divided between Caroline Zuber as Recording Secretary, and Beverly Hoonhout as Corresponding Secretary.

In 1977 John and Dot Gould also resigned from their official duties but have continued to be genial presences at every regatta. They have been made honorary members along with Cyrus Hamlin, Bill Danforth, Albert and Betty Roberts, Ernst Wiegleb, and David Graham.

The scope of the Society's activities outside Friendship has broadened considerably. In 1975 four sloops, *Cockle*, *Schoodic*, *Mary Anne*, and *Eastward*, participated in the reenactment of the Arnold expedition to Quebec, transporting a group of colonially-clad "soldiers" from Newburyport up the Kennebec River to Pittston.

In 1980, several sloops, including *Ollie M.* and *Eagle*, participated in OPSail in Boston Harbor, and in 1984 the Society was invited to join the Donald McKay Tall Ships Parade in Boston and the Boston Harbor Festival. Friendship sloops are urged to enter the Arundel Yacht Club's Boon Island Race and to rendezvous at the Isles of Shoals in June and September. The customary Marblehead race is, of course, still held each August.

In 1976 the flagpole was erected overlooking Friendship harbor to memorialize departed members and friends of the Society. The pole is a retired mast and topmast from *Tannis*, standing on land donated to the Society by Al and Betty Roberts. A plaque on the base was provided by Ernst Wiegleb and Bruce Morang. The flagpole

*A Friendship sloop and a cat boat among the tall ships in Boston.*

was dedicated on July 29, 1976, to the music of the Society's piper, Donald Duncan, with appropriate literary exercises in the presence of a large assembly.

Not only has the size and complexity of the racing program increased, but also shoreside problems have multiplied and claimed the attention of people like Douglas Lash, Bill and Caroline Zuber, John and Dorothy Gould, and Elbert and Connie Pratt. When a large number of spectators suddenly invades a small town with only one narrow road along the shore, traffic problems abound. A field is donated in which to park, but even so, parking facilities must be provided elsewhere and shuttle cars arranged. Traffic must be directed to move only one way and signs lettered. There must be an information booth and a first aid center. Public toilets must be provided. A communication center must be established with which ham radio operators from the Yankee Radio Club, in boats following the race, can communicate and the information announced on a public address system. Sloop owners, crews, and spectators must be provided meals ashore, from breakfast to a lobster bake and a chicken barbecue. The gift shop must be manned. And finally, afterwards, the whole mess must be cleaned up, trash collected, borrowed items returned, and reusable material put away for the next year.

But the most important part of the Friendship Sloop Society is people. In the beginning, it was Bernard MacKenzie, John Gould, Carlton Simmons, and Herold Jones who, with their infectious enthusiasm and incredible energy, started the organization. Al and Betty Roberts, Doug Lash, Ernst Wiegleb, Bill Danforth, Lincoln Ridgway, the elected officers, and a variety of others kept the Society growing. Today, many of these people have left us, drifted away or died, but others are taking their places. As long as a shared enthusiasm for the handsome, able, Friendship sloop endures, and with it the capacity for cooperation and unselfish effort that its name implies, there will be a Friendship Sloop Society.

8

# *H*ome Builders and Rebuilders

*I* *n side yards, garages, barns,* and shops all over the country, people build their own boats. Some projects are propelled by dreams of tradewind passages to tropic isles. Others, less romantic, think that they can save money by building a boat themselves; and others simply like building things and see that a boat, a Friendship sloop perhaps, is one of the loveliest things ever conceived by the mind of man and executed by his hand. For whatever reason, they start, and some of them finish. Building a seagoing vessel is a monumental undertaking, yet we know of at least 30 Friendship sloops built by their owners between 1960 and 1984.

Every one of these builders deserves to be chronicled in this book, for every one faced unique problems as well as some common to the others and solved them by hook, crook, subterfuge, or personal resourcefulness. But there is neither time nor space to mention all of them. The best we can do is discuss a few in detail. The others will, to some extent, see themselves reflected.

To begin, one can scarcely do better than repeat Ed Coffin's account of building *Ray of Hope,* which Al Roberts included in *Enduring Friendships.*

I once read somewhere that rowing away from your boat and looking back in pride at your accomplishment of wood to water is the height of love afloat. Naturally, this point of view is very strongly shared by all dockside loafers. As one of Maine's leading dockside loafers, my appetite always becomes strangely full when viewing the gaff rig and the powerful sheer of a Friendship Sloop. This always led to a fierce desire, which, in my case, started to slacken when we began to build a replica of the famous 25-foot *Pemaquid*.

We ordered her plans by Chapelle from the W.W. Norton Publishing Company at a cost of $12. Our boat shop on western Penobscot Bay, where we are building, measures 38 x 22 x 12 feet, with windows on the whole east and south walls. It is a grand building in which to build small craft. From the 25-foot-long workbench, one can see Heron Neck Light, on Vinalhaven, and the outer ledges and islands of the Muscle Ridge Channel, where the Friendship Sloops long ago used to earn their keep.

For earlier boat building projects before our shop was built, we used a friend's barn floor for lofting lines and built outdoors in a pole shed made of scrap boards covered with tar-paper and canvas and open on the north side.

Our biggest incentive for building the *Pemaquid* model came from a friendly duck hunter, who, having built one for himself, offered me an extra cast iron keel of 2,000 pounds for $352. It came with eight hull molds and patterns.

The planking of native one-inch cedar was ordered first, to allow for drying time. It cost $138 for 950 feet, of which 250 feet was an an inch-and-a-quarter thick for planking around the turn of the bilge where you have to hollow out to fit the curve of the frames. This amount of planking allows for numerous mistakes.

I would have liked to use galvanized nails for planking, but the friendly duck hunter insisted I use Everdur screws. "You will have potential buyers visit with you longer that way," he said. It has taken 20 gross of inch-and-a-half by No. 12 screws for planking. This cost $99.

I drew out to full size on the shop floor the shape of the keel and all the deadwood. This controlled the fit of the wood to the tapered 1-ton keel and gave me two sore knees! The red oak keel is 6 by 8 inches by 18 feet long and cost $25. This is the same good Maine red oak used in yacht and fishing dragger construction and by all lobster pot builders. Contrary to popular thinking, many knowledgeable marine architects hold it in high regard.

The deadwood and keel bolts are three-quarter-inch galvanized iron and were found in a local junkyard. With threading and fitted with washers and nuts, they came to $27.

Once the oak backbone was fitted and sized and the rabbet cut, the whole assembly was treated for about a week to a daily brushing of a mixture composed of half linseed oil and half turpentine, to prevent checking of the backbone and deadwood. The oak keel, to be bolted to the iron keel, was first redleaded on the bottom and a 30-pound-weight sheet of tarpaper fitted in between to insulate the oak from the iron keel. After the backbone was blocked up and plumbed to grade, a hole was bored two inches deep or more in the stemtop. A funnel was inserted into which was poured the turps and linseed mixture until it ran out the bottom of the stem, showing full saturation. This is necessary in a warm shop, as the wet oak when drying out would pull off line and crack.

Now that the backbone was up and trued to a center line, the molds were placed on station from the plan and braced off from the shop roof and walls. At this point of construction I would suggest that every night before turning in, in addition to reading the Bible, the amateur boatbuilder read Chapelle's book on boatbuilding. This volume will give good simple directions for tomorrow's step in assembling the "ark."

Two of the most difficult areas of construction that caused strain in my brain were: one, the curved transom with its quarterblocks, and, two, the proper cutting of the changing angle of the stern deadwood rabbet. I was fortunate in being able to visit Sloops under construction in the area and to see how professionals handled these sections. I found that all were most willing to help me when in trouble with a difficult task. Never hesitate to ask advice.

The transom of the *Pemaquid* model is of handsome line and, if properly executed, is a beautifying complement to the whole boat. It was laid out of one-and-three-quarters-by-five-inch oak on a curved rack built up of two-by-eight-inch

*The tank made for boiling timbers for* Ray of Hope. *Harry Remsen, Francis Nash, and Jeff Coffin from the left. (Ed Coffin)*

spruce to hold the boiled oak transom frame to shape. Once assembled, the transom was bolted to the horn timber with a knee.

The molds being in position and the rabbets roughed out, we were ready for the spruce ribbands to be sprung around the molds to hold the shape rigid. Once they were nailed in position and braced off from the floor, we then turned to fashioning the one-by-two-inch frames.

The oak frames were cut from a flat grain; they cost $30. These were placed eight at a time, in a mixture of one gallon of permanent anti-freeze and a quantity of water and were boiled for about 30 minutes, or until pliable. The anti-freeze additive, for some reason, leaves the frames a natural color, whereas boiled water will usually turn oak black. The boiling tank was built of two old galvanized hot water tanks, which were found on the local dump. They were welded together with a supporting frame fixed to the front end so as to allow a fire of scrapwood to be built underneath. It took almost two days to frame the boat. Why hurry what should be an enjoyable process?

'T is a wonderful thing to have a sympathetic helper. Francis Nash, my superintendent of the Tug and Grunt Boat Yard and only employee, is my third arm. He provided the incentive for much of the difficult work on this boat. When a wrong cut was made, or a piece fitted poorly, his well-chosen comments gave new hope. I recall how I ruined part of the stern deadwood early in the job and Nash's comment was, "Never mind, there is plenty of wood still growing in the forest. Let's go get us another chunk."

*Garboard plank in place on* Ray of Hope. *(Ed Coffin)*

One of the greatest contributions by the plastics industry to wooden boat builders is the new blue car body putty. This costs about $1.80 per quart and may be obtained in an auto store. But if you buy it from a marine shop, the same thing costs $8.00. This putty sets up like iron and is workable by file or plane. Using this on many holes and voids I found gave one the feeling of being a sculptor. This thought can become rather dangerous, if you start thinking, "Maybe I can build the whole boat of blue putty and just use wood for fuel in the stove."

As of March, 1970, the Sloop was two years under construction and was all planked with the clamp and shelf in. Looking back at the time spent working on the boat — weekends and some weekdays — we found ourselves tentatively drawing a name on the handsome transom: *Ray of Hope!* This will not necessarily be the final name, but it reflects the attitude of the builder and his family. The cost that we see to date is about $1,200.

We amateur boat builders are like good English tea — our strength really shows when we get in hot water. After Bill Payne bought *Ray of Hope* from Ed Coffin, he sailed parties in her on Monhegan. She is now named *Eden* and sails parties out of Bar Harbor under Capt. Peter Thompson.

Kent Murphy's experience building *Ollie M.* is also worth recording. Kent had had no experience building boats, although he had done some radical reconstruction on an old schooner. He had it vaguely in mind to build a boat some day, for he loved sailing. One day, he and his wife Ollie were sailing with Don Huston in *Eagle* off Nahant, Massachusetts. A summer squall built up. Says Kent, "We hurried around like two monkeys, taking everything down. My wife was really calm. If that's the way she's going to act in a squall, that's the boat for me."

Kent became a "Friendship bum" for the next several years, sailing in many different sloops and talking with owners. *Eastward* appealed to him, so he tried to buy her plans from Jimmy Chadwick, the builder. But Jimmy did not own the plans — they are the property of the designer — so Kent and Don Huston visited Murray Peterson in South Bristol. Murray was reluctant; he said he was not in the business of selling plans. However, after several hours' conversation in which he was impressed with Kent's serious intentions to build the boat in traditional style, he sold a set of *Eastward*'s plans, making Kent promise to study both Chapelle's and Steward's books on boat building and further, to loft the boat out full size as evidence that he really was going to build her. This was on December 7, 1972.

Kent found a motel in Swampscott, Massachusetts, that was closed for the winter but that kept a dining room open for occasional functions. He pasted together lengths of brown paper to make a sheet, 50 feet by 12 feet, spread it out on the floor, and began his lofting, using 50-foot battens to make fair curves. He had to roll up his mold loft to leave the room clear for the Rotary Club or Lions, but nights, weekends, and holidays he plotted points and drew lines.

On March 17, 1973, he realized with a jolt that there were no more points to plot, no more lines to draw. So he bought a house with a level backyard, a big garage, and a long, flat driveway. He borrowed a band saw with a four-foot throat from a Nahant resident who had just finished building a lobster boat, and he was ready to begin.

Now Murphy, who works for the Board of Health in Swampscott, has a close friend who is a tree man. They noticed that a developer, in filling some low land, had filled in around a red oak about 28 inches in diameter and had damaged it so badly that it was dying. Murphy condemned the tree because it had measles, and the tree department concurred. They cut it down and on the same day sawed out 1½-inch stock for planking.

Then, again accompanied by Don Huston, who has a most persuasive tongue, he visited Sargent's Mill in East Kingston, New Hampshire. Sargent was reluctant to saw boat lumber; boat builders are unduly fussy. At length, however, he agreed to saw lumber in even quarters and presently became interested in the project. He cut 2,000 feet of pine in 17-foot lengths, picked it over, and piled it with sticks between each layer so it would season. Only three or four pieces of the whole lot were unusable for planking. Oak for frames he cut as green as possible so they would bend easily. There are 52 frames in *Ollie M.*, and only the last few in the tumble-home at the stern gave any trouble.

Kent made patterns for molds and backbone by rolling out the brown paper mold loft on the driveway, covering the relevant part with waxed paper, and transferring the pattern to boards so that it could then be cut out on the band saw and assembled. With the help of his three sons, Kent set up and assembled the backbone. A tight wire was run from stem to transom as a reference line to which molds were trued up.

Construction proceeded steadily, the shipwright working from 6 to 10 p.m. every evening he could, the boat illuminated by a fluorescent light after dark. He made it a rule, however, never to drive a nail after nine o'clock, lest he disturb sleeping children in the neighborhood.

Lead for the keel was melted in an old bath tub, borrowed from the last man in the area who had cast a lead keel.

By the summer of 1976, *Ollie M.* was well along. The mast was stepped as she stood

Ollie M. *framed out. (Courtesy of Kent Murphy)*

in the yard, and a pipe scaffolding built around it. Iron work and rigging were thus easily attached to the mast without having to swing about in a bosun's chair. Sails, made by Clarence Hale in Sargentville, Maine, were bent one quiet day, and *Ollie M.*, with topmast and bowsprit, was substantially complete. Then she was unrigged, the mast was unstepped, and she was finished out below during the winter, after the whole inside of the boat was thoroughly treated with water gas, a residue from natural gas tanks that is excellent for controlling dry rot. Kent's sons installed the ceiling, ripped out of 2" x ⅜" pine, and varnished it.

The rudder post was a piece of bronze shaft working through a tube set in the horn timber.

In June 1977, *Ollie M.*, brave in new paint, was carefully jockeyed between the trees, around the corner of the garage, and skidded on to a trailer. Escorted by a strong representation of Swampscott's leading citizens, she was skidded off the trailer below low-water mark, the cradle ballasted. When the tide came in on June 23, 1977, *Ollie M.* floated clear, with champagne dripping from her bow.

Two fire-department pumps had been provided lest she leak unduly, but to her builder's delight, she leaked scarcely at all, no more than her own bilge pump could handle, although the skipper slept aboard that night to be sure.

She was taken to Nahant where the tree man's cherry picker could step her mast. Rigged, her sails bent, and "in all respects ready for sea," she sailed out on Boston Bay, welcomed by *Tannis* to the Friendship sloop fleet.

That July, while six miles outside the Isles of Shoals early in the morning, she was running east for Friendship, single reefed before a brisk southerly, when suddenly, she would not respond to the wheel. Murphy looked in the wheel box – no rudder. No rudder post either! He got the sail off her, anchored in 180 feet of water, and called the Coast Guard in Portsmouth. They arrived in less than an hour and towed *Ollie M.* to Ted Brown's in Kittery, Maine. On inspection, it appeared that the rudder, laminated of two pieces of plywood joined with resorcinal glue and built bigger than Peterson's design, had flexed under strain, gained enough slack to jump out of the bearing on the keel, pulled clear of the gudgeons, and dropped off. Murray Peterson would never countenance the use of plywood in any shape or form for any purpose, and Murphy admits that Peterson knew best.

Ollie M. *under way. (Courtesy of Kent Murphy)*

With a new rudder, *Ollie M.* has behaved well. To be sure, she lost two topmasts, one when the mainsail gybed over against a taut backstay and one in a race at Friendship when , with Malcolm Barter as tactician, she was well up with the leaders of the fleet. The spar let go at about 1 p.m. By 3 p.m., *Ollie M.* was alongside the wharf, the broken spar on deck. By five o'clock Murphy had found a rough stick of spruce in the yard of Doug Lash, who was building Friendship cats. By nine o'clock he, Doug, and a helper had made it into a topmast, the butt squared, fid hole cut, and all completed with a coat of priming. At 6 a.m., they gave it another quick coat of paint, had it stepped, rigged, and the sail set in time to start the race at 12:30. Unfortunately, the race was called off when fog shut down, so the story cannot end with the report of the victory cannon.

*Ollie*'s engine has occasionally gone on strike, but the sloop is so good under sail that loss of power occasions little trouble. She beat against a 25-knot southerly from Isles of Shoals to Gloucester in reasonable comfort and the next day ran home to Swampscott before a brisk northeaster without her skipper ever feeling that she was in trouble. She has been an enormous satisfaction to her builder and has given many people a good time.

John Chase built *Noahsark* in 1972, easily recognized by her flat-cut mainsail. Chase made a regular practice of coming east for the regatta by sailing offshore, direct from Cape Ann to Monhegan. We welcomed him to Monhegan one day in a brisk north-wester after a rather wild night during which he had slammed around in the Gulf of Maine under very short sail. He and his crew were dead tired, but confident in the design and construction of their sloop.

Red Jacket. *(Courtesy of Don Huston)*

In the early 1970s in eastern Massachusetts, John Chase was building *Noahsark*, Charlie Burnham was working on *Maria*, Jim Hall was working on *Renascence*, and Bob Gardner had *Red Jacket* under construction, using a plan provided by Phil Nichols. Each man helped the others. Charlie Burnham gained a reputation as a caulker, Bob Gardner as a rigger. All the sloops were at length completed, and all joined the regatta at Friendship to be welcomed and admired by other skippers. Sad to report, neither Jim Hall nor Bob Gardner lived long after their sloops were finished, but both sloops survive their builders and are a delight to many.

Bruce Lanning did not build *Schoodic* from scratch, but there is a great deal of him in the boat. When Elmer Collemer died, he left in his shop a planked-up hull designed by Geerd Hendel. A boat is less than half finished when she is planked, as Lanning found out when he bought her "as is" and moved her to his Winter Harbor shop in the fall of 1970. He was running a marine electronics business as a retirement project, so work on *Schoodic* was only a spare-time occupation. Nevertheless, by spring, *Schoodic* was decked. Lanning worked alone most of the time, which often made the job move slowly, for two men can do more than twice as much as one. He laminated the rail, cut a 60-foot spruce for the mast, and fabricated many of the metal parts himself, parts no longer available in marine supply stores. He did an elegant job of cabinet work in finishing *Schoodic*'s cabin, and, by late April 1973, she was launched. She leaked impressively to begin with, because she had dried out badly while under construction, but after pumping Winter Harbor through her several times, Lanning reported her tight as a cup.

*Schoodic* appears at Friendship regularly and has often been to the Massachusetts Bay races. She has taken Bruce and Mary south once and made a start for Bermuda once, but gales and heavy seas drove her back. Nevertheless, she behaved as well as one could expect any 31-foot boat to behave in the confused waters of the Gulf Stream.

*Schoodic* certainly is a compound triumph for Geerd Hendel, Elmer Collemer, and Bruce and Mary Lanning.

A number of other amateurs purchased old wooden boats and rebuilt them. One who undertakes such a project has often been swept away by the classic grace of a particular Friendship hull, her keen bow, quick sheer, and powerful, graceful stern. Some, indeed, buy their boats without ever inspecting them critically.

In the winter of 1932, Hugh Kelly walked out on the ice of Long Island Sound at Whitestone to where he saw a mast protruding. It looked like a Friendship spar. He stuck his knife in it, found it sound, and bought the 36-foot *Osprey* as she lay on the bottom for $200. When she was raised, she could only be kept afloat by pouring pails of sawdust into the quiet water around her so that it would be sucked into her thirsty seams. That and constant pumping got her to the railway where she could be hauled. Kelly found that her stem, stern, keel, planking, and lock streak were sound, but her timbers were rotten on top and bottom and hard and brittle as glass in the middle. They bent new frames on forms, took off a few planks to get C-clamps in, and put in 80 new 2" x 2½" frames. They rebuilt the deck, finished out the cabin, rehabilitated the engine, rerigged the boat, and had new sails made. After many vicissitudes, Alice Kelly wrote in the August 1946 *Rudder:*

We set sail! Surely there is never another time so full of beauty as when the spotless canvas goes up and up for the first time. Just a steady light breeze we had for that first trial. A black pigeon with a message fastened to his leg alighted on the cabin deck, and kept us all breathless for a moment. We thought he was looking for something, so Ruth poured herself like slow molasses down the companionway for a cup of water. The bird took a drink, rested a moment more, then as we watched him he took off and flew west. We saw him swiftly dwindle to a speck against the sunset and felt that a seal of perfection and a good omen had been set.

Joe Richards, in his book *Princess,* told of rebuilding his 26-foot Wilbur Morse dream ship. Let him tell the story:

I was looking over a little weekender with bilges like a coffin . . . when I caught a glimpse of *Princess.* It was perhaps the sheer of her deck, the clipper bow, the gentle reverse curve of her forefoot or the well-fed look of her fat-bellied chine that did it. I was a goner . . . .

It was a lovely morning. I sat with the hammer dangling in my hand, leaned back against the ceiling, and gave the old girl an affectionate rap. "Holy Cow!"

The hammer went through her ceiling like a one-inch auger bit through cheese . . . . I began to tear away at the ceiling. It came off in black rotten masses . . . .

The pitiful evidence of framing came loose in long sections to the touch or broke apart like toasted muck.

"Whatever held her together up to now?"

"Force of habit and a bit of paint . . . . Frame her up and she'll give you a lot of pleasure . . . ."

The following weekend there were 30 frames bent over a form that followed the curve of *Princess* . . . . Each frame was dragged down into the damp hull and set into a notch in the keel. The curve of the contour was a great big beautiful S. The frames were bent to fit perfectly amidships, and as I moved forward, a different part of the S fitted into place . . . . The pieces I cut off the bottom of the S to make it fit were longer as I moved forward. But always by the same amount. Small wonder that this was one of the finest designs for a hull that man has ever known.

What with her years and odd bulges, *Princess* was a little out of line . . . . The curved frames had to be pressed into position. I rigged automobile jacks to do the job . . . . Bronze screws were used to lock the frames in place. When I released the jacks, they went off like the crack of doom . . . . Working all day Saturday and most of Sunday, I broke my record, the Sabbath and all of my fingernails. I installed three frames . . . .

I was getting suspicious of a patch of cement on the inside of her stem . . . . Probing pay dirt in the stem, I reached clear through and felt the warm sunlight on my empty hand . . . .

The [new] stem fell into place. I borrowed a big auger and . . . drilled up for the bolts. Then I cut new knightheads and fastened them to the stem. There didn't seem to be anything you couldn't do on a boat if your back was as strong as the obsession . . . .

The fever that drives a man to rebuild a sixty-year-old vessel can make him lose sight of the reason for doing it . . . . A new part added to the vessel made the old parts look worse . . . . The hardest thing about rebuilding an ancient ark is the decision you have to make about the things you are not going to do . . . . I wanted to launch *Princess* by the first of September . . . . A couple of floors fashioned out of two-inch oak were lagged deep into the keel with bronze . . . . I developed a personal method of caulking that would have got me fired from any fourth-rate yard . . . . My *Princess* looked really lovely with her chain plates and bowsprit back on and a gleaming white coat of gloss on her topsides . . . . It was no trick to get the engine going . . . .

From the early days of spring I had watched the boats go down into the water . . . . Now at last it was her turn. My heart beat fast. The boys came over, put down the greased planks, and snatched her away . . . .

There followed a ritual, however, that has persisted down through the years. It is symbolic of the length of work and the shortness of time . . . . She had me chasing after her into the water with a last brushload of paint.

. . . I pumped. The third night it rained. The fifty-year-old planks, now firmly tied with bronze to the new frames, squeezed themselves together and closed the last remaining gap.

The sails were bent on . . . . I raised her staysail, freed her lines, and moved out into the bay . . . . *Princess* cut through the water like a thing alive. She pivoted on a point, and clawed into the teeth of the wind . . . . She was slippery all right and there was hardly a ripple aft. I had myself a boat! . . . I swung in between the moorings and the two dolphins and came about smartly by the floating dock. There was a man standing there, alone, watching. It was the man who sold me the boat.

*Princess* was first a fisherman and in 1925 was used as a yacht by Robert Ayer. At that time she had no forestay and was rigged with a balanced jumbo, a popular rig with fishermen in eastern Maine.

This sail was set flying, without a stay. The foot was laced to a boom that was hooked down to the bowsprit about 18 inches aft of the tack, thus leaving the tack of the sail projecting to windward. The mast was supported by a jibstay to the end of the bowsprit, on which Ayer set a big jib in light weather.

When Ayer owned her, *Princess* had a big cockpit, accommodations for two below, a stove that he remembers as being so efficient it sometimes drove him out of the cabin, and a one-cylinder, two-cycle Lathrop engine that all but shook her to pieces. He had to strengthen her with extra oak around the engine beds. Ayer sold her in about 1934 to a Long Island yachtsman, presumably the man from whom Richards bought her. She was a little nail sick when she went to Long Island.

One of the most interesting and best documented accounts of a rebuilding is that of *Estella A.*, rebuilt by Newbert and Wallace at Thomaston, Maine, between 1970 and 1973. Her history is outlined briefly in Chapter 4. She was launched in 1905, used as a workboat out of Matinicus until 1930, and used as a yacht until 1957. During her yachting career, she was converted to a marconi rig, her bowsprit shortened, her house raised, additional floor timbers installed, a lead shoe added outside, and lead ballast substituted inside for the iron she had always carried. In 1957 she was donated to Mystic Seaport, where she was returned to her original rig and kept as a floating exhibit. By 1967, however, she would no longer float and was stored ashore. There is nothing harder on a boat than staying ashore, baking in the sun, drying in the wind, and being soaked down with fresh water. By 1969 planks were literally falling off, and it was decided to have her rebuilt. She was trucked to the yard of Newbert and Wallace in Thomaston and, under the supervision of Maynard Bray, was carefully taken apart and re-assembled with sound material.

It was considered important to retain her original construction plan and her original shape. Her lines had been taken off by her former owner, Duncan Selfridge, but they were now taken off again and found to be essentially unchanged. Then her cockpit and deck were removed, leaving a few deck beams to hold her together, and the cement that had been poured into her bilge to the height of the keelson when she was built was chipped out, revealing a sound keel notched for the foot of each frame.

Three molds were now made and put in and the planking nailed to them enough to hold her shape. The garboards, the bottom planks next the keel, were taken off and every third plank removed, the others being retained to preserve her shape. The old frames were then removed one by one, each being replaced by a new one, 1½" x 2¾", installed in the keel notches, bent to the inside of the planking, and clamped to it where the planks had been removed. The new frames, like the old, were bent on the flat side and slit crossways in the way of the sharpest bends so they wouldn't break.

During the framing process, it had become evident that the old planking had deteriorated too much to be saved, so the sloop was replanked, the old planks, which had served as ribbands, being removed one by one to make room for the new. She was fastened with bronze screws instead of the galvanized iron nails that had been used originally. These nails were found in remarkably good condition, although the galvanizing was mostly gone, because they were iron, not steel.

With the boat planked, the molds were removed and a deck clamp sprung in. This is a long timber running from bow to stern and bolted to each frame near its top. On it rest the deck beams. These are notched to let in the lock streak, which is then fastened down to the deck beams and drifted through the heads of the frames. The illustrations show this clearly.

One reason that *Estella A.* was believed to be worth restoring was that her stern was so strongly built that rot had not yet caused it to sag and destroy her sheer line. As the photographs and construction plans show, the sternpost comes up to the deck, and ear pieces run from each side of it aft to the counter, making a well for the rudder head. All this timbering was carefully replaced.

Also, there were several grown floor timbers in her that survived. The stem, breast hook, and knight heads were replaced piece by piece.

Her old mast was used, but the other spars were replaced, and all the rigging was replaced as accurately as could be ascertained from Newell McLain, son of the builder, and Oscar Ames, who had fished in her with his father. A few of these rigging details will be enough to demonstrate the simple and direct approach of the builders.

The eyes in the stem to which forestay and bobstay were attached were rod iron, galvanized, bent into an eye, and the shaft drifted through the stem. A heavy washer was placed on the inside and a slot cut through the rod into which an iron wedge was driven to lock the iron in position. The bowsprit was mortised to fit over a tenon cut on

**Above:** Estella A.'s *reconstruction showing stem keel, floor timber, and deck clamp in place. One deck beam rests on the clamp. (Mystic Seaport)* **Below:** *Estella A.'s reconstruction looking aft. At the left the ear pieces are bolted to the sternpost and carried aft to the counter and up to the deck. The deck framing rests on the clamp, and the lock streak appears at the right. She is partly sheathed with an air streak left between the sheathing and the clamp for ventilation. (Mystic Seaport)*

the stem head and its butt held between the bitts with a pin over the top. There was no gammon iron. The topping lift was spliced into an eye at the masthead and into the becket of a single block a short distance above the boom. A line ran from the boom, through this block, through a slot in the boom, and forward to a cleat on the starboard side of the boom about over the tiller. Halyards were belayed on cleats under the collar on which the boom jaws rested when the sail was lowered. This collar was made in three pieces and was simply nailed to the mast.

Nathaniel S. Wilson of East Boothbay made her a suit of cotton sails, cut with the cloths parallel to the leech in the original way, hand roped, and with the corners and

*Estella A.'s restoration complete. (Mystic Seaport)*

reef cringles reinforced with hand stitching. As the photograph shows, they set beautifully.

Of Rob McLain's *Estella A.* all that remains is the keel, several of the grown floor timbers, the sides of the house, and the coaming. Yet could he step aboard her, he would recognize everything else as authentic, so carefully was she rebuilt. She is on exhibit, afloat, at Mystic and is well worth an hour's careful inspection.

One other tale of rebuilding will have to suffice. *Chrissy*, built as *Sonny* in 1912 by Charles Morse, had been repaired as she needed it through the years, but in 1969 Ernst Wiegleb, her owner since 1945, whacked her quite hard on a ledge off Crotch Island. The incident helped him to the conclusion that the time for substantial rebuilding had come.

First, he cleaned out all the furnishings and sheathing below and set braces under the deck beams at each end of the house, where bulkheads had been. Then, starting from the bow, he removed the old frames and the many short pieces that had been sistered in to reinforce them, tackling no more than 18 inches at a time so she would not change shape. This was not difficult; many of the pieces came out almost of themselves, although he left five white oak frames put in only 10 years before and still hard as iron. Wiegleb then plugged all the nail holes and lathered everything with Cuprinol. On a wide oak plank 1¾" thick, he laid out each old frame, drew around it, and set in 1-inch iron pins where the curves came so that a new piece of steamed 1¼" x 2" oak could be bent into the same shape as the original frame. A board strap was tacked to the ends of the new frame to prevent its straightening out when it was removed from the pins, and it was then slipped into its notch in the keel. Two planks were removed where the bends were the sharpest and several slots cut in the remaining planking, thus sacrificing it where necessary so the new frame could be pulled tightly to the old planking and clamped. The board strap was removed and the new frame fastened in with bronze screws.

Amidships, where the frames were too long to be worked in under the deck, Wiegleb made each one in two pieces with a 10-inch lap. The lower section could be steamed and pulled in with clamps, but the upper part had to be prebent and held with a strap like the ones forward. Far aft, where the bend is very short, he laminated frames from thin pieces glued together and nailed with holdfast nails. He put in 66 new frames. He replaced all butt blocks at the same time and refastened them with Everdur screws. He then sprung in a 1" x 4" bilge stringer on each side, fastened to each frame through the places where they were lapped, and he added two lengths of 1" x 2" oak from sternpost to mast. He then set in a new floor timber for each pair of frames and built a new lock streak out of black locust.

With the hull thus strengthened, it seemed that *Chrissy* could carry an outside lead keel. She had an oak keel. Using a proper length of this for a pattern, a box was made, caulked with asbestos and coated inside with waterglass, a silicate of sodium or potassium that, when dissolved in water, forms a waterproof coating. The box was buried in the ground and backfilled solidly to be sure it would hold its shape under the pressure of the molten lead. The new 2,000-pound keel was exhumed and bolted in place.

Sixteen pieces of decayed planking were removed and replaced, including, of course, the ones that had had slots cut in them for clamping frames. These were fastened, bunged, planed, and sanded, and finally a professional was called in to recaulk *Chrissy* with cotton and polysulfide. The unused slots in the keel and spaces between timbers at stem and stern were filled with Sakrete or pitch and a coat of primer applied. All this was done between when *Chrissy* was hauled in September and when the weather turned cold in December. The next spring, *Chrissy* was ceiled and fitted out below and appeared as formidable as ever at the regatta, much better able to carry sail.

Many other Friendships have been resurrected, and their rebuilders deserve mention. Ralph Stanley rebuilt *Morning Star*. Jarvis Newman and Ralph Stanley rebuilt *Venture* and *Dictator*, discussed in the next chapter. H.C. Vibber and his son Jaxon rebuilt *Ancient Mariner*. Robert Vaughan of Seal Cove Boatyard rebuilt *Chance* for Alan Goldstein, who gave her to the Maine Maritime Museum. James Rockefeller rebuilt *Sazerac* on the slopes of Bald Mountain for George Morrill. Don Huston bought *Eagle* with no stem in her, her bow gaping open, and rebuilt her into a champion.

Bill Zuber at Friendship is even now rebuilding *Gladiator* so she will last longer than any of us. He has hauled her up next to his barn in Friendship, built a plastic shed

Chrissy. *(Irving Nevells Photographs)*

Venture *before she was rebuilt.*

Eagle *as she stood when Don Huston bought her. (Courtesy of Don Huston)*

Eagle *reconstructed. (Courtesy of Don Huston)*

West Wind's *new keel showing the old frames, sternpost, and stern knee and a bit of the old planking.*

around her, and cleaned off layers of old paint. He has also chipped all the cement out of her bilge, revealing several grown floor timbers, and bent in a number of sister frames where the original frames and later sister frames had deteriorated. Once he gets her structurally strengthened, Zuber plans to cover her with cloth soaked in epoxy and then with pine sheathing, making her practically indestructible short of a major shipwreck.

John Fassack is rebuilding the big *Westwind* at Nahant. David Nutt is entirely rebuilding *Depression* at West Southport for Lloyd Oleson. *White Eagle* lies in a shed behind Peter Throckmorton's shop in Newcastle, awaiting attention. Every one of these will no doubt be handled differently, but the examples we have seen should suggest what can be done by a devoted and imaginative person with ingenuity, persistence, some money, and a supportive family.

# 9

## *Fiberglass and Fer-a-Lite*™

*J*     *arvis Newman from the town of Manset* on Mt. Desert Island early took the lead in
       the development of Friendship sloops in fiberglass. Educated as an engineer, he
had molded fiberglass yachts for Henry R. Hinckley, Inc., in Manset for several years
and had developed a popular fiberglass dinghy when in 1968 he decided to build a
fiberglass Friendship sloop. The cost of building wooden boats had soared almost out of
reach, and fiberglass techniques had been developed to produce much less expensive
boats.

He decided to start with the popular Pemaquid model, partly because James
Rockefeller had recently built a wooden one, *Old Baldy*, whose owner, Mahlon
Hoagland, was willing to lend her for a plug.

In September 1968, her mast was taken out, and she was hauled to Newman's shop
on a trailer. He and his helper, Roland Stanley, removed all trim and fittings and
sanded her down to the bare wood to produce a perfectly smooth and fair surface. Then
she was turned on her side, heavily waxed, and sprayed with a gel coat. Layers of
fiberglass were added to make a female mold. The mold was sprung off, *Old Baldy*
rolled to her other side, and the same procedure followed. A flange was built on each
mold so that the two molds fit together precisely.

To build the fiberglass boat, each mold is waxed, sprayed with gel coat, and coated
with 10 alternate layers of fiberglass cloth and roving, each saturated with resin, rolled
down and cured, producing a homogeneous hull about ½" thick. Then the two molds,
each with its half of the boat, are bolted together so that inside the two molds, the two
halves of the boat are matched exactly to each other. From the inside, then, fiberglass

---

™ Registered trade mark of Aladdin Products

**Above:** *The mold for a new generation of Pemaquid sloops coming off* Old Baldy *at Jarvis Newman's shop. (Jarvis Newman)* **Below:** *The first hull out of the mold. Notice the place left for the ballast keel and the deck mold in the background. (Jarvis Newman)*

putty is worked into the joint, followed by a layer of "choppings," short lengths of fiberglass mixed with resin to a putty-like consistency. Thus, any angles where the two halves meet are filled and flattened out. Then 4-inch-wide layers of alternate mat and cloth are rolled on, followed by several layers of 12-inch mat and cloth.

When the joint is completely cured, the molds can be removed. A shelf is built inside of the hull all the way around, reinforced with five double layers of cloth and mat below it, to receive the deck.

The deck, which has been molded in the same way, all in one piece, is then lowered on the shelf, landing on a layer of wet fiberglass, and is bolted down to the shelf with stainless steel bolts. Deck and trim cover the bolt heads, and the side of the boat projecting above the deck provides a toe rail.

A space for a lead ballast keel has been left in the mold, and this is bolted on. Bulkheads are installed from keel to deck and firmly glassed in all the way around. From here, it is a matter of finishing out the cabin and trimming up the deck and cockpit with nicely finished wood.

The first hull was molded in the spring of 1969 and taken to James Rockefeller's yard on Bald Mountain to be finished out. Another was started at once and towed on a trailer, incomplete in some details, to Friendship for the 1969 regatta as an eyecatcher. Newman lived aboard during the three days of the regatta. She was finished up for George Lauriat of Southwest Harbor, launched, christened *Salatia*, and sailed in company with the repainted and rerigged *Old Baldy* in September, the first of 18 fiberglass Pemaquids to sail.

The model proved very popular. In 1984, 15 were registered with the Society, and most had raced in the regatta at one time or another.

While many who are accustomed to wooden boats and the traditions surrounding their building and rebuilding consider a fiberglass Friendship sloop a contradiction in terms, owners of the new boats have found them as solidly built and as handy and seaworthy as wooden boats. In fact, the racing records suggest little difference. Furthermore, the wood finish is so complete and so well done, and the hull is so heavy, that there is none of the corky, bubbly feel characteristic of many modern fiberglass yachts.

While Jarvis Newman was developing *Old Baldy* in fiberglass, the firm of Bruno & Stillman in Newington, New Hampshire, was developing a 30-foot fiberglass Friendship sloop. Instead of building a mold from an existing sloop, Bruno and Stillman had a design drawn by Marbridge Associates and built a plug of plaster that conformed to the design. From this, a female mold was made. The mold was waxed, sprayed with gel coat, and the fiberglass laid up inside. In two days, the mold could be removed, and a Friendship hull was built. Removing the mold was said to have been quite exciting because static electricity charged the whole area, including the hair of the workmen.

Building the boat from two molds, as Newman does it, makes it much easier to do a good job of laying up the narrow parts in the after sections, but it is not quite so fast a process as the Bruno & Stillman method.

The Bruno & Stillman sloop had 3,800 pounds of lead inside the fiberglass hull and 860 square feet of sail, including topsail and jib topsail. She was finished in quite elegant style, with Sitka spruce spars, lignum vitae cleats, a black locust pin rail, teak deck, mahogany trim, and plexiglass hatches for light below.

The design departed somewhat from the traditional. She carried a little more freeboard and a higher house than the old-timers to provide headroom below. The cabin extended farther aft for greater cruising accommodation, and the cockpit was comparatively small and self-bailing to make her more suitable for offshore work. In

Salatia, *the second hull and the first fiberglass Pemaquid to sail. (Jarvis Newman)*

fact, Al Beck raced *Phoenix*, Bruno and Stillman's second hull, from Marblehead to Halifax. The mast is farther aft than in a traditional Friendship to make a smaller mainsail and bigger staysail, and the topmast is stepped on a bracket fastened to the forward side of the mast rather than on the traditional trestle trees.

The first Bruno & Stillman sloop was *Perseverance*, registered with the Society in 1969 as No. 83 by Harold E. Kimball of Concord, New Hampshire. Since then, 14 others have been registered. As the firm is no longer in existence, figures on how many were built are not easily available.

About the same time, George and Chester Harris of Passamaquoddy Yachts used a sloop built by McKie Roth for a plug and produced several fiberglass sloops, of which two, *Ellen Anne* and *Magic*, have been registered with the Society.

Impressed with the success of the Pemaquid model, Jarvis Newman undertook in 1971 to develop a fiberglass model of the 31-foot *Dictator*.

*Dictator* had been built in 1904 by Robert E. McLain for Stephen Gray, a Deer Isle fisherman. She was used by a succession of fishermen until she was purchased in about

**Above:** Perseverance, *the first Bruno & Stillman sloop.* **Below:** Dictator *as Jarvis Newman bought her. (Courtesy of Jarvis Newman)*

Dictator *being rebuilt. The new backbone is in place.*

1930 by Alan Chesney of Deer Isle for use as a yacht. By 1971 Chesney had died, and *Dictator* was in sad shape. A garboard on one side was missing, and her starboard bow was stove in. Yet her fundamental shape was preserved. Jarvis Newman, always willing to try a desperate move — he had pumped *Venture* from Friendship to Manset — replaced the missing garboard, nailed a rough patch of boards and canvas over her stove-in bow, stuffed several logs of styrofoam into her cabin, and towed her, almost awash, to Southwest Harbor. Then he rebuilt her.

First, he took off her lines very carefully, leveling her up with a transparent hose filled with water to the height of her designed waterline fore and aft. Then, supporting her by her bilges, he cut the keel clear of the rotted ends of the frames, dropped it out, and made a new keel, stem, and stern assembly to the patterns of the old ones. With the new backbone in place, every other plank was removed; then every other frame, one at a time, was replaced with new wood. Once framed, she was replanked, each old plank being removed as the new plank was prepared. She was then strengthened with floor timbers at every other frame and with the usual clamps and shelf. She was finished out elegantly below and on deck, and in 1973 she was launched. In 1974, with a new suit of Hood sails, she won both the Governor's Cup and the Eda Lawry trophy, for she is classed as an original, even though the only piece of wood in her that Robert McLain ever touched is a piece of the old keel, set into the new one as a symbol of her ancestry.

Even before the rebuilt *Dictator* was launched, in the spring of 1973, Newman made molds for a glass Dictator and molded the first one that year for Winthrop Bancroft of Boothbay Harbor. The bare hull was trucked to the shop of J. Ervin Jones in East Boothbay. He put on a wooden deck and finished her out below. Murray Peterson designed her rig, moving the mast aft a little, increasing the hoist of the mainsail so as to keep a generous area without putting the end of the boom out of reach, and adding a gaff topsail and jib topsail. In 1974 she won the Class D trophy in the regatta, and, until Bancroft's son-in-law Murray McQuade took her to Florida, she was a good bet in any Friendship sloop race.

Other hulls followed quickly, all being fitted with wooden decks. In 1975 Ralph Stanley finished out Richard Salter's *Liberty*, and her wooden deck was used to make a mold for a glass deck, first used on James Genthner's *Endeavor*, finished out by her owner in 1978.

The details of construction on the Dictator hull are about the same as those on the Pemaquid, but everything is heavier, 14 layers being used instead of 10, and the minimum thickness being about ⅝ inch. The Dictator may be had either with inside ballast or with an outside lead shoe like the Pemaquid's.

The glass Dictator is, as glass boats go, a heavy boat, displacing about 17,000 pounds of which 5,500 pounds are lead ballast. She is a stiff boat that will stand up to her work, and like her namesake, she will hold her own in any fleet with sheets started. Her cockpit, while big enough for day sailing, is not so big as to be dangerous should she fill it. She is not only a pleasant day sailer but is a capable offshore cruiser.

A one-off, fiberglass 22-footer, *Seal,* was finished by Alvin J. Zink, Jr., of Andover, Massachusetts. He bought the outer shell, lined the inside of it with blocks of end-grain balsa set in resin, covered the balsa with another layer of glass, and finished her out elegantly. A friend carved a lovely wooden seal's head for a figurehead. He launched her in May 1984, sailed her to the regatta at Boothbay, and found her a delight. Al Zink talks of selling his larger boat and keeping *Seal.*

Next to *Seal* in Andover, Jim Hamilton built the lovely wooden 22-foot *Ansa,* a sister ship. She sails out of Islesboro, Maine.

Other materials than wood and fiberglass have been used. Two sloops, *Medusa,* owned by Ron Nowell of Marshall, California, and *Annie Pode,* are built of ferro-cement.

Dictator *rebuilt. (Courtesy of Jarvis Newman)*

*Anna B.,* the first fiberglass *Dictator, and* Matelot, *a Pemaquid type. (Boutilier Photos)*

Wire mesh is stretched over a grid of pipe frames and rod stringers and spread with cement. The cement is worked through the wire so the whole metal structure reinforces the cement hull.

An improvement on this method is being used by Harry D. Quick of Wiscasset. He is the author's dentist, and because said author's teeth have a way of breaking off or caving in at frequent intervals, the following saga has been assembled while waiting for the anesthetic to take effect or for the fillings to harden:

Quick served in Korea with Lou Alley, a South Bristol lobsterman. After the war, Lou took him out lobstering one summer day, and Harry saw *Depression* sailing by.

"What's that?" he asked.

"You damned fool, that's a sailboat."

"I know that. What kind of a sailboat?"

"It's a Friendship sloop."

Quick liked sailing and determined to build a Friendship sloop, but he could not find plans, and what he read about lofting sounded difficult. So he looked at old sloops. He found that rebuilding would be about twice as much work as building, what with taking apart and putting together again. Meanwhile, he tried lofting out a Pemaquid and found it less difficult than he had feared, but he also found that she was not just what he wanted.

Then Quick offered to trade a repair job on a broken tooth for my opinion on a new kind of construction. He took me to visit Platt Monfort, who was building a 45-foot ketch of Fer-a-Lite. Platt is a chemical engineer, a most ingenious man, and the sort of man who *must* try out an idea at once, if not sooner. He was impressed with the simplicity of building such a complex form as a boat out of ferro-cement, but he didn't like the cement. It was heavy and would not bond to itself, so it had to be applied to the wire all in one day. To get around this, Platt invented Fer-a-Lite. This is a mixture of reinforced cement with fiberglass resin and hardener. It is mixed to the consistency of a mashed potato, sets in a few hours, is almost light enough to float, is waterproof, has the flexibility and resilience of aluminum, and, best of all, bonds to itself so that the boat can be plastered bit by bit. Then, to improve on wire as a base, Monfort invented "wire plank." This consists of eight parallel strands of 14- or 16-gauge wire held 7/16" apart by light transverse wires. It comes on a roll 500 feet long and 3½" wide. Because the wires are not held rigidly to each other, they will take compound curves readily. We were much impressed with the progress of the ketch, and Quick resolved to use Fer-a-Lite on his Friendship sloop.

Then someone sent him to Phil Nichols. Quick got on beautifully with Nichols, who had drawn plans for a 30-foot boat to which Robert Gardner had built *Red Jacket*.

"How much do you want for a set of plans?" Quick asked Nichols.

"Nothing."

"I don't want to take them for nothing."

"If you don't want to take them, the hell with 'em," replied Nichols with a characteristic twinkle.

So Harry helped him move a lumber pile, cut firewood, and do some of the heavy work around the place, all on an informal basis. In the course of their acquaintance, to see what he would think of Fer-a-Lite, Harry took Phil to see Platt Monfort's boat, then still under construction. Phil didn't say anything at all about it except to observe, "The fella's a fine craftsman."

Weeks later, they drove to Belfast to look at *Red Jacket*. Phil declared she needed more sheer and said he would redraw the plans. While they were standing on the wharf, a fiberglass sloop sailed by. Two other observers made disparaging remarks about fiberglass, and Phil agreed, adding, "Sailing a bath tub. Every time I see a fiberglass bo't, I look around for the soap dish. But," he added, "if you have to use fiberglass, you want to look at this Fer-a-Lite. Steel-belted fiberglass is what it is." And he continued with a full and accurate encomium on the new material. Harry gaped.

With the plans redrawn, Harry asked how much space he would need to loft the boat. Phil suggested they haul that pile of boards by the barn down to the boat shop. They did. Harry asked why.

"You damned fool, that's for the molds. What do you think we brought 'em down for?" – all this with the delighted twinkle in the eye of a man who loves surprises.

With the lines laid out on the floor, Phil laid down along the line of one of the sections a row of small nails with the heads carefully laid to the line. Then he laid a board over the nails and walked on it. The nail heads made dents in the board, which he connected in a fair curve. He then took an axe and chopped out the mold quite close to the line and bade Harry plane it down. The next one he told Harry to cut out himself.

"Oh I couldn't. I'd split it."

"Well, then we'll make another," observed Phil mildly.

In one day they made a whole set of molds and nailed them together, and Harry carried them home on his truck.

Quick next set up a backbone, using a ⅝" piece of steel, 5 inches wide and 20 feet long for the keel. A piece of 2-inch, heavy-wall pipe bent on a pipe bender was welded to it for a stem, and a piece of T-bar made the horn timber. On the keel he set a stress box with ¾" iron wiggle-bars in it and filled this with lead for ballast. The transom was laminated of plywood, cedar, and Fer-a-Lite covered with fiberglass cloth. Working alone, Harry bolted it in place on the horn timber, using a tackle to the barn roof, both hands, and his head. Tabs were welded on the stem and drilled. Ribbands were bolted to these and run through notches cut in the molds so the outside of the ribband was flush with the outside of the mold, for the ribbands were to remain part of the hull. Deck clamps and shelf were put in the same way. Floor timbers of steel were welded to the top of the stress box and bolted through the ribbands to tie the two sides of the boat together. Then the whole structure was covered from gunwale to gunwale with wire plank, stapled into every ribband it crossed. Another layer of wire plank was laid from bow to stern, wired to the first layer at its many intersections, and stapled to the ribbands. Next a layer of 3-foot-wide stretch mesh was laid from gunwale to gunwale and stapled to the ribbands. Stretch mesh is like hardware cloth but with no galvanizing, so it can be twisted and bent into compound curves as the wires slide by each other. The mesh was covered with a final layer of the same material 4 feet wide so that the seams would not come in the same place.

Now that the form of the boat was rigidly established, Quick mushed Fer-a-Lite through the wire and jiggled it to be sure all voids were filled and it adhered to the wires. Then he climbed inside, smoothed it off, and ran around outside to be sure it hadn't sagged and to apply another dose.

When the whole boat was done and cured, he covered the boat inside and out with fiberglass cloth set in resin, working it around and over the ribbands. Thus, he had a smooth, fair surface inside and out. From this point on, she was finished like a wooden boat with oak deck beams, plywood decks covered with Fer-a-Lite and fiberglass, laminated beams for the house top, and cedar sheathing inside. She was almost complete in 1984, needing only the cockpit framing and planking. The cockpit floor is removable to provide easy access to the engine. The steering gear is a worm gear out of *Emmie B.* – much too heavy, but then the whole boat is overbuilt, Quick says.

He has been at the job now for eight years, and he is in no hurry to finish, although he keeps working at it. He likes building a boat. He is doing a good job and is justly proud of it. "If you want to go sailing," he says, "buy a boat; if you want to build a boat, build a boat." She will be done some day, and the doctor will enjoy sailing her, but his patient is willing to bet a good shirt that about that time, he will be starting another.

# 10

## *Exploits and Disasters*

### *DUFFER II*

*T his tale centers* on Frank Pallow (or Palow or Pollo), alias George Miller, a pirate as ingenious and as ruthless as any villain of fiction. He was a seaman on a Pacific coast freighter and eventually landed in Spain. There he stole a small boat and sailed her across the Atlantic in the winter of 1930, apparently with the intention of smuggling aliens into the United States, However, he was wrecked on the coast of Cuba.

In June 1931, he was issued a chauffeur's license in New York. On July 2, 1931, he mailed a package from a Boston post office.

Later in July, Pallow invited one Albert Hitchcock to go for a boat ride with him. He told Hitchcock that he had been smuggling aliens and had come to Massachusetts to steal another boat in order to return to the business. Apparently, he and Hitchcock broke into a number of yachts, stole canned food and marine supplies, and cached them on Peddock's Island in Boston Harbor, where they hid out.

William Kemp of the Quincy Yacht Club noticed unusual activity on the island, informed the police, and with them searched the island. They caught Hitchcock but failed to find Pallow or the cached supplies. As they returned to the mainland, Hitchcock pointed to *Duffer II*, a 29-foot Friendship sloop lying off the Quincy Yacht Club, as the boat they had planned to steal. The police thought he was bragging and ignored him.

Hitchcock was given a three-month suspended sentence for stealing a canoe.

On the night of July 29, 1931, *Duffer II* disappeared. So did Hitchcock. *Duffer's* owner, Clark Saville, at once notified the Coast Guard and spent several days investigating every harbor and cove between Quincy and New York in search of his boat, but he found no trace of her.

On August 25, George J. Wemyss was kidnapped while swimming off Hough's Neck, Quincy Bay, Massachusetts. On September 4, Wemyss staggered into a Long Island police station, badly beaten up and exhausted, telling how he had been held captive on a yacht and had been taken ashore to a hut, from which he had escaped when his guards got to fighting among themselves.

On September 9, off Long Island, two men boarded the yacht *Penguin*, owned by Benjamin F. Collings. The men tied Collings up, threw him overboard, and attacked his wife. They demanded transportation to the Connecticut shore for a wounded man. Mrs. Collings's description of the two men corresponded to Hitchcock and Pallow.

In early October, a British vessel in the English Channel hailed a small sailing yacht, whose skipper said he was sailing around the world on a wager.

On October 14, 1931, *Duffer II* was wrecked on the shore of Schiermonnikoog Island off the Dutch coast. There had been three men aboard. Apparently, they had anchored off the shore the night before. An onshore gale came on, and the anchor began to drag. The crew fought hard to save the sloop. They slid the stove down the anchor line to act as a spring and even lifted the engine off its beds and added that to the weight of the stove and anchor; but *Duffer* at last dragged ashore. The body of Pallow was found aboard, but the other two bodies, if there were two others, were never recovered.

In the wreckage was found a trail board inscribed "Wilbur A. Morse, builder, Friendship, Me."

The American Consul reported the details to the Secretary of State and, in reply to a letter from the Chief of Police in Quincy, to that official. While the connection with the kidnapping of Wemyss and the murder of Collings is tenuous, the police and the newspapers regarded it as likely. There can be no doubt of the identification of *Duffer II* as the wreck on the Dutch coast. Her engine serial number checked out. Also, there seems little doubt as to the identification of Pallow, as he had the chauffeur's license and the receipt from the Boston post office in his pocket.

This unusual tale is supported by evidence in the Friendship Museum.

## OCHITO

*Ochito* was a big sloop, 36 feet long with beam and draft in proportion. She was said to have been a Wilbur Morse boat, and her owner, J. Edward Crowley, Jr., described her as having a rather more sweeping sheer than most Friendships and an exceptionally clean run. She had a long house, a small cockpit, and the longest gaff and shortest hoist on her mainsail I have ever seen on a boat her size.

In the fall of 1931, Crowley and his wife left Gloucester for Bermuda. The experience of many yachtsmen confirms the generally held opinion that autumn is no time to be at sea in the North Atlantic. The 600-odd miles that Bermuda racers cover in four days in June took the Crowleys 21 days.

They spent the winter in Bermuda and then started for the Azores and Europe. At the very start, they met a heavy head wind and ran into St. Georges to wait it out. But as their big mainsail drove them rapidly up Town Cut, *Ochito* stubbed her toe heavily on a wire stretched across the channel to a barge on the far shore, fell forward, and fetched up on another wire. She leaked some, so they hauled her out, recaulked her strained garboards, took on an enthusiastic lad named Cuddy, and struck out again.

Cuddy proved "more ornamental than useful," but with a fine fair wind for the first week, his services were not vitally needed. That was just as well, because he could neither steer a compass course nor cook a meal. He was assigned to do the resting while the skipper and mate steered and cooked by turns.

After a week of running before a fair wind and a lumpy sea under double-reefed main and staysail, they were tired. They hove *Ochito* to under a trysail and two sea anchors, cones of canvas extended by 30-inch-diameter iron hoops. She lay comfortably thus, and after a day of hard beating against a heavy easterly, they hove to again. The fair wind soon returned, however, and *Ochito* pressed on across the Atlantic. After a day or two of calms enlivened by the near presence of water spouts and another day escorted by friendly whales eager to exhibit to each other and the Crowleys their ability to hurl themselves clear of the water, they made Castello Branca and picked up a mooring in Horta that night in a spatter of rain. Crowley writes:

. . . We were carrying too much canvas for entering a strange port, but we could not have shortened before we made the best of our daylight, and we wouldn't shorten after that with our harbor furl less than an hour away . . . . After we tied up . . . doused sails and hung out our yellow flag for the morning, we went below and finished what delicacies were left in the stores and enjoyed the fact that it was getting to be a nasty night outside.

They went on to Ponta Delgada, beating a local coasting schooner on the voyage, had a rough passage to Cape St. Vincent because the Portuguese trades were not acting as predicted, and finally slipped into Lagos, "fastened to the mainland of Europe at last."

We next catch sight of the Crowleys in Piraeus. George Weller, a *New York Times* writer, saw *Ochito* as an inexpensive ride home. Crowley said "December is a terrible month for sail in the Med, but we have to get my capital home, and I can't start the engine." Cuddy was still aboard, but Mrs. Crowley was to meet them at Ischia, off Naples, Italy.

Crowley, Weller, and Cuddy sailed from Piraeus on December 4, mistook the entrance to the Canal of Corinth, and grounded on the weather side of a breakwater in the rainy dark. Weller held her off the breakwater by superhuman determination while Cuddy and Crowley got out lines and warped her clear.

They continued past Parnassus above Delphi, past the scene of Lord Byron's disillusionment, past Ithaca and Corfu, and beat across to Italy in two weeks of heavy westerlies. In the Strait of Messina, dead tired, hungry, dizzy from a diet of rum eggnogs and potato chips, they hove to with a light at the mast head, careless of whether or not they were run down by the procession of steamers from Europe to Suez.

After a brief stop at Reggio Calabria, a desperate night fighting to keep clear of the Lipari Islands where Mussolini maintained a concentration camp, an unhealthy spot for an American journalist, and a week under trysail, they made Ischia. Mrs. Crowley joined the ship, and Weller left to go home on a tramp steamer.

From Ischia, *Ochito* made Gibraltar with only one storm, ran down to the Canaries, and raised Sandy Hook in 44 days from the Canaries. For 18 days in the tradewinds, *Ochito* sailed herself.

Crowley was unable to sell *Ochito*, and she disappeared, last seen in a marina near Neponset, Massachusetts.

*Gladys D.* Rose *in Carver's Harbor working as a fisherman. Notice the high rails for carrying a deck load of fish. (The Mariners' Museum)*

## SUSANNAH, ex-*GLADYS D. ROSE*

Wilbur Morse's yard built the 36-foot *Gladys D. Rose* in 1904 to haul fish gurry to a glue factory, an unsavory occupation she pursued for a number of years. For this trade, she was built with a large hold and a small cuddy. She was sold to a Vinalhaven fisherman, several of whose acquaintances claimed that she had once, by virtue of her high bulwarks, brought in 12 tons of hake.

She fished commercially until World War II, the last of her career being under Bert Andrews, who went handlining in her. It is said that he would anchor her in deep water, fish until he was exhausted, chop the anchor line with an axe, and sail home. If fish were cheap in those days, so also were anchors.

About 1940, just before the war, Boyd Guild bought her and took her up to Sargentville. He did not use her much because of the war and sold her to Joe Tapley, who hauled her out for the duration. Several years on the bank in the sun, wind, and rain did her no good.

In 1946 Paul Coolidge bought her. By virtue of a coat of roofing paper, she was floated to Frank L. Day's yard in Sedgwick to be rebuilt. The rebuilder, Orrin L. Oles of Noank, Connecticut, chipped the cement out of her bilge and found that most of her frames could be removed with a shovel. To preserve her shape, he supported her hull from outside with a forest of stocks and rebuilt her entirely except for keel, sternpost, and a few frames forward. He also installed a Jeep engine in place of her old, two-cylinder Palmer.

In 1948 she was launched, renamed *Susannah,* and taken off to Ringtown Island in Jericho Bay, where she was ballasted with beach rocks and pobblestones, small, round rocks about the size of softballs. Even with her 2,000-pound iron keel, these proved inadequate, so the rocks were replaced with 5,400 pounds of galvanized bolts, rivets, and clinch rings.

Coolidge, her new owner, a talented pianist, was a student at Harvard and at the New England Conservatory of Music. He had a Steinway concert grand piano installed in *Susannah*'s fish hold. It was such a tight fit that the key board extended into the fo'c's'le, where he had his piano stool. Aft of the instrument he built accommodations and planned to live aboard in New York harbor winters while continuing his studies at Columbia. During the summers he sailed day parties out of Boothbay Harbor with Captain Chester Lovett as skipper. He did his practicing in the evening to the delight of Boothbay's music lovers.

In 1953 Coolidge sold her to John S. Dickerson, Jr., who ran a boatyard in Essex, Connecticut. Dickerson removed the piano, reballasted her with three tons of lead in the bilge, rebuilt her accommodations below, and painted her dark green. The photograph shows her as she was under Captain Dickerson's command.

She survived Hurricane Carol in Port Jefferson, lying to a 28-pound Danforth anchor with 250 feet of 1-inch line, and was one of the few vessels left afloat when the skies cleared.

Susannah *when she was owned by John S. Dickerson. (Courtesy of Capt. Robin Colcord)*

Late in the 1950s, *Susannah* was again for sale. E. Pierson Richardson of Brookline wrote, " . . . it was a case of love at first sight . . . from a picture." The picture was in an advertisement by John Alden in the brokerage section of *Yachting*. Richardson at once drove to Saybrook, sailed *Susannah* up and down the Connecticut River between the bridges, and bought her that day. For several years, he used her with great pleasure for family cruising down east and in 1961 had her keel replaced by Richard Price in Marblehead. Rot had been found in the mast step. "I wanted to do absolutely everything I could to keep her going indefinitely," he wrote.

In the summer of 1962, Richardson and his family cruised to the eastward, stopping to visit Murray Peterson at South Bristol, then going on to Blue Hill, Isle au Haut, and Tenants Harbor. The family went home by land, leaving Richardson with a strong and experienced university student named Steve to bring the sloop back to Massachusetts. Despite fog, calm, and a balky engine, they got as far as Jewell Island in Casco Bay on the night of August 28. They missed the anchorage in the fog, anchored in the lee of the island, and stood anchor watches that night.

The morning brought ragged, dark, low-flying clouds and a strong northeast wind in the wake of storm Alma. The forecast, however, was for improving weather as the wind shifted to the north and northwest. Because time pressed, they double-reefed the mainsail, set the staysail, and had a fast trip to Cape Elizabeth and Wood Island with the sloop making seven knots or better and behaving beautifully. There was no sign, however, of a shift of wind.

Off the Cape Porpoise whistle buoy, *Susannah* gybed inadvertently with the boom broad off. When it fetched up violently on the sheet, the boom broke at what later appeared to be a rotten spot. They hove to under the staysail and managed to wrestle aboard the broken boom, lower the mainsail, and make all secure. They ran on under staysail and turned their attention to the engine. Despite the engine's having run for much of the day before, the battery seemed weak, and the wires were wet. Although they dried her off as best they could, she refused to come to life.

With the wind still fresh northeast and the day waning, they decided to try for York Harbor.

Beneath a lowering sky, at about six o'clock that afternoon, they bore down on the lee shore before the wind and sea under staysail alone, tired from standing anchor watches and from a long day at sea and discouraged by their failure to start the engine. Although they knew they could not sail up the narrow channel against the ebb tide under staysail alone, they hoped to get under the lee of the northern point enough to anchor until someone could tow them in.

They negotiated a furious breaking sea on the bar, a bad place with an onshore breeze and an ebb tide, then swung around the northern headland and into the lee where the water was not nearly so rough. The wind was fluky here, and an eddy of tide set *Susannah* toward the southern shore. They dropped their biggest anchor, a 50-pound kedge, ready on the bow; at first, it took hold. Soon, though, it began to drag, bumping over the rocky bottom. They hastily launched their skiff, planning to carry out another anchor, but just then she struck. The surge hammered her on the bottom. The dragging anchor let her bow swing around, and despite the vigorous efforts of volunteers on the shore and the Coast Guard boat from Portsmouth, *Susannah* drove broadside up on the rocky beach.

The next morning at low water, it was evident that she had sailed her last voyage. Her starboard bow was stove in, and her keel was split. With the help of local people, her gear was salvaged, much of it eventually finding its way into other Friendship sloops. Fortunately, no one was hurt, and Richardson, incurably infected with Yachtsman's Disease, in the same letter in which he described the accident, asked Murray Peterson to design him the schooner *Serenity*, which he now sails out of Mt. Desert Island.

# *MANDALAY*

In Chapter 6, we told how *Mandalay* was designed with a Friendship sloop hull and a ketch rig by Wilbur Morse and built in 1938 by Scott Carter. Her early years were spent in Florida waters under several owners until she was bought in 1950 by James S. Rockefeller, who later was to run the Bald Mountain Boat Works and build *Old Baldy* as well as several other Friendships. His account of *Mandalay*'s last years follows:

Bringing her up to Stamford, Connecticut, I outfitted her for a world cruise. She was in awful shape with dry rot rampant all through her. With the help of Bob Kingett of Freeport, Long Island, we replaced the rotten timbers and altered the sail plan. We cut the area down from 1,000 square feet to 800. We cut four feet off the bowsprit, made the sails loose-footed (no boom whatsoever), put a roller reefer on the jib, added permanent backstays, and fitted her with twin spinnakers for tradewind passages.

In November of 1951, we took her around Hatteras and got blown clear the other side of the Gulf Stream by one gale after another. She leaked badly. On Cumberland Island, Georgia, it took another six months before she was seaworthy enough to tackle the Pacific. Half a keg of boat nails in her bottom and pounds of caulking and iron straps on her weaker ribs helped the leaking to some extent.

From Georgia, we wandered down through the Bahamas to the Virgin Islands. From there, I took her to Panama through the canal to Galapagos, Marquesas, Tahiti, the outlying islands of Moorea, Huahine, Raitea, Bora Bora, on to Suvarov, Samoa, Fiji, and finally the New Hebrides. She was a good sailer downwind and, with the twin spinnakers, would do up to 180 miles a day with a good wind. It took six days from the Virgin Islands to Panama, three weeks to Galapagos in the oil calms, 26 days to make the 3,000 miles from Galapagos to the Marquesas.

By the time I reached the New Hebrides, two-and-a-half years had elapsed since leaving the states, and *Mandalay*'s bottom was getting weary. So I sold her to a French planter in Santo who was going to use her for carrying supplies for his cocoa and copra plantation and to go in search of native labor on the nearby islands. Lately, I have learned she has struck a reef and been lost — a fitting end, I think. Much better to go that way than to rot out her remaining years on a forgotten beach.

She was a wonderful sea boat, with a motion as easy as a rocking chair. She would sail herself until the wind worked abaft the beam. She went to windward like a lard can, and she was top heavy with her extra stick and the raised deck. Outside she had an iron keel of two tons and inside another ton or two of sash weights, which I bedded in concrete to stiffen the hull. She was a gallant boat, and I wonder if she didn't travel further from her downeast home than any of her kin.

In the Marquesas, she lived up to her *Friendship* name by rescuing a dismasted 38-foot Dutch sloop, *Anna Elizabeth*, from going on the rocks. Under full sail (the motor was never dependable), *Mandalay* towed the crippled yacht safely away from the booming rocks and into a little harbor where we repaired the mast of the Dutchman and restepped it using *Mandalay*'s mainmast as a derrick.

## *TINQUA*

*Tinqua* was a Bruno & Stillman fiberglass sloop built in 1971 and owned by Warren A. Locke of Milton, Massachusetts. He kept her in Hadley's Harbor on Naushon and annually sailed her east to join the regatta at Friendship.

In 1977, somewhere to the south of Seguin, after an overnight voyage from Massachusetts, *Tinqua* lost her steering. The bronze rudder post was sheared off in the tube that carried it up through the hull. There was no way to get hold of it, so, steering with the sails, Locke headed *Tinqua* toward shore. He intended to run in to the Kennebec River, but wind, tide, and the difficulty of steering with the sails conspired to set him close to Whaleback Ledge. He anchored at last, but the anchor failed to hold in the rocky bottom and *Tinqua* grounded on the ledge. Locke and his crew saved some of their personal possessions and some of the vessel's gear, but she broke up quickly. The crew got safely ashore from the lee of the ledge, but *Tinqua* was a total loss. As the rock is awash at high water, most of the equipment that would float came ashore on Stage Island later.

## *ANNIE B.*

*Annie B.* was a 40-foot sloop built in 1912; she might be identified as the *Alice A.*, the only 40-foot sloop Wilbur Morse built in that year. All we know for sure is that she was a Morse boat and so could have been built by Charles or Albion. She had been rebuilt during World War II. With oak frames, pine and cedar planking, and galvanized fastenings, she had been covered with Celastic. The description circulated by a broker in 1955 declared her "sound throughout; no leakage at all; boat in excellent condition — ready to sail around the world." She had somehow made her way to Charlotte, Vermont, on Lake Champlain, where she lay off the home of her owner, Luther H. Bridgman.

Bridgman's account of *Annie B.*'s loss follows:

> It was a funny thing, but the last time we saw her whole, Boots [his wife] remarked how good she looked framed in our window. The next morning about 5:30, Boots woke up, looked out, but the boat was gone.
>
> Boots roused me and we both went tearing down to the shore, thinking that she had sunk at her mooring. I took the dinghy and grappled for her, and, not finding her, we began to search the Vermont shore. Later, we noticed the mooring line and an extra safety line had broken loose, and we decided to drag the area, feeling sure the boat had sunk because the buoy had.
>
> After dragging up and down the Vermont side, we gave up. We were sure she had gone down.
>
> Then the telephone rang. It was Alan Carter, director of the Vermont Symphony, who has a summer residence near Essex, New York. He said a boat answering the description of mine was literally shipwrecked about three miles down the coast. I went right over on the ferry, and sure enough, the boat was the *Annie B.* her bow in two feet of water, her stern in five.
>
> After I came back, Paul Aschenbach, three hired men, and I barraged the Coast Guard for help, and, equipped with line, pumps, ground tackle and aqualung, we set out for the shipwreck.
>
> We tied an anchor to the high side of the boat and used block and falls between the anchor line and the boat to raise her enough to make underwater repairs.

Slowly, but with a creak of triumph, the boat was partially righted, and we went under and tacked canvas over the holes with strips of wood. Then I rowed a 5-inch hawser from the Coast Guard boat . . . to the *Annie B.* . . . but she was more than the Coast Guard boat could handle.

So then, with my rusty knowledge of semaphore, I managed to get across to the Coast Guard captain, Chief Bothwell, that we would have to get her alongside his boat to use its big pump. That pump was our main staff of life, but we had to use another small one at the same time. When we finally sighted Shelburne (Vermont) harbor, we were pretty sure we had succeeded.

But just then the big pump conked out and the little one was forced to go it alone. But it was too much; we knew it couldn't last. We cut loose the bow line, ready to give up and let her go.

We were in for another shock, however. Just as suddenly as it had stopped, the pump got going again. Boots, meanwhile, had contacted Shelburne harbor and told them we were approaching in a state of distress. We held our breath and headed north to Shelburne Point, but the pump now going beyond its capacity went out again, this time for keeps. Somehow we wouldn't give up, and all of us pitched in, bailing water like mad, using anything we could find, even waste baskets, and finally we got up to Shelburne Shipyard,.

Before we could establish communications, she sank. And there was nothing more we could do to save her. I'll go down in the aqualung, pick her bones dry, and save what I can. After that, she belongs to the lake.

However, Bridgman did not give up. He wrote later, "I spent the next two months patching her underwater and decking over the cockpit. I finally succeeded in floating her and put her on the marine railway at the shipyard. As soon as her bowsprit crossed the shoreline, she suffered her last indignity. The cradle broke. The fall finished her."

## *COMESIN* and the Bridge of Lions

*Another Friendship,* Comesin, nearly lost her life in a frightful incident under a drawbridge. Marjorie Wilder recounted in *Yachting*, May 1980:

It's not easy to get on a boat and sail away, but we did it. *Comesin* had never been more ready or more beautiful. But now, her fate was in the hands of an inattentive bridge-tender and we were barely three days into The Cruise – 40 minutes from home if returning by car after shipwreck.

We had been anchored in Salt Run at Conch Island – soaking up boat life at last, enjoying being part of the show for the thrice-daily sightseeing boat, and gradually letting off the pressures of winter and spring. Our next easy hop down the ocean would be to Ft. Pierce. After lunch on what now appeared to be Doomsday, we had motored around the bend to St. Augustine for gas, water, some groceries, and laundry. In our leisured mood we did not mind when the clothes weren't dry in time for us to make it through the Bridge of Lions by 1630. Rush hour would pass tranquilly for us.

A Canadian sloop, a little bigger than we were, came up the waterway and anchored nearby to wait for the bridge. She was something to watch idle-eyed, with her foreign flags and sunbrowned, shorts-clad, longhaired crew. When the minute hand rose to the hour for the bridge to open again for yachts, the laundry was on board and adieus were done. Without a moment's anxiety, in fact ecstatic over a sea bag of dry clothes, we powered in a smooth curve to the channel, waving at a young crewman hand-over-handing the big Canadian boat's anchor rode.

We turned for the bridge, sounded our horn, and heard the sirens answering, saw the gate lights flashing, and three boys getting off their bicycles to stand by the parapet opposite the control tower on the bridge. So far, so perfect. Just through the bridge and around the island into our cove, and we would anchor for sunset and supper. The only obstacle – the bridge that had sometimes failed to respond, where sometimes a shrimp boat was a-comin' on the other side – was raised wide and clear.

Then the bearded skipper of the big boat behind us was dramatically sounding a ram's horn for the bridge. And he was gaining on us. Incredibly he did intend to go first, and both diplomatic courtesy and prudence called for letting him. The tidal currents there are awesome, and there was neither time nor room for maneuvers. Slowing as much as we could, we veered off, then, almost at the fenders, swung back into his wake as he sped beneath the bascule we thought *we* had raised. A lot more heart-in-mouth than we expect in the non-competitive cruising we do. But we shrugged an allowance for flower children manners, thinking "Peace to you, too, fella, and sorry for any unintended offense!" We were still gulping and trying to smooth our ruffled feelings while steering straightly in the turmoiled waters of the bridge when he gave two mighty blasts of the ram's horn at his lips and the bridge with alacrity began cranking down! We stared up, dumbfounded in new disbelief. But it was coming down and there was no way for us to stop, back up or go sideways. I saw my own horror showing on the faces of the boys on the bridge. Though our skipper sounded the unfailing horn and I shoved open the throttle, they were pygmy acts, no match for the screaming sirens and gnashing gears of the lowering bridge.

We had once seen a boat that over-anticipated a bridge opening. She was at our boatyard for a new mast and other repairs. Her captain was in the hospital. Except in the nursery rhyme, we had never heard of a bridge coming down on top of a fair lady, a bonny boat, a United States documented vessel given extraordinary love and care. Still, this bridge's worst was about to be done – and done quickly – splintering *Comesin*'s stubby mast, chewing up her shrouds, crunching her hull against its finders in sudden towers of swooped inundation. The nightmarish *What if?* of that imagery persists.

But the boy ran. However many giant steps were needed to reach the bridgetender, he took them, and in time. The bridge stopped in glorious midair.

The wonderful boy reappeared, gazing down at us as we came safely through. I think I may have waved numbly at him. He deserved a hero's salute.

As for the bridgetender, our narrow escape must haunt him, too. If we're more careful, surely so is he. Now when following another boat through, we prefer to first see the whites of the bridgetender's eyes – even when we are the boat that signalled the opening and should have been noted, a Friendship being a distinctive-looking boat in our waters and rarely mistaken for another boat choosing to go first. And we think it best never to two-toot that we're through if there's a boat behind us.

Who was that boy? I still want to thank him.

## *SCHOODIC* Towards Bermuda

On June 24, 1979, Bruce Lanning, Dick Salter, and Tom Hanna, aboard *Schoodic*, left Winter Harbor, Maine, for Bermuda, intending to return in time for the regatta in late July. After a stop in Southwest Harbor to repair the engine, which was needed for charging batteries to operate loran and lights, they had a slow and comparatively uneventful passage, with light head winds for the most part, until the evening of Saturday, June 30. By then they had covered less than half the distance to Bermuda, and Tom, who had undertaken to cook, was out of action with seasickness, requiring Dick and Bruce to stand alternate four-hour watches.

About 2100, a screaming rain squall struck, followed at intervals by others. They kicked up a confused and lumpy sea. In one of the intervals between squalls, the

Schoodic. *(T. Gray)*

dinghy, which they were towing, drifted under the bow and was swamped when *Schoodic* came down a sea on top of it. They tried to lie to it as if it were a sea anchor, but with double-reefed main and staysail, she did not lie well.

The next day, Sunday, they bailed out the dinghy and dropped it astern on 150 feet of line, but they continued to make slow progress through lumpy seas with light airs against the Gulf Stream. That evening, with Tom still suffering from seasickness and Dick and Bruce all but exhausted, still less than half way to Bermuda, they decided to up helm and run in for Nantucket, 215 miles away. If they had continued to Bermuda, they would have had to start back before they had time to refit and rest, to say nothing of enjoying the island.

Then, early on Monday morning, they were struck again. *Schoodic*'s log reads:

*Monday, 2 July '79*
*0000* Wind WSW 15-18 knots, S 4-5. Seas running 12-15 ft. Very sloppy going. C 350° SW horizon full of ominous black clouds. Lower ones blackest. It appears we are in for another bad night. Bruce & Dick getting dangerously low on sleep.
*0030* Dick on watch – called Bruce to come on deck to assist as squall line approaches. Double reefed mains'l and stays'l. Jib furled on roller. Wind picked up suddenly. Worst gusts estimated to be over 70 kts. Very, very heavy rain. Furled jib torn from forestay – it did *not* unfurl. Port jib sheet, ½" dacron parted 1 ft. back from clew, leech of jib shredded, tabling gone. Altered course to keep wind close on port bow to barely hold wind in sails to retain control. Suspect a staysail also blown out, but now unable to see in darkness and heavy rain. Seas breaking over port bow and running down deck, shooting over stern. Stbd side down so far water is half way between top of cabin side and companionway. Cockpit flooded. Speed 6 knots plus – and we're trying to spill wind out of the sails! Cook got out of his bunk, put on life jacket and pulled out abandoned ship supplies. Dick and Bruce wearing life lines (the night watch standers always wear lifelines) are very much concerned for the safety of the vessel. Bruce said conditions now much worse than he experienced in

100 kt. winds off Delaware coast a few years ago. All hands speaking directly to their Creator. Above weather conditions lasted for an hour. By the time two hours had passed, winds were down to 20 kts. again. Dick went forward and furled the stays'l, which was damaged, but not blown out. Dinghy wallowing astern, swamped and capsized. Our eyes burning from salt in water.

*0330* Wind now 15-20 kts. southerly. Furled mains'l and relashed water and fuel stores on foredeck. Bilges again check to be dry. Amazed that we did not ship any water during the "black squall." Vessel laid-to using the capsized dinghy as a sea anchor until first light. Bruce and Dick absolutely exhausted. Rolled Tom out of his bunk to stand watch for ships. He can be just as seasick on watch as he is laid out in his bunk. Bruce and Dick try to get some shuteye.

At 1000 on Wednesday, they arrived in Nantucket, very glad indeed to be in, to wash off the salt, and to rest up after a very considerable adventure.

It is interesting to note that the vessel weathered the storm well. As in most cases, it was the exhaustion of the crew that was the limiting factor.

# *PERSEVERANCE* ex-*DOTTIE G.*

*Dottie G.*, a 27-foot Friendship sloop, was designed by Eldredge McInnis for Joseph Plumb and built at Simms Yacht Yard in Scituate, Massachusetts, in 1962. Plumb already had a magnificent schooner yacht, *Dorothy G.*, built on the lines of a Gloucesterman, and he built *Dottie G.* as her little sister. She is all of the best: She is planked with African mahogany, and her deck, transom, and all her bright work are teak. Her trail boards are gold-leafed, capped with a cast bronze eagle head. Her hollow spars were made by the Pigeon Hollow Spar Co., and by Simms. All her hardware was designed especially for her and cast by the Taylor Foundry. Turnbuckles on the shrouds are hidden by deadeyes and lanyards for an authentic, antique look. Her transom is decorated with a carved and gold-leafed eagle and surrounded by what appears to be a rope cast in bronze. Below, she was elegantly appointed. Indeed, on deck, below, or from a distance, she was a gem of a Friendship sloop.

Plumb kept her on a mooring in Marion, Massachusetts. Now it happened that on the shore of Marion Harbor was a Tabor Academy student named Bill Reed. Sailing and rowing around the harbor, he was much attracted to *Dottie G.* and hoped some day to own her.

After college and a cruise to the Pacific with Phineas Sprague of Cape Elizabeth, Reed found himself in a position to buy a boat. Plumb had died, and *Dottie G.* had been sold. Finally, he traced her down to a New Jersey yard and bought her. She had been neglected as to paint and varnish, but her fundamental structure was sound. He cleaned her up, named her *Perseverance*, and sailed her up to Mystic, Connecticut.

In September 1977, Reed was exhibiting her in the Stamford, Connecticut, in-the-water boat show as part of a display to promote *Maritime Quarterly*. There he met Kevin Latady who asked to sail back to Mystic with him on Sunday night, September 18-19.

The wind was generally fair but light and variable, and *Perseverance* eased along under full sail. A little after midnight, about six miles east of Stratford Shoal, while Latady steered, Reed was lying on the cockpit floor, contemplating the heavens. The light breeze had steadied on the port quarter. He noticed a mistiness about the stars, stood up, and saw a darkness over the New York shore that looked like a bank of haze. Even though it did not appear to be anything serious, he took in the main topsail and went out on the bowsprit to take in the jib topsail, having some trouble controlling halyard, sheet, and tack line. He had the sail down to the point where he could reach the tack when a terrific squall hit from the northwest, tore the sail out of his hand, and sent it to the masthead. The sloop broached to and lay broadside to the wind, flat to the water, half her gaff submerged. Reed picked his way aft, afraid the rigging might part, feeling that his place was at the wheel. As he passed the hatch, he thought to go below and start the bilge pump. He saw that the water in the cabin lay at the same height as the water in the cockpit – *Perseverance* has no bridge deck – and realized with a shock that the immediate problem was survival. *Perseverance* felt dead under his feet and he knew she was going.

He ordered Latady into the inflatable Zodiac towing astern and, out on the counter, tried to clear the painter. But when the squall struck, Latady had let the main sheet run, and it had become fouled on the quarter bitt from which the Zodiac was towing. So Reed reached for the bowline on the other end of the painter, tied into the Zodiac's towing bridle, to untie it. He said afterwards, "As I was bringing the fall out of the bight, it was taken out of my hand by the boat sinking. I was sitting on the stern, and the other fellow was in the boat, and by the time I finished, I was treading water."

Fortunately, he kept hold of the bridle and climbed into the Zodiac. It was still blowing very hard. The motor and the oars had been stolen at the boat show. There was no time to get life preservers. They were adrift, blowing like a bubble before the wind.

Reed untied the bridle, passed it through their belts, and tied it again to the boat so that if the boat capsized, they would stay with it. They drifted all night, in some distress lest wind and tide carry them out through The Race. However, about 8:30 in the morning, a helicopter passed over; they signalled it by waving oil coats, and it picked them up. Three yachts had been reported missing that night, but the crew of *Perseverance* were the only survivors.

As soon as he got ashore, Reed organized a search for the missing sloop, despite fall gales and rough water. Dragging with a wire was unsuccessful. At last he found the boat with a Klein Side Scanning Sonar. By running carefully down loran lines, they combed the area thoroughly and, after two-and-a-half days, found *Perseverance* on October 5, lying in 90 feet of water.

Reed hired a barge and several Navy divers from New London, who were each permitted a limited amount of spare-time diving. Because of the depth and temperature of the water, the divers used Morgan masks. These are like motorcycle helmets supplied with air from tanks on the barge and with a telephone set for communication with the surface. The "umbilical" also carried a high-pressure air hose for pneumatic tools and a high-pressure water hose.

The first attempt to put straps under *Perseverance* failed because of the soft, silty bottom. Not only did the slightest movement reduce visibility to zero, but also the bottom was so soft and shifty that even with a high-pressure jet the divers could not get a strap under her.

Therefore, they unbent the sails, brought up boom and gaff, and cleared all rigging aft of the mast. They put a strap under the counter and another around the mast, with a line to the forward bitt to prevent its riding up. An air bag was attached where the two lines joined to support the sling so it would not foul anything on deck. The derrick on the barge was attached to the sling, and for five minutes the operator jiggled and tugged gently, rocking *Perseverance* in the mud to break the suction. Once clear of the bottom, she came up easily. With her deck above water, she was quickly pumped out, towed into Milford, and hauled out.

Perseverance, *ex*-Dottie G.,
*as she was being raised.*
*(Courtesy of William Reed)*

She had been 47 days on the bottom and was hung with weed and marine growth of various kinds. Her engine had nearly disintegrated from corrosion. The pressure had driven water deep into the wood, so she was very heavy. The week after she was hauled, it snowed and froze hard, freezing the trapped water. For a year after her resurrection, it was impossible to keep varnish on her because the water in the wood lifted the varnish as it came out.

Rehabilitating *Perseverance* was a long job, but in 1984 she will be in top condition, clean, rebuilt below, with a new engine, and much new gear and rigging.

We learn from this experience that the sea, even Long Island Sound, is an environment hostile to man; that only an inch of plank or a skin of fiberglass stands between him and drowning; that a Friendship sloop with a large, open cockpit cannot afford to fill it; but that a bridge deck or a tight companionway might help. We also cannot escape the conclusion that in addition to foresight and caution, a seaman needs a little more than his share of good fortune.

# 11

# $H$ow to Sail a Friendship Sloop

$A$ *Friendship sloop was designed* to carry a cargo of fish or freight and not, like a modern racing yacht, simply to go fast. Therefore, she is to be sailed quite differently from a modern, light-displacement yacht with a tall, narrow rig.

In light weather, you must "put the duck to her," for she is a broad, deep, heavy boat and needs a great deal of sail to move her. The old-timers carried a huge mainsail, over that a topsail, and over the jib a jib topsail. A 32-foot Friendship sloop even nowadays may carry nearly 900 square feet of sail.

Going to windward in light airs, the main sheet should be eased off quite well over the quarter and the boat sailed no closer than six points (67½°) from the wind. If the sails slat in a chop, one can rig a vang or a boom tackle, but often just having someone lean against the boom with everyone else sitting to leeward will be sufficient.

As the boat begins to gather way, and she will do it slowly, little by little one can take in the main sheet and creep up toward the wind, perhaps as much as a point (11¼°); for as she gathers speed, she makes her own wind. Therefore, do nothing to disturb her momentum. Steer gently and sit still.

She should balance pretty well in gentle weather, perhaps even have a slight lee helm. Therefore, the headsails should be trimmed quite slack, their principal value in light weather being to funnel wind by the lee side of the mainsail. To trim them too flat is to kill her dead on her feet as the bow is forced to leeward, the drag of the rudder increased, and the mainsail backwinded by the draft off the leeches of the jibs.

As the breeze increases and the sloop begins to heel a little, the mainsail can be

Jolly Buccaneer.

trimmed a little flatter and the headsails trimmed so they luff just as the luff of the mainsail is beginning to lift. Still, the mainsail must not be trimmed flat amidships or she will
just stand still and nod at you. It must be eased off a little over the quarter. A traveller
long enough to hold the sail *down* as well as *in* will help the mainsail set better. Also, the
peak halyard needs constant attention. When the sail is first set, the peak should be
swayed up until there is a little wrinkle from peak to tack. As the sail fills, this will disappear, and the draft of the sail will be well forward where it belongs. However, as the
halyard stretches, even a little, a slight hard spot or tightness will appear from throat to
clew. This is best seen from the lee side of the sail. This hard spot spoils the draft of the
sail completely, so the boat will neither foot fast nor point high. She must be at once
luffed and the halyard swayed up again.

If the mainsail is rigged in the old-fashioned way, with jaws on the boom to hold it to
the mast, it is well to rig a tack downhaul to keep the luff of the mainsail tight. If a rigid
gooseneck is used with no vertical adjustment, it will be necessary to slack the peak,
sway up the throat halyard for a tight luff, and reset the peak.

At the same time, you are likely to notice that the headsail halyards have stretched
too, letting the luffs sag away from the stays and developing bags between the hanks.
Not only does this make a slack luff, but it lets the clew sag and encourages the leech to
tighten and backwind the mainsail. So keep everything swayed up snugly.

Someday, when you are well clear of the shore with a smooth sea and a gentle steady
breeze that gives the boat something less than hull speed, try her on different points of
sailing, perhaps every 5°, from as close as she will sail to dead before the wind and
make a diagram like the one in the illustration. Keep her on each course for about five
minutes, for her momentum or lack of it will affect her speed for a little while until she
settles down. The illustration was made for *Eastward* and gives a good idea of her effi-

ciency both to windward and off the wind. Notice that she actually gets to windward faster by sailing four-and-one-half to five points from the wind than she does by pointing higher, and she does better by tacking down wind about two points either side of the course than she does running dead before the wind. However, as the wind increases so the boat makes hull speed running dead before it, she can go no faster by bearing up; and if she will sail at hull speed pointing four points, she better do it.

Sailing a Friendship sloop hard on the wind in a good breeze is a delight. She carries a slight weather helm, so all that is needed is to ease off on the helm a little, let her feel her way up to the verge of a luff, bear off a whisker, and gently crowd up again. Her sharp bow, driven by a press of sail and her considerable heft, slashes through the chop, and the water closes astern with scarcely a scar on the surface of the sea.

If the chop increases and the wind eases off so she jumps twice at the same sea and then goes around it, motor sailing is the best way of getting in before dark. Sheet everything hard amidships and head about three points from the wind, as high as you can, and keep the sails full. Taking the seas at this angle with both sails and engine working will get you to windward faster and more comfortably than plugging head-on into a steep chop. Before the advent of marine engines, when the wind went soft at the end of the day and the sea smoothed out, it was common practice to rig a long oar on the lee side, row gently with one hand and steer with the other, thus maintaining a steady progress and urging the bow gently to windward.

As the strength of the wind increases, new factors begin to affect the boat's perform-

Chrissy *leading* Black Jack. *Notice that* Black Jack *is pointing higher but not sailing so fast.*

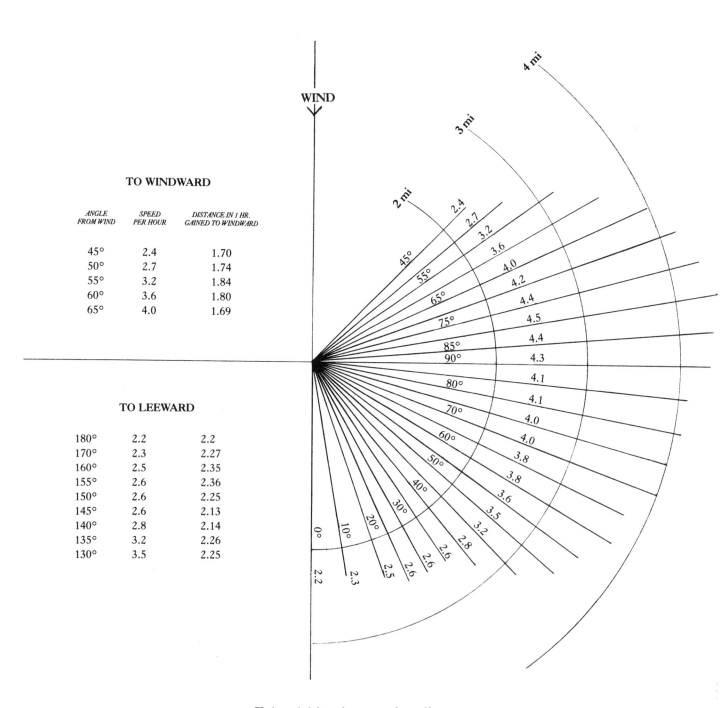

## TO WINDWARD

| ANGLE FROM WIND | SPEED PER HOUR | DISTANCE IN 1 HR. GAINED TO WINDWARD |
|---|---|---|
| 45° | 2.4 | 1.70 |
| 50° | 2.7 | 1.74 |
| 55° | 3.2 | 1.84 |
| 60° | 3.6 | 1.80 |
| 65° | 4.0 | 1.69 |

## TO LEEWARD

| | | |
|---|---|---|
| 180° | 2.2 | 2.2 |
| 170° | 2.3 | 2.27 |
| 160° | 2.5 | 2.35 |
| 155° | 2.6 | 2.36 |
| 150° | 2.6 | 2.25 |
| 145° | 2.6 | 2.13 |
| 140° | 2.8 | 2.14 |
| 135° | 3.2 | 2.26 |
| 130° | 3.5 | 2.25 |

Friendship sloop polar diagram

ance. On almost any point of sailing except a dead run, she will heel. As she ceases to sail on her bottom and begins to sail on her side, she is pushing an entirely different shape through the water. No longer does her sharp bow part the water, pass it aft by the easy turn of her bilge amidships, and leave it cleanly under her flat run. Now she rams her broad shoulder down into the sea, presenting a surface that skids her bow to windward and moves her center of lateral resistance forward, giving her such a weather helm that she wants to turn around and look you in the eye. This requires a strong pull on the tiller to hold her off and causes the rudder to drag heavily and act as a brake. At the same time, she shoves her broad and buoyant side into the water and instead of a flat run now presents a rounded, more nearly spherical shape. She now drags the ocean behind her, as you can see by noticing the big quarter wave astern.

To help counter the weather helm, trim headsails a little more tightly and let her come to the wind a little in the puffs, enough to lift the rail out of the water and luff the mainsail a little but not enough to shake the sail and bring her to a standstill, cold meat for the next heavy puff. It depends upon the characteristics of your own boat, but in general, sailing consistently with a luff in the mainsail takes the drive out of your most powerful sail and should be practiced gingerly and only in the heavy puffs.

As the wind increases and the boat heels further, the sails become less efficient. The drive of a sail depends on its acting as an airfoil and developing a lift on the lee side like an airplane wing on end. When the boat is upright, the lift is horizontal, parallel to the surface of the water. As the mast inclines to leeward, the lift increasingly develops a downward vector, tending to bury the bow rather than drive the boat ahead. Furthermore, the wind, instead of moving across the sail from luff to leech as it does when the boat is upright, now begins to blow off the top of the sail, moving more from tack to peak, and accordingly lessening the effect of the airfoil.

As the sloop heels further under the increased pressure of the wind, she drags her rail and lee deck through the water, which offers more drag than a bucket towed astern. At the same time, sailing on her round bilge, she skids off to leeward because the keel, no longer vertical, gets less grip on the water. Also, severe strains are developed in the hull, which, especially in the case of a heavily ballasted, old, wooden boat, can cause serious damage.

The original sloops were usually ballasted with rocks, which are not nearly as heavy as iron. This gives the boat a relatively high center of gravity and an easy motion. A load of fish on top of the rocks would raise the center of gravity still more. Accordingly, the boat would heel comparatively easily and would be reefed when the rail was awash before it began to blow really hard. Also, the shrouds, if carried, were set up with lanyards, not with turnbuckles, and stretched a little under tension. Thus, an old-timer always had a little slack in the lee rigging in a strong breeze. This meant that the mast itself was bending and taking some of the athwartships strain.

An old wooden sloop, especially if built according to the usual Morse construction plan and then fitted with an iron shoe and ballasted with iron or lead in the bilge, would suffer badly in a breeze. With no floor timbers to hold the boat together at the keel, with the mast stepped directly on the keel, and with a strong, heavy deck structure at the partners where the mast goes through the deck, there would be a tendency to pry the keel to windward and, when the boat tacked, to pry it the other way, loosening up the garboards. If the rigging were set up rigidly and tightly with turnbuckles, the mast would bend less and the horizontal strain would be converted into a compression strain, a downward push on the mast against the keel, which again would encourage leaks along the garboards. Also, the upward strain on the chainplates would develop a hogged look along the rail abreast the mast, a common sign of old age in wooden boats.

Mar-Gin *lugging her sail. If she were not in a race, she would have reefed before this.*

Therefore, the considerate skipper, when the wind gets up, when his sloop begins to make a great smother of foam under her lee bow, when she drags a heavy wave under her quarter, when her lee deck is consistently buried, when he has to carry a luff in the mainsail to keep her on her feet, and when a dispassionate look at the wake shows little forward progress and a slick to windward, will heave to and reef his mainsail. The fire-eating young racing hand with more guts than brains and perhaps imbued with false courage from reading tales of racing fishermen out of Gloucester may object, and the man used to sailing modern fin-keeled racing boats designed to sail well on their sides may think the skipper hasty; but a Friendship sloop was designed to sail on her bottom. To drive her through the water on her side is to abuse her.

Experience has shown the author that the easiest way to reef is to take in the jib, sheet the staysail down hard, and let the main sheet run with the helm hard down to leeward. The rudder will hold her bow to windward while the staysail pushes it to leeward, and she will hang with the wind just forward of the beam, sliding sideways, making a nice slick to windward, and lying quite peacefully. Then set up the topping lift and lower the mainsail so the gaff is about two feet off the boom. The heavy gaff brings the sail down, and the mast hoops do not bind as some sail tracks do when the boat is not heading into the wind. Now trim the main sheet. The sail will flap around some, but ignore it and tie down the tack earring tightly to the boom. Then pass the clew earring. A piece of ⅜" line with a splice in one end, carried for this express purpose, is passed around the boom outboard of a cheek block, the end carried through the splice, up through the reef cringle, down through the cheek block from aft forward exactly as modern boats do it with "jiffy" reefing, a new name for an old technique. Now haul hard on the reef earring, setting it up with a tackle if the sail is a heavy one and working from forward to aft along the reef band to be sure the sail is as far aft as it can be hauled and lies smoothly along the boom. Make fast the earring, which should have hauled the cringle down to the boom and out to the cheek block. Tie in the reef points around the bunched-up sail, not around the boom, using a single bow so they can be shaken out quickly. It is important to tie each one tightly, for if one is too slack, it will tear the sail at the reef points on either side of it. Now slack the main sheet, hoist the mainsail, and go on your way.

The sloop will sail on her feet, will have less weather helm with the center of effort moved forward under the reefed mainsail, and will be faster and more comfortable, efficient, and pleasant. The whole process should take no more than 15 or 20 minutes, and even our fire-eating friend will enjoy the result.

If one is suddenly overwhelmed by a squall or has only a short way to go in a heavy breeze, he can quickly reduce the area of the mainsail by scandalizing it, setting up the topping lift, and dropping the peak. This reduces the mainsail to a leg o' mutton sail or a trysail with the gaff and the upper part of the sail sagging off to leeward.

There is another real danger, heretofore unmentioned, of driving a Friendship sloop too hard. Many have large cockpits that extend nearly to the side of the boat. They were designed thus to make it easy to lift fish and lobster traps over the rail and to provide working space for the crew and space for bait barrels, fish boxes, and other gear. If such a sloop is pushed so far that her coaming goes under, she will fill very quickly. The weight of water on her lee side will hold her down, the rudder, now nearly horizontal, can have little effect, and she will sink very quickly indeed. William H. Taylor commented on this situation in the December 1946 *Yachting:*

Ruth Logan, *built in 1908 by Wilbur Morse, sailing comfortably reefed. (Courtesy of William Peterson)*

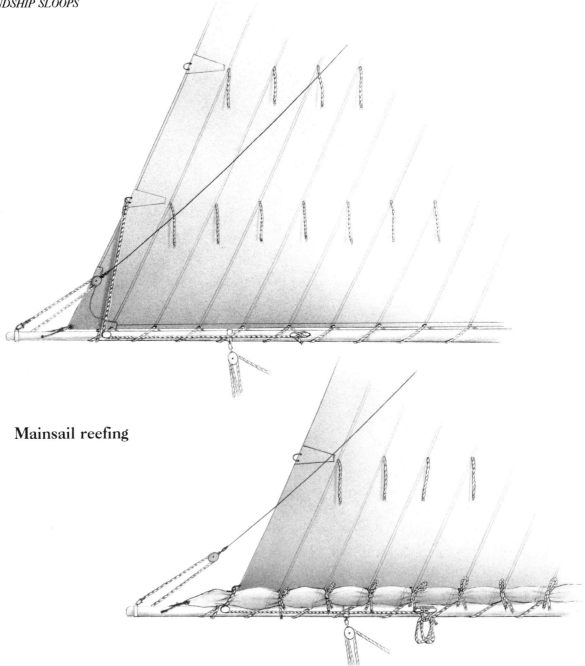

**Mainsail reefing**

While nobody will ever know for sure, I have always believed that this [filling the cockpit] was what caused the loss of the *Sea Fox*, with eight persons aboard, on Long Island Sound in 1931. I had owned *Sea Fox* for several years, and an abler boat, if you sailed her with reasonable judgment, you couldn't ask for. But she had inside scrap-iron ballast and a huge cockpit which, while self-draining, had five hatches in it, including a big box over the engine. As long as you sailed her on her bottom, or at least kept her coaming out of the water, she'd take you anywhere, yet in the end she went down so quickly that the skiff was still made fast to her stern when she was located and raised, months later. They must have lugged full sail on her too long, and held her down to a hard puff that drove her coaming under too deep. Once that big cockpit took in a load of water, a hatch probably fell or floated off and she went down like a rock.

Eastward *"wung out." (Al Perrin)*

Off the wind, the Friendship sloop does well in light weather with so much of her sail area in her large mainsail and topsail. It is well to slack the peak halyard just a grind — a grind is a little more than a whisker but not so much as a dight — to get a little more fullness into it and let the sheet right off so the boom is against the rigging. People in a hurry will pole out the clew of the staysail and thus skid the wind from main to staysail to jib. The jib topsail can often be persuaded to wing out too, if the wind is far enough aft. A neat trick for winging out the staysail is to rig a line from the bitt through a block at the end of the bowsprit and back to the clew of the staysail. Haul it out to windward, where it will draw nicely and not slam back and forth on its traveller all afternoon. If there is a brisk breeze, all the weight of the wind in the sails forward will drive the fine bow down and raise the stern, which makes for a cleaner run unless carried to an extreme by putting all hands on the foredeck and burying the bow.

The old-timers, especially those to the eastward, around Mt. Desert, often used a balanced jumbo. They carried only one headstay, which ran to the end of the bowsprit. The staysail, or jumbo, was set flying, without a stay, and instead of being made fast forward at the tack, was tacked down about 18 inches from the forward end of the staysail boom. Thus, the tack of the sail stuck out beyond the stay and was said to set much more steadily than the conventional jumbo, especially off the wind.

A Friendship sloop runs easily off the wind, for her long keel and large rudder prevent her from yawing about unduly and her broad counter lifts easily to a following sea. She may be a bit hard-headed, but she will behave herself a lot better than her modern cousins and will sail nearly as fast under working sails as modern boats will sail under spinnaker.

A Friendship sloop had to be a handy boat, not only to haul traps among the ledges, but also to make her mooring under sail, to come alongside wharves and floats, to set off dories, pick up trawls, and make life easy for her crew. Albert Cushman, who used to haul traps under sail in the 34-foot, Morse-built *Wawenock*, said, "Lead out the . . .

*The balanced jumbo on a Southwest Harbor party boat early in the century. (Courtesy of Jarvis Newman)*

sheet of the mains'l quite a way and trim the jib tight when you're hauling. The sloop will lay good then. The trap will come to the top of the water quite a way off, so you can pull it to you."

A Friendship sloop is so heavy and has such easy lines that she holds her way well. If you keep the mainsail full, so that there is always water going by the rudder, she will thread a needle for you. She won't turn very short, but you can count on her to turn through the eye of the wind if she is moving ahead at all. A sure way to get in trouble, though, is to let her stop in a light air and a tight spot. It takes time and space to get her heft moving again. If you have to beat up a narrow passage in a light air, make each tack as long as you dare, let go of your jib sheet before you tack, put the helm over gently, and sail her very full, even if it means several more tacks. If it looks as if she is going to hang in stays, push the staysail out to what will be the new windward side. It will check her forward speed, but it will help her to turn.

In making a mooring or a landing at a float, remember that she will range a long way right into the wind if the weather is moderate. I usually drop the staysail before rounding up so that she will turn more easily and lie alongside more comfortably when we get there. As she ranges ahead, the slower she goes, the longer she will keep going, so don't give up on her if you think you may be coming short until a range taken abeam almost stops closing up. Then, put the helm over with the last of your steerage way, set the staysail, back it to what will be the windward side, and try again. While this is somewhat ignominious, it is not nearly as bad as coming in too fast, straining everything, and slamming into the float. A heavy boat takes a lot of stopping! At best, you will look clumsy; at worst, you may break something or even hurt someone. Your foredeck hand will soon learn to take a turn with his bow line; and quarter bitts take strain better than jib sheet cleats.

In heavy weather, though, you may be surprised to find your sloop will not range nearly so far despite her greater speed because the resistance of wind and sea is so much greater. Furthermore, a miscalculation in heavy weather is much more likely to cause damage or injury. To make a float or mooring when it is blowing hard, come in with the wind well forward of the beam, staysail sheeted hard, and mainsail eased off. A pull on the main sheet is like stepping on the accelerator; it pushes you ahead and to windward. Thus, you can control your speed to come in at a moderate pace, heading half a boat length to leeward of your mark. When very close and travelling slowly, drop the staysail, trim the main sheet hard, head into the wind, and slide alongside. Your deck hand must move smartly to get a line ashore and catch a turn, but he will have to make no death-defying leap, and the boat will be under control all the way.

In connection with this maneuver and others involving headsails, note the importance of a downhaul. This is a light line made fast to the head or top hank of a jib, leading down through several hanks, through a block at the foot of the stay, and aft to a cleat on the foredeck. With a downhaul, one need never go out on the bowsprit to muscle down a flogging sail while leaving the halyard adrift, and one is never tempted to yank a sail down by the leech. Throw the halyard coil on deck so the line passes over your shoulder and take in the downhaul with both hands. If the halyard fouls, you can grab it before it goes up the mast in a wad (it's a wise precaution to belay the bitter end of the halyard temporarily); and the sail comes down quickly, is smothered, and stays that way.

Another piece of old-time gear that is useful is a reef tackle ready to rove off and a boom tackle to hold the boom out when running off the wind or by the lee. A vang such as is used by modern boats with short booms may cause more trouble than it cures. A

*The jib downhaul in action aboard* Eastward. *(Harold Prenatt photo)*

big mainsail with a long boom and a heavy gaff swinging about will put tremendous strain on a vang, which must be attached well forward on the boom. Also, the strain on the boom and the deck is great. Surely, the deck pad must be through-bolted and heavily backed up. Should one have the misfortune to gybe all standing in a breeze with a conventional vang set up, something would be pretty sure to let go – probably the most expensive thing to repair.

A Friendship sloop doesn't gybe easily as the gaff holds the sail well out to leeward. She can go a point at least by the lee before you feel the wind in what was your leeward ear, the leech begins to curl, the boom begins to rise, draws back like a man with a maul, and slams across, fetching up with a savage jerk and a rattle of gear. It is possible, with a high-peaked gaff, to perform, inadvertently of course, a Chinese gybe, where the boom comes over but the gaff does not. The leech of the sail holds the boom nearly vertical and the resultant tangle of sail and gear is a real hurrah's nest. It can usually be straightened out by gybing the boom back again unless it has fouled itself or the main sheet in shrouds or spreaders. Once I saw a gybe in which the peak halyard fouled on the masthead. Sorting out the resulting tangle took an hour's heavy work in a bosun's chair.

To gybe in a more controlled fashion, it is just possible to get the boat sailing well by the lee and then to put the helm hard up and turn the boat fast enough so that by the time the boom gets across, it brings up not on the main sheet but on the wind. A controlled gybe with the sheet trimmed flat aft is no very frightening experience in ordinary weather, but the sheet must be held with a turn around a quarter bitt or a stout cleat, for the heavy boom and gaff come over with considerable authority.

A Friendship sloop is not fast to windward by modern standards, although with sheets started she will stay with the fleet. She is not the boat to take on a transatlantic passage without extensive remodeling to close in her cockpit and shorten her rig. She is not "easy to handle" in the sense meant by the salesmen of modern yachts. But she *is* fun to sail. She has the feel of a real vessel under sail. She has the power to drive through a chop and the weight to tread it down. She is dry and comfortable, handy, able, and reasonably fast if you treat her properly. Abuse her and she will balk, beat you about the head, try to drown you, and perhaps end by jamming herself ashore. Treat her like a lady, with respect and affection, and she will be free with her favors.

*The* Hattie *and the* Eliza, *ob-*
*viously ice bound. (The*
*Mariners' Museum)*

*Appendix* A

*Sloops Registered*
*with the Friendship Sloop Society*

1. *Voyager*– 30 – A – Charles Morse, 1906 – John Kippen, Ipswich, Mass.

   For an account of *Voyager*'s contribution to the foundation of the Friendship Sloop Society.
2. *Dictator* – 31 – A – Robert McLain, 1904 – George Pappas, Tarrytown, N.Y.

   *Finette* – See *Right Bower*, no. 55.
4. *Golden Eagle* – 26 – A – A.F. Morse, 1910 – William Haskell, Marblehead, Mass.
5. *Content* – 25 – B – Stuart Ford, 1961 – Robert Edwards, Naples, Fla.

   *Content* sails out of Boothbay Harbor.
6. *Eastward* – 32 – B – James Chadwick, 1956 – Roger and Mary Duncan, E. Boothbay, Me.
7. *Tannis* – 38 – B – W.S. Carter, 1937 – John D. Cronin, Sturbridge, Mass.

   *Tannis* sails from North Shore, Massachusetts, ports.
8. *Banshee* – 30 – A – Morse

   *Banshee* was owned by Benjamin Waterworth in New Bedford for many years before 1976, but at about that time she was found to be too far gone to repair. She is the ancestor, in a way, of John Wojcik's *Banshee*, no. 180.
9. *Amity* – 30 – A – Wilbur Morse, 1902 – James R. Wiggins, Brooklin, Me.

   Wiggins has owned *Amity* since before 1961 and sailed her in several early regattas.
10. *Mary Anne* – 31 – B – Lash Brothers, 1958 – Joseph Griffin, Damariscotta, Me.

    *Mary Anne* was built for John Dallett.
11. *Shulamite* – 24 – B – Gannett, 1938 – James and Pauline Doolittle.

    She sails out of Five Islands, Me.
12. *Friendship* – 29 – A – Wilbur Morse, 1902 – Robert Cavanaugh, Compton, R.I.
13. *Easting* – 29 – B – Charles Morse, 1920 – James R. Pierpont, Milford, Conn.

14. *Vigor* – 30 – B – Wilbur Morse, 1946 – Robert K. Emerson, Hancock Pt., Me.

The builder was not the "original" Wilbur Morse but his grandnephew, grandson of Jonah Morse.

15. *Vida Mia* – 30 – C – E.L. Stevens, 1942 – George Loos, N. Cape May, N.J.

16. *Retriever* – 22 – B – Gannett, 1942 – John and Clarice Rice, Scituate, Mass.

17. *Jolly Buccaneer* – 45 – A – Eugene McLain, 1909 – sunk

18. *Chrissy* – 30 – A – Charles Morse, 1912 – Ernst Wiegleb, Friendship, Me.

19. *Black Jack* – 33 – A – Wilbur Morse, 1900 – Wilson Fletcher, Bar Harbor, Me.

In 1960, owned by the estate of Dr. Jackson of Winchester and Searsport. Sold to William Pendleton in 1961 and in 1977 to Fletcher. She sails parties out of Northeast Harbor, Me.

20. *Moses Swann* – 30 – A – Morse, 1910

In 1966, named *Wanderer* by Robert Trayes of Beverly, Mass. In 1967, sold to J. Hubbard; in 1979, to Charles Newman and named *Joeanna;* in 1971, to Roger Mercaldi; in 1972, to Roland Barth *et al.*, and named *Moses Swann.*

21. *Wilbur Morse* – 30 – B – Carlton Simmons, 1947 – Karl Heiser, Cundy's Harbor, Me.

22. *Ellie T.* – 25 – B – John Thorpe, 1961 – John Collins, East Hampton, N.Y.

Thorpe sold her in 1974 to William Hunter, who sold her in 1975 to Dwight Foster. In 1980 the present owner bought her.

23. *Depression* – 30 – A – unknown, 1900(?) – Lloyd and Tina Olson, Boothbay, Me.

Myron Hahn picked her off the shore during the Depression for $15. On his death in 1974, she went to Mel Burns, who sold her to Larry Hanes. In 1979 the Olsons bought her, and she is being rebuilt by David Nutt at Southport, Me.

24. *Ancient Mariner* – 25 – A – Wilbur Morse, ca. 1900 – Holt and Virginia Vibber, Waterford, Conn.

She has been in Waterford, Conn., in the process of rebuilding for a number of years.

25. *Sea Duck* – 25 – Charles Morse

She was owned for some time by Lawrence Bershad of Marblehead, Mass. She is rigged as a ketch.

26. *Virginia M.* – 28 – A – Wilbur Morse, 1910 – destroyed

Formerly *Swan*, she was owned in 1962 by George Owen, sold in that year to George Garrity and Robert Steinberger and in 1967 to Jaxon Vibber. Owen bought her from Irving D. Miner of Long Island in 1954.

27. *Sarah E.* – 25 – B – Robert MacKean and Sid Carter, 1939 – Eldon and Elizabeth Homesey, Wilmington, Del.

28. *Bounty* – 22 – Gannett, 1932 – Richard Bailey, Peekskill, N.Y.

George McFadden owned her in 1961-1968; Ray Gumpell bought her and sold her to Bailey in 1973.

29. *Susan* – 41 – Wilbur Morse, 1902

Formerly *Ocean Belle*, she was owned by Paul Eykel in 1965, sold to N. Bradford Mack of South Miami, Fla., in 1966, and is now believed lost.

30. *Kidnapped* – 21

Formerly named *Fly-a-way*, she was owned by Julian Dodge of Danvers, Mass., in 1965 and in 1966 was believed lost.

31. *White Eagle* – 28 – Wilbur Morse, 1914 or 1917 – John de Sousa, Friendship, Me.

32. *Nomad* – 33 – A – Wilbur Morse, 1906 – Craig Rowley, Amston, Conn.

Owned in 1972 by James Ford; by L. Hazard Knowles, 1972-1973; by Ray Gold, 1973-1975; and by Montague Miller, 1975-1982. Sold to Rowley in 1982.

33. *Smuggler* – 28 – Philip J. Nichols, 1942 – Sinclair Kenney, Edgewood, R.I.

34. *Pal O' Mine* – 27 – B – Gannett, 1947 – James Lane, Winchester, Mass.

35. *Mary C.* – 20 – N.D. Clapp, 1962 – Nathaniel Clapp, Pride's Crossing, Mass.

*Mary C.* is rigged with a marconi mainsail.

36. *Mar-Gin* – 25 – William Blodgett, Waldoboro, Me.

Owned 1961-about 1971 by Gerald Kinney of Waldoboro and raced in early regattas.

37. *Chance* – 31 – A – Wilbur Morse, 1916 – Maine Maritime Museum, Bath, Me.

Owned for many years by Dr. Files and sold to Alan Goldstein in 1976. He had her rebuilt by Robert Vaughan at Seal Cove Boatyard and gave her to the museum in 1982.

38. *Eleazar* – 38 – B – W.S. Carter, 1938 – Captain David Smith, Marshfield, Mass.

    Named for Eleazar Wheelock, founder of Dartmouth College. Bought in 1970 by H.C. Marden and named *Gold Ivy*. Smith bought her in 1971 and renamed her *Eleazar*.
39. *Downeaster* – 30 – B – Lash Brothers, 1963 – Virginia Grew, Dover, Mass.
40. *Comesin* – 32 – B – J. Ervin Jones, 1962 – Carlton Wilder, Green Cove Springs, Fla.

    Designed by Murray Peterson and built for Winthrop Bancroft as *Elicia III*. Sold to Wilder in 1967. Her picture is in the foreground on the dust jacket of this book.
41. *Snafu* – 35 – Alfred Gastonguay, Beverly, Mass., since 1961.
42. *Selkie* – 26 – C – Carlton Simmons and J.P. Hennings, 1963 – Albert McDougal, Byfield, Mass.
43. *Gypsy* – 23 – C – Judson Crouse, 1939 – Robert Lash, Orland, Me.
44. *Sazerac* – 35 – A – Wilbur Morse, 1913 – Roland Barth *et al.*, Alna, Me.
45. *Flying Jib* – 30 – B – W.S. Carter, 1937 – Kevin Crowley, Newburyport, Mass.
46. *Dirigo* – 30 – B – Lash Brothers, 1964 – Bill Leavenworth, Searsmont, Me.
47. *Galatea* – 30 – McKie Roth, 1964 – John Kapelowitz, Mountain View, Calif.

    Built by Roth in California for Richard Muenzer, sold to her present owner in 1970.
48. *Channel Fever* – 33 – C – F.A. Provener, 1939 – Jim Nesbit, Ft. Myers, Fla.
49. *Surprise* – 33 – B – Philip J. Nichols, 1965 – Robert Phaneuf, Chelmsford, Mass.
50. *Heritage* – 29 – C – Elmer Collemer, 1962 – Bill and Barbara Hadlock, South Freeport, Me.

    Designed by Murray Peterson on the idea of a sloop used to haul granite, she is a little different from the traditional Friendship, but close enough to deceive most observers. She was built for the Hadlocks.
51. – 32 – Wilbur A. Morse – Robert Morrison, Metuchen, N.J.
52. *Rights of Man* – 30 – B – Lash Brothers, 1965 – Philip Cronin, Cambridge, Mass.
53. *Eagle* – 31 – A – Wilbur Morse, 1915 – Donald Huston, Nahant, Mass.
54. *Echo* – 22 – B – Lee's Boat Shop, 1965 – William Thon, Port Clyde, Me.
55. *Right Bower* – 47 – Wilbur Morse, 1915 – Thomas K. Baldwin
56. *Iocaste* – 33 – A – Charles Morse, 1907 – Charles Currier, Jr., Washington, D.C.
57. *Old Baldy* – 25 – B – James Rockefeller, 1965 – Dorothy Ahlgren, Kittery, Me.

    She was built for Mahlon Hoaglund; sold in 1970 to Louise Millar; in 1972, to Dick Salter; in 1976, to Frank West; and in 1977, to her present owner.
58. *Tern* – Jerry Maxwell, 1969 – Michael Bull, Stratford, Vt.

    Jerry Maxwell kept *Tern*, then registered under No. 85, until 1974. He sold her to Frank Perkins, who registered her under No. 58. At the same time, Perkins sold *Departure* and took her number for *Tern*. No. 85 went to Maxwell's new boat, *Ann Frances*.
59. *Sarah Mead* – 30 – B – Newbert & Wallace, 1963 – Ted and Consuelo Hanks, Jefferson, Me.

    She was built for Henry White and named for his daughter; sold in 1976.
60. *Old Salt* – 32 – R. McLain, 1902 – Leon Knorr, Rowayton, Conn.
61. *Windward* – 25 – James Rockefeller, 1966 – Ruth and David Westphal, Northeast Harbor, Me.

    She was built for Skip and Jane Bracy, who cruised in her on their honeymoon. In 1973 she was sold to George Dowley and in 1980 to the present owners.
62. *Columbia* – 23 – Lester Chadbourne – Bill Steig, Portsmouth, N.H.

    Lee Green sold her to the present owners in 1980.
63. *Kochab* – 28 – B – Speers, 1953 – Janet Hyland, Jamaica Plain, Mass.

    Before 1968, owned by Stanley Kanney and was the subject of classification discussion among Peterson, Hamlin, and Lash. Sold to Ted Charles in 1971, to Robert Morse in 1975, and to Holbrook Smith of Boothbay, Me., in 1976. Smith did considerable work on her and sold her in 1980 to the present owner.
64. *Amicitia* – 33 – B – Lash Brothers, 1965 – Jeff and Susan Pontiff, Plymouth, Mass.

    Built beside *Voyager II* for Dr. Colpoys of Scituate, Mass. Sold to Emerson Stone in 1969 and to the present owners in 1976.
65. *Gallant Lady* – 33 – Wilbur Morse, 1907 – James Smith, Toronto, Ont.

    Anthony Mankel rebuilt her in 1971. The present owner had her in 1980.

66. *Venture* – 27 – A – Wilbur Morse, 1912 – R.S. Kleinschmidt

   In 1944 V.A. Hicks of Boston sold her to Pane Wemmerwesser, who sold her to Emmet Carver. He owned her for many years and sold her to Robert Thing in 1954. He traded her to Jarvis Newman, who rebuilt her for John Porteous of Cape Elizabeth. In 1971, he gave her to the Penobscot Marine Museum, which sold her to Kleinschmidt in 1971.

67. *Hieronymus* – 33 – B – Ralph Stanley, 1962 – Albert Nielson, Southwest Harbor, Me.

   The Nielsons still own her and have cruised in her as far as Bras d'Or.

68. *Robin L.* – 25 – B – James Hall, 1967 – Pat and Robin Ferrin, Southport, Me.

   Kept by Jim Hall 1967-1974. Sold to Otis Maxfield in 1974 and to present owners in 1980.

69. *Coast O' Maine* – 30 – B – Vernell Smith, 1967 – John Rutledge, Kittery, Me.

70. *Spirit* – 30 – B – Roger Morse, 1967 – Christopher Beebe, Friendship, Me.

   Built as *Margaret Motte* for Michael Grove of Milford, Conn., she was sold in 1980 to the present owner, renamed *Symbolon* and then *Spirit*.

71. *Gladiator* – 32 – A – Alexander McLain, 1902 – William Zuber, Friendship, Me.

   There are articles on *Gladiator* in the 1977 and 1982 yearbooks.

72. *Temptress* – 33 – Philip J. Nichols, 1934 – Sea Scouts, Westerly, R.I.

   Built as *Result*, she was owned by Charles Hedge and by Philip Mason before coming to the Sea Scouts.

73. *West Indian* – 26 – Pamet Harbor, 1951 – Richard Faredy, Naples, Fla.

   She was formerly owned by Philip C. Morse, Jr. Formerly *Dauphine*.

74. *Patience* – 30 – B – Malcolm Brewer, 1965 – John Arens, Milton, Mass.

   Built by Brewer for his own use, she was sold to Blair Lamont, who registered her with the Society in 1969. He sold her to Philip Peterson of Worcester, Mass., in 1971. He sold her to Francis Hagerty in 1976 and she passed to the present owner in 1979.

75. *Omaha* – 35 – Wilbur Morse, 1901 – C.F. Hansel, Cranford, N.J.

76. *Packet* – 26 – Charles Morse, 1925 – Michael Reidy, Vineyard Haven, Mass.

   Tom and Bob Denny registered her with the Society in 1969. She was sold to Matthew and Ed Spaulding in 1972, to Donald Ives in 1974, and to the present owner in 1977.

77. *Beagle* – 28 – C.A. Morse, 1905 – Mrs. John Glenn, Centre Island, N.Y.

   Mrs. Glenn registered *Beagle* with the Society in 1969.

78. *Emmie B.* – 37 – B – Reginald Wilcox, 1958 – burned

79. *Nimbus* – 32 – A. Chenault III, 1954 – Fred Swigart, New Orleans, La.

80. *Headway* – 35 – Buck & Adams, 1941 – Christopher Head, Stow, Mass.

   Built as *Dickie II*, she was a fisherman at first and about 1950 was converted to a yacht, named *Gray Dawn*, and blessed with a new engine and a doghouse. Andrew Fetherston bought her in July 1970, named her *Sepoy*, and registered her with the Society. In 1971 she was owned by Robert Fairbanks. In 1980 she was owned by Perry Hood of Richmond, Va., who changed her name to *Sunshine*. In 1981 she was sold to the present owner and given her present name.

81. *Regardless* – 38 – B – Fred Dion, 1963 – William Williams, Swansea, Mass.

   Built as *Friendship* by Dion, she was owned by Donald Priestly in 1969 and by her present owner in 1970.

82. *Morning Star* – 28 – A – Albion Morse, 1912 – Robert Wolff, Cambridge, N.Y.

   In 1969 she was registered with the Society by B. John Heinstein and rigged as a ketch. In 1970 she was owned by Ronald Ackman of Oyster Bay, N.Y. In 1974 she was owned by her present owner, who subsequently had her rebuilt by Ralph Stanley and restored to her original rig.

83. *Perseverance* – 30 – D – Bruno & Stillman, 1969 – Robert Jacobson, Buckingham, Pa.

   She was the first of the Bruno & Stillman fiberglass hulls. She was built for Harold E. Kimball of Concord, N.H.

84. *Philia* – 22 – Kennebec Yacht, 1969 – Richard Condon, Atkinson, N.H.

   She was built for Bruce Myers of Alexandria, Va., and disappears from the record in 1976; but she appears under the name of her present owner in 1982.

85. *Ann Frances* – 38 – B – J.D. Maxwell, 1974 – J.D. Maxwell, Sprucehead, Me.

86. *Allegiance* – 24 – Albert M. Harding, 1970 – A.M. Harding, Kennebunkport, Me.

87. *Eagle* – 22 – McKie Roth, 1969 – Henry S. Goodwin, Avon, Ct.

Built for Philip Groetzinger.

88. *Apogee* – 30 – Bruno & Stillman, 1969 – H.M. Landemare, Toms River, N.J.

She was built for A. Marshall Smith, was passed on to his son, and came to the present owner in 1973.

89. *Avior* – 22 – B – McKie Roth, 1970 – Julia and Bertha Chittenden, Edgartown, Mass.

90. *Salatia* – 25 – D – Jarvis Newman, 1969 – Lauriat family, Southwest Harbor, Me.

91. *Phoenix* – 30 – D – Bruno & Stillman, 1970 – Anne and Al Beck, Exeter, N.H.

92. *Puffin* – 25 – B – Rockefeller & Day, 1970 – K.S. Axelson, Waldoboro, Me.

Built for A. Carl Maier and named *Victory*, she came to her present owner in 1973 or 1974.

93. *Anna R.* – 25 – Kenneth Rich, 1970 – Kenneth and Anna Rich

It is reported that she is now owned by the Richs' son.

94. *Diana* – 25 – D – Jarvis Newman & Rockefeller, 1970. – Ebenezer Gay, Hingham, Mass.

95. *West Wind* – 40 – Charles (?) Morse, 1902 – John Fassack, Cincinnati, Ohio

Rebuilt in 1970, she was registered with the Society in 1971 by Frank and Marcel Savoy and sold to Herbert Crocker in 1977. She passed to her present owner in 1983. He is having her rebuilt.

96. *Voyager* – 32 – B – Lash Brothers, 1965 – Bernard MacKenzie, Scituate, Mass.

MacKenzie did all the finish work and rigging on *Voyager*. She is the successor to *Voyager*, no. 1.

97. *Gannet* – 27 – A – 1903 – Willis Collier

Registered with the Society as *Gay Gamble* in 1970 by Francis P. Hardy, she was sold to Rodgers Pierce of Derry, N.H., in 1976, and her name changed to *Gannet*. In 1983 she came to her present owner.

98. *Down East* – 30 – Bruno & Stillman, 1970 – James Beatty, Westerville, Ohio

She was built for Edward Dodd. On his death, she was passed to his family, owned briefly by Frank Glover, and sold to her present owner in 1976.

99. *Buccaneer* – 27 – Wilbur Morse, 1890 – Eugene Tirocchi, Johnston, R.I.

The present owner acquired her in 1968.

100. *Morning Watch* – 26 – Backman's Boatyard, 1970 – Donald Starr, Boston, Mass.

She was built for Philip Whitehouse and was sold to the present owner in 1972.

101. *Minerva* – 30 – Bruno & Stillman, 1971 – David Hotelling, Freeport, Me.

She was built for Richard Flinchbaugh and named *Sea Fever*. In 1972 she was named *Inverary* and owned by Norman MacNeil of West Newton, Mass. In 1978 she came to her present owner and her present name.

102. *Augustus* – 37 – Tim Bliss – Tim Bliss, Coconut Grove, Fla.

103. *Solaster* – 25 – D – Jarvis Newman, 1970 – Curtis Ruff, Butler, Pa.

104. *Cockle* – 28 – C – Elmer Collemer, 1950 – Widgery Thomas, Portland, Me.

*Cockle* is a round-bowed sloop listed as Class C. It is reported that Thomas sold her in 1981.

105. *At Last* – 30 – D – Bruno & Stillman, 1971 – George Kwass, Andover, Mass.

She was built for Roger Merriman and named *Victory Chimes*. In 1972 he sold her to Thomas Reisley, who renamed her *At Last*. She went to her present owner in 1978.

106. *Hold Tight* – 25 – D – Jarvis Newman, 1970 – John Cassidy, Bangor, Me.

107. *Magic* – 22 – Passamaquoddy Yachts and Johnston, 1970 – Nancy Kandusik

She was built by and for Bill Johnston and named *Magi*. In 1983 she was sold and her name changed.

108. *Loon* – 35 – Wilbur Morse, 1905

She was owned by Hugh Jacob of Darien, Conn., in 1971. About 1974 she was destroyed, and a new *Loon* was built for the Jacobs by Newbert & Wallace and was listed in 1975 as No. 108. In 1966 the new *Loon* appears as No. 168 with the same owners.

109. *Petrel* – 31 – G. Cooper, 1933 – Michael Brown, Dorchester, Mass.

About 1977 Earl White sold her to the present owner.

110. *Amistad* – 23 – Robert White, 1971 – Robert C. Lee, Houston, Tex.

Her builder sold her to her present owner in 1976.

114. *Pearle* – 30 – D – Bruno & Stillman, 1971 – Maine Maritime Museum, Bath, Me.

Built for John Chadwick as *Solaster*. In 1974 she was sold to Morris Goldsmith and her name changed to *Pearle*. In 1979 she went to the Apprenticeshop at the museum.

115. *Kittiwake* – 30 – D – Bruno & Stillman, 1971 – Gardner Mason, Killingworth, Conn.

Built for George D. Jackson, she was sold to her present owners in 1983.

116. *Tinqua* – 30 – D – Bruno & Stillman, 1971

She was lost on Whaleback Ledge.

117. *Leading Light* – 30 – Bruno & Stillman, 1971 – John and Eve Crumpton, Oxford.

Built for George Shaw, she was sold to her present owners in 1978, her name unchanged.

118. *Wenonah* – 30 – D – Bruno & Stillman, 1971 – Scott and Beth Newsham, Solomons, Md.

Built for Richard Sonderegger of Marquette, Mich., she was sold to the present owners in about 1979.

119. *Valhalla* – 30 – Bruno & Stillman, 1971 – Paul D. Wolfe, Pittsburgh, Pa.

120. This number is reserved for Carlton Simmons.

121. *Island Trader* – 27 – Elmer Collemer, 1960 – Pamela Mckee, Seattle, Wash.

Designed by Murray Peterson, she was built for Dean Walen and sailed in Massachusetts. Tom Peterson bought her from Walen and changed her name to *Island Trader*. She went to Bob Mosher in San Diego, then to Land Washburn in Washington, and then to present owner.

122. *Ray of Hope* – 25 – B – Nash and Coffin, 1971 – Peter Thompson, Bar Harbor, Me.

Ed Coffin built her as *Ray of Hope* and sold her to Bill Packer in 1977. Bill Payne was registered as her owner in 1982 but almost certainly bought her before that. He used her sailing parties from Monhegan and sold her in 1983 to her present owner.

123. *Resolute* – 28 – B – Charles Burnham, 1973 – Charles Burnham, Essex, Mass.

124. *Callipygous* – 30 – D – Bruno & Stillman, 1971 – Richard Sharabura, Toronto, Ont.

She was built for James Gibson of York, Me. Her name means in Greek "beautiful stern." In 1975 her owner was Henk Vanderkolk of Ontario. In 1983 she was listed as belonging to her present owner.

125. *Billy Budd* – 25 – Al Paquette, 1969 – Fred and Anne Holbrook, Rochester, Mass.

In 1972 she was owned by Edward Lewis of Falmouth, Mass., and named *Jacataqua*. In 1981 she was listed to her present owners with her present name.

126. *Whim* – 20 – Chester Spear, 1939 – William Flanders, Abingdon, Mass.

Her present owner registered her with the Society in 1972.

127. *Lucy S.* – 28 – 1890 (?) – Jonathan Smith, Concord, Mass.

Her present owner listed her in 1972.

128. *Schoodic* – 31 – C – Collemer and Lanning – Bruce and Mary Lanning, Winter Harbor, Me.

129. *Gisela R.* – 25 – A.P. Schafer, 1969 – Andrew P. Schafer, Rosedale, L.I.

130. *Narwhal* – 25 – Jarvis Newman, 1972 – Jim Rosenbaum, Whitefish Bay, Wis.

131. *Noahsark* – 30 – John Chase, 1972 – Richard Willis, Ipswich, Mass.

She was sold in 1982 to her present owner.

132. *Vogel Frei* – 30 – Wilbur Morse, ? – Herman Samitsch

Samitsch is reported to have sailed her to the Canary Islands and the Azores.

133. *Independence* – 30 – D – Bruno & Stillman, 1973 – Frederich Schwartzman, Far Hills, N.J.

134. *Four Sons* – 22 – Charles Collins, 1973 – David Hussey, Marblehead, Mass.

Shortly after she was launched, Collins sailed her to Friendship outside the Cape. The story is in the 1974 yearbook. She was then named *Angelus*. She is first listed under Hussey's name in 1975.

135. *Green Pepper* – 25 – Newman and Morris, 1973 – Harper Sibley, Miami, Fla.

She was built for John Jurkowski and named *Tremolino*. James Wilmerding owned her in 1974 and gave her her present name. In 1981 she was listed by her present owner.

136. *Squirrel* – 28 – Charles Morse, 1920 – Larry Moxon, Mystic, Conn.

She was first listed by John Harrington of Moody in 1973. In 1975 she went to Dick and Theresa Dixon of Stonington, Conn., and in 1980 to her present owner.

137. *Friendship* – 46 – Wilbur Morse, 1900 – William Van Zee, Miami, Fla.

Her name was at one time *Wild Dutchman*.

138. *Red Jacket* – 25 – Robert Gardner, 1973 – Christopher Day, Islesboro, Me.

There is a good article about her building in the 1974 yearbook. The present owner bought her in 1977.

139. *Covenant* – 25 – J. Newman and T. Morris, 1973

She was built for John Jurkowski and first named *Tremolino*. In 1977, her name unchanged, she was owned by

Windward, *Number 61, sailing well with her owners, Skip and June Bracy, off on their honeymoon.*

Catherine Dickey. In 1981 her name was changed to *Covenant,* and she was owned by Douglas and Michelle Jacoby of Marblehead, Mass. It is reported that she has again been sold.

140. *Brandywine* – McKie Roth, 1968 – Paul Johnson, Campbell, Calif.

141. *Renascence* – 25 – James Hall, 1974 – Malcolm and Lucy Myers, Deerfield, N.H.

She was originally named *Recovery* by her builder. Hall died that year, and the sloop was listed the next year under the name *Renascence* by Anna Hall. In 1976 Mrs. Hall gave her to her son-in-law, Dr. Myers. In 1981 she was registered by her present owners.

142. *Albatross* – 21 – Peter Archbold, 1976 – Stephen and Annette Locke, Rochester, N.Y.

The builder christened her *Psyche* and sold her to the present owners in 1980 or 1981.

143. *Matelot* – 25 – J. Newman and T. Morris, 1974 – Gerard Miller, Perrysburg, Ohio

144. *Ribbit* – 25 – Newman and Morris, 1974 – W. Mark Murphy, Buffalo, N.Y.

145. *Deliverance* – 31 – Newman, Purslow & Partridge, 1974 – Gerald Purslow, Hancock, Me.

146. *Fiddle Head* – 25 – Newman and Chase, 1970 – Harry and Rebecca Jackson, Groton, Conn.

She was built for Eugene Myer of Baltimore, who owned her until 1978.

147. *Anna B.* – 31 – Newman, Ervin Jones, 1974 – C. Murray McQuade

148. *Sloop Out of Water* – Joe Vinciquerra, Andover, Mass.

This boat is probably gone now.

149. *Fiddler's Green* – 25 – Roy Jenkins, 1978 – Roy Jenkins, Waterville, Me.

150. *Woodchips* – Deschenes & Willett, ca. 1975 – E. Thomas Willett, Holden, Mass., and Jean Deschenes, N. Grafton, Mass.

151. *Departure* – 15 – Gregg Reizran, Mystic, Conn.

Frank Perkins of Ogunquit owned *Departure* for a number of years and cruised in her to Friendship annually. Perkins sold her to W.G. Heath of Hammondsport, N.Y., who brought her all the way from Hammondsport to Friendship on her bottom once.

152. *Ollie M.* – 32 – Kent Murphy, 1977 – Kent Murphy, Swampscott, Mass.

153. *Angelus* – 22 – Charles Collins – Charles Collins, Bass River, Mass.

Her builder owned her in 1980. It is reported that she has a new owner.

154. *Muscongus* – 28 – Albion Morse, 1909 – Albert and Jennie Lindquist, Wilton, Conn.

155. *Queequeg* – 25 – Newman and Morris, 1975 – Mark Roman, Riviera Beach, Fla.

She was built for Frank Shaw of Youngstown, Ohio, and christened *Wisdom of Solomon*. In 1981 she was registered by her present owner under her present name.

156. *Departure* – 31 – Newman and Morris, 1975 – James A. Russell, Philadelphia, Pa.

She was built for Paul Lacouture of Dayton, Ohio, and christened *La Perouse*. In 1980 she was registered by the present owner under her present name.

157. *Liberty* – 31 – Newman and Salter, 1980 – Alice and Dick Salter, Manchester, Mass.

158. *Eva R.* – 33 – E. Robinson, 1906 – Robert Bruneau, Stamford, Conn.

She has been converted to marconi rig.

159. *Pacific Child* – 31 – Bruno & Stillman, 1969 – John and Doreen Nosworthy, San Diego, Calif.

160. *Spring A Leak* – 23 – McKie Roth, 1973 – Morgan and Vita Hendry, Wilmington, Del.

It is reported that she was formerly named *Defiance*.

161. *Jenney* – 22 – Sam Guild, 1976 – Gordon Towle, Landenburg, Pa.

She was built for Didier Dorot and named *Damien*. In 1979 she was listed as *Jenney*, owned by Roland Shepard of Brunswick and in 1981 by her present owner.

162. *Irene* – 38 – Charles Morse, 1917 – John and Mary Clarke, Vineyard Haven, Mass.

She was owned by Captain Boyd Guild about 1940 and named *Sea Bird*. She was sold south to New Jersey, where she was sailed for years by an old gentleman who lived aboard. Warren and Grace Huguley bought her and had her replanked in the early 1970s. The present owners, John and Mary Clarke of Vineyard Haven, bought her in 1977 and use her as a party boat out of Vineyard Haven. In the winter of 1983-1984, Clarke took her south to Georgetown and the Exumas and found her fast and able, sailing from Walker's Key to Charlestown in three days and Charlestown to the Cape Fear River in 17 hours. Some of her former names are: *Sea Bird*, *New Moon*, *Hel-Don*, *Fudee 3d*, and *Southern Cross*. She has been registered under the Coast Guard out of Boston, Cleveland, and New York.

163. *Reward* – 25 – William Greene, 1975 – William and Jean Greene, Rocklin, Calif.

164. *Jessie May* – 30 – Charles Morse, 1906 – Doreen and Dennis Mayhew, St. Clair, Mich.

165. *Reunion* – 25 – Niederer, 1975 – Mason Stober III, Alameda, Calif.

166. *Schoodic* – 25 – Concordia Co., 1967 – Gerald Zee, N. Dartmouth, Mass.

167. *Freedom* – 28 – Ralph Stanley, 1976 – Richard and Helen Dudman, Ellsworth, Me.

168. *Loon* – 30 – Newbert & Wallace and Hugh Jacob & Sons, 1974 – Hugh and Ruth Jacob, Bath, Me.

169. *Defiance* – 22 – Dowd Dias, 1976 – Bill and Beth McCallum

She was built for Frank Phinney of Brewer, Me., and was owned by Lorenzo Creamer of Salisbury Cove in 1981.

170. *Lady of the Wind* – 31 – Jarvis Newman – William Manookian, New York, N.Y.

171. *Golden Anchor* – 31 – D – Newman and Morris – Golden Anchor Inn, Bar Harbor, Me.

172. *Amnesty* – 25 – Jim Drake, 1981 – Jim Drake, Carlisle, Pa.

She was first christened *Fool Star* but her name was changed in 1983.

173. *Medusa* – 25 – Ron Nowell (ferro-cement) – Ron Nowell, Marshall, Calif.

174. ? – Newman & Standish – Arnie Standish and Jill Paperno, Port Alberni, B.C.

175. *Edelweiss* – 15 – B – David Major – David Major, Westminster, Vt.

176. *Trumpeter* – 28 – Charles Morse – Gale York, Jackson, Miss.

177. ? – 20 – New England Yacht and Kirk Rogers – Kirk Rogers, New Gloucester, Me.

Irene, *Number 162, up on the ways. A Charles Morse boat built in 1917. Her name at the time this photo was taken was* Sea Bird.

178. *Essential* – 25 – Newman and Chase, 1977 – Robert Stein, Huntington, N.Y.
179. *Celene* – 22 – G. Hargrove, 1977 – Bruce Robinson, St. John, N.B.

Hargrove kept her for several years.

180. *Banshee* – 25 – D – Newman and Wojcik – John and Carol Wojcik, Norwell, Mass.
181. *Surprise* – 20 – Patrick Ahearn, 1975 – Richard Brownlie, Nahant, Mass.
182. *Charity* – 22 – Apprenticeshop, 1977 – Ted Watson, S. Dartmouth, Mass.

She was raced by the Apprenticeshop and won Class C in 1977, first across the finish line of the whole fleet. However, she is a Muscongus Bay sloop with a centerboard. She was sold to Leo and Sue Campbell of Reading, Pa., before her present owner bought her.

183. *Silver Heels* – 25 – Newman and Morris, 1978 – Ed and Karen Carroll, Fort Collins, Colo.
184. *Perseverance* – 27 – W. Simms, 1963 – William and Elizabeth Reed, Mystic, Conn.
185. *Calypso* – 27 – J. Philip Ham, 1978 – J. Philip and Beverly Ham, Holden, Mass.
186. *Ragtime Annie* – 27 – Bolger & Apollonio, 1975 – Barry and Julie Stoodley, Unity, Me.
187. *Peregrine* – 27 – Ralph Stanley, 1977 – Peter Blanchard III, Short Hills, N.J.
188. *Maude* – 32 – H. Gamage, 1939 – G.R. Axelson, Newburyport, Mass.

Ed Collins sold her to Robert M. Bartlett, who sold her to her present owner.

189. *Tradition* – 31 – Newman and Nehrbass, 1981 – Roger and Donna Nehrbass, Port Washington, Wis.

A good article about his experiences finishing out *Tradition* appeared in the 1982 booklet.

190. *Aikane* – 31 – Newman and Chase, 1978

She was burned in 1983 in the Billings shipyard fire at Stonington, Me.

191. *Bauneg Beg* – 22 – Apprenticeshop, 1978 – Ann and John Boswell, Hanover, N.H.

    Launched as *Pearle* for Steve McAllister. Sold to John and Nancy Gruen of North Berwick and given her present name. In 1983, sold to present owner.

192. *Kerwin Riggs* – 22 – McKie Roth, 1977 – John Chase, Carrboro, N.C.

    Owned in 1980 by Steve Williams and Roy Bouchard.

193. *Lady* – 32 – Harvey Gamage, 1978 – Linwood and Robin Gamage, South Bristol, Me.

    Harvey Gamage, builder of big fishing vessels, built her for his own use but died before she was finished. She is reported to be sailing parties out of Rockland.

194. *Huckleberry Belle* – 25 – Niederer, 1977 – John Nofzinger, Florence, Ala.

195. *Princess* – 25 – Wilbur Morse, ca. 1910 – Joe Richards, Smyrna, Del.

    Richards has rigged *Princess* with a marconi mainsail.

196. *Endeavor* – 27 – Ralph Stanley, 1979 – Betsy Holzman, Southwest Harbor, Me.

197. *Christania* – 31 – Newman and Davis, 1978 – William Davis, Five Islands, Me.

Phoenix, *Number 91, a Bruno & Stillman boat.*

198. *Bay Lady* – 31 – Newman and Lanning, 1979 – Captain Robert Fish, Boothbay Harbor, Me.

 She was built for Gary B. Mohr and sailed parties out of Bar Harbor. Captain Fish bought her in 1983 and sails parties out of Boothbay Harbor.
199. *Trinity* – 31 – Newman and Liberation Yachts – Doug and Michelle Jacoby, Marblehead, Mass.

 She was built as *Liberation*. Leo Thompson of Hope, R.I., finished her from a Newman hull.
200. *New Venture* – 25 – Newman and Foster, 1980 – Robert Foster, Mt. Desert Island, Me.
201. *Endeavor* – 31 – Newman and Genthner, 1979 – James Genthner, Fairhaven, Mass.
202. *Arrival* – 31 – Newman and Niedrach, 1981 – Robert and Anne Niedrach, Amherst, N.H.
203. *Aurora* – Claus Dietrich, Boston, Mass.
204. *Marie-Anne* – 27 – Jason Davidson, 1977 – Diana Echeverria, Jamaica Plain, Mass.
205. *Day Star* – 28 – Richard Mosher – Richard Mosher *et al.*, Kalamazoo, Mich.

 She was under construction in 1983.
206. *Mary Eliza* – 31 – Newman and Clark, 1979 – Wyndham Clark, Washington, D.C.
207. *Daisy Nell* – 30 – Herbert Melquist, 1980 – Captain Scott Edington, Gloucester, Mass.

 Formerly *Lanette M.*, she is currently used as a day-party boat.
208. *Ladyship* – 31 – Newman and Lanning, 1981 – Tony Dewsnap, Ladyship Cruises, Boothbay Harbor, Me.

 She was built to sail parties in the Virgin Islands. She was sold to Capt. Bob Fish in 1982, and to her present owner in 1984. She sails parties out of Boothbay Harbor, Me.
209. *Friend Ship* – 31 – Newman, 1981 – Captain Hank Warjonin

 She went south in the fall of 1981 to sail parties in the Virgin Islands.
210. *The Sloop John B.* – 23 – Elio Oliva, 1974 – Al Perrin, Canandaigua, N.Y.

 Christened *Betsey Darlin*. The owner is an outstanding photographer of Friendship sloops.
211. *Ansa* – 27 – James Hamilton, 1981 – James and Ann Hamilton, Andover, Mass.
212. *Achates* – 22 – Nick Roth, 1980 – Richard Leigh, Nashville, Tenn.
213. *Amie* – 25 – Bob Holcomb, 1978 – Hal and Pauline Hanson and Perry Lovelace, Edmonds, Wash.
214. *Gaviota* – 31 – Newman and Pettigrew, 1982 – John and Barbara Bush, Cotuit, Mass.
215. *Ellen Anne* – 31 – Passamaquoddy Yachts, 1968 – Dave and Ellen Colinan, Lincoln, R.I.
216. *Amity* – 47 – W.S. Carter, 1941 – John F. Nichols, New York, N.Y.
217. *Odyssey* – Shoreline Boats, 1972 – Peter Haynicz, E. Stroudsburg, Pa.
218. *William M. Rand* – 22 – John B. Rand, 1982 – William Rand,Jr. and John B. Rand, Lincoln Center, Mass.
219. *Yankee Belle* – 23 – Paul Edwards, 1983 – Paul Edwards, Matituck, N.J.
220. *Aikane* – Moore & Pettigrew, 1984 – Hal Marden, Wilmington, Del.
221. *Seal* – 22 – Ahern – Alvin J. Zink, Andover, Mass.

Other sloops not registered with the Society but believed to be still sailing:

*Amity* – W.S. Carter – Benjamin Plotkin, Norwalk, Conn.

*Annie Pode* – (ferro-cement)

*Angus* – Elio P. Oliva, Centerville, Mass.

*Aurora* – Richard Steel, Rockport, Me.

*Ayesha* – 37 – Charles Morse, 1900

*Betsy Darling* – 23½ – D. Elio Oliva

*Black Watch* – H. Rider – Donald Davis, Newport Beach, Calif.

*Carolyn* – A.J. Rousseau, Warwick, R.I.

*Duchess* – Sims, Scituate, 1898 – H. Reese Mitchell, Houghton, Mich.

*El Yanqui* – Wilbur Morse – Gene Peltier, Wilmington, Calif.

*Estella A.* – R. McLain – Mystic Seaport, Mystic, Conn.

*Maria* – Charles Burnham

*NorEaster* – Wilbur Morse – Robert Synnestvedt, Jenkintown, Pa.

*Pemaquid III* – George McKennor, Sillery, Quebec

*Red Wing* – Wilbur Morse – Marjorie Debold, Middletown, Conn.

*Sea Gull* – W.S. Carter – Mike Dolan, Hollywood, Fla.

*Spirit of Joshua* – James Tazelaar, McLean, Va.

*Spoondrift* – Harold Tweedy, New Rochelle, N.Y.

*Surprise* – Peter Boback, Fairfield, Conn.

*Tecumseh* – Wilbur Morse – Museum, Fort Lauderdale, Fla.

*Volunteer* – Gannett – Brian Neri, Buffalo, N.Y.

*Wild Wind* – Robert Standen, Manhattan Beach, Calif.

*Stella Maris* – Ted Wells, Duxbury, Mass.

*Appendix* B

# *R*ace Winners

| Governor's Trophy<br>Overall Winner A & B | | Eda Lawry Trophy<br>Class A Saturday | | Lash Brothers Trophy<br>Class B Saturday | |
|---|---|---|---|---|---|
| 1961 | *Voyager* | 1962 | *Amity* | 1961 | *Eastward* |
| 1962 | *Eastward* | 1963 | *Jolly Buccaneer* | 1962 | *Eastward* |
| 1963 | *Downeaster* | 1964 | *Chrissy* | 1963 | *Eastward* |
| 1964 | *Eastward* | 1965 | *Chrissy* | 1964 | *Eastward* |
| 1965 | *Dirigo* | 1966 | *Chrissy* | 1965 | *Dirigo* |
| 1966 | *Eastward* | 1967 | *Fog* | 1966 | *Eastward* |
| 1967 | *Dirigo* | 1968 | *Chrissy* | 1967 | *Fog, no race* |
| 1968 | *Rights of Man* | 1969 | *Eagle* | 1968 | *Rights of Man* |
| 1969 | *Eagle* | 1970 | *Gladiator* | 1969 | *Echo* |
| 1970 | *Eastward* | 1972 | *Chrissy* | 1970 | *Rights of Man* |
| 1972 | *Ellie T.* | 1973 | *Dictator* | 1972 | *Tannis* |
| 1973 | *Sarah Mead* | 1974 | *Dictator* | 1973 | *Patience* |
| 1974 | *Dictator* | 1975 | *Amos Swan* | 1974 | *Tannis* |
| 1975 | *Dictator* | 1976 | *Dictator* | 1975 | *Sarah Mead* |
| 1976 | *Loon* | 1977 | *Eagle* | 1976 | *Tannis* |
| 1977 | *Eagle* | 1978 | *Dictator* | 1977 | *Noahsark* |
| 1978 | *Rights of Man* | 1979 | *Dictator* | 1978 | *Rights of Man* |
| 1979 | *Tannis* | 1981 | *Chrissy* | 1979 | *Tannis* |
| 1980 | *Resolute* and *Tannis* | | | 1981 | *Resolute* |
| 1981 | *Noahsark* | | | | |
| 1982 | *Sarah Mead* | | | | |
| 1983 | *Liberty* | | | | |
| 1984 | *Tannis* | | | | |

**Morrill Trophy**
**Class C Saturday**

| | |
|---|---|
| 1965 | Heritage |
| 1966 | Channel Fever |
| 1967 | Fog, no race |
| 1968 | Channel Fever |
| 1969 | Channel Fever |
| 1970 | Cockle |
| 1972 | Channel Fever |
| 1973 | Channel Fever |
| 1974 | Channel Fever |
| 1975 | Cockle |
| 1976 | Gypsy |
| 1977 | Charity |
| 1978 | Heritage |
| 1979 | Schoodic |
| 1981 | Heritage |
| 1982 | Schoodic |

**Bruno & Stillman**
**Class D Saturday**

| | |
|---|---|
| 1970 | Phoenix |
| 1972 | Salatia |
| 1973 | Magi |
| 1974 | Hold Tight |
| 1975 | Salatia |
| 1976 | Anna B. |
| 1977 | Anna B. |
| 1978 | Anna B. |
| 1979 | Anna B. |
| 1981 | Phoenix |

**Jonah Morse Trophy**
**Class A Overall**

| | |
|---|---|
| 1966 | Chrissy |
| 1967 | Black Jack |
| 1968 | Chrissy |
| 1969 | Eagle |
| 1970 | Black Jack |
| 1972 | Chrissy |
| 1973 | Chance |
| 1974 | Dictator |
| 1975 | Dictator |
| 1976 | Dictator |
| 1977 | Eagle |
| 1978 | Dictator |
| 1979 | Dictator |
| 1980 | Dictator and Gladiator |
| 1981 | Chrissy |
| 1982 | Chance |
| 1983 | Chance |

**Anjacaa Trophy**
**Class B Overall**

| | |
|---|---|
| 1969 | Friendship |
| 1970 | Eastward |
| 1972 | Ellie T. |
| 1973 | Sarah Mead |
| 1974 | Rights of Man |
| 1975 | Hieronymus |
| 1976 | Loon |
| 1977 | Loon |
| 1978 | Rights of Man |
| 1979 | Tannis |
| 1980 | Resolute and Tannis |
| 1981 | Noahsark |
| 1982 | Sarah Mead |
| 1983 | Sarah Mead |

**Palawan Trophy**
**Class C Overall**

| | |
|---|---|
| 1964 | Mar-Gin |
| 1965 | Heritage |
| 1966 | Channel Fever |
| 1967 | Channel Fever |
| 1968 | Heritage |
| 1969 | Channel Fever |
| 1970 | Cockle |
| 1972 | Channel Fever |
| 1973 | Channel Fever |
| 1974 | Gypsy |
| 1975 | Cockle |
| 1976 | Heritage |
| 1977 | Charity |
| 1978 | Heritage |
| 1979 | Schoodic |
| 1980 | Heritage |
| 1981 | Heritage |

**Class D Overall**

| | |
|---|---|
| 1970 | Phoenix |
| 1972 | Phoenix |
| 1973 | Callipygous |
| 1974 | Hold Tight |
| 1975 | Anna B. and Salatia |
| 1976 | Anna B. |

## Jarvis Newman Trophy
### Winning Pemaquid Design

| | |
|---|---|
| 1972 | *Ellie T.* |
| 1973 | *Salatia* |
| 1974 | *Hold Tight* |
| 1975 | *Salatia* |
| 1976 | *Salatia* |
| 1977 | *Diana* |
| 1978 | *Salatia* |
| 1979 | *Hold Tight* |
| 1980 | *Salatia* |
| 1981 | *Salatia* |
| 1982 | *Salatia* |
| 1983 | *Salatia* |

## Seiler Trophy
### Friendliest Skipper

| | |
|---|---|
| 1969 | *Chance* |
| 1970 | *Tannis* |
| 1971 | *Vida Mia* |
| 1972 | *Sarah Mead* |
| 1973 | *Gypsy* |
| 1974 | *Magi* |
| 1975 | *Black Jack* |
| 1976 | *Eastward* |
| 1977 | *Tannis* |
| 1978 | *Schoodic* |
| 1979 | *Resolute* |
| 1980 | *Resolute* |
| 1981 | *Salatia* |
| 1982 | *Resolute* |

## Gould Trophy
### Youngest Crew Member

| | |
|---|---|
| 1970 | *Gladiator* |
| 1972 | *Tannis* |
| 1973 | *Dictator* |
| 1974 | *Schoodic* |
| 1975 | *Tannis* |
| 1976 | *Tannis* |
| 1977 | *Morning Star* |
| 1978 | *Salatia* |
| 1979 | *Venture* |
| 1980 | *Ragtime Annie* |
| 1981 | *Ragtime Annie* |
| 1982 | *Christania* |
| 1983 | *Ragtime Annie* |

## Gladiator Trophy
### From Greatest Distance

| | |
|---|---|
| 1970 | *Sepoy* |
| 1972 | *Vogel Frei* |
| 1973 | *Sepoy* |
| 1974 | *Tannis* |
| 1975 | *Eagle (A)* |
| 1976 | *Departure* |
| 1977 | *Apogee* |
| 1978 | *Ollie M.* |
| 1979 | *Endeavor* |
| 1980 | *Ellie T.* |
| 1981 | *Calypso* |
| 1982 | *Banshee* |
| 1983 | *Headway* |

## Pemaquid Trophy

| | |
|---|---|
| 1979 | *Fiddler's Green* |

## Owner-Built-and-Sailed

| | |
|---|---|
| 1979 | *Noahsark* |
| 1980 | *Resolute* |
| 1981 | *Resolute* |
| 1983 | *William Rand* |

## Bequia Trophy

| | |
|---|---|
| 1980 | *West Wind* |

## Loon Trophy

| | |
|---|---|
| 1980 | *Surprise* |

## President's Trophy
### Second Overall

| | |
|---|---|
| 1982 | *Loon* |
| 1983 | *Sarah Mead* |

## Homecoming Trophy

| | |
|---|---|
| 1983 | *Phoenix* |

Golden Anchor, *Number 171,*
*a Newman and Morris boat*
*owned and sailed by the*
*Golden Anchor Inn, Bar Har-*
*bor, Maine. (Photo by James*
*A. Moore)*

In 1982, awards restructured as follows:
Governor's Trophy – 1st Overall Classes, A, B, C, D
President's Trophy – 2nd Overall
Seiler Trophy – 3rd Overall
Jonah Morse – 1st Overall in Class A
Anjacaa – 1st Overall in Class B
Morrill – 1st Overall in Class C
Herold Jones – 1st Overall in Class D
Others unchanged, but no Eda Lawry
or Lash Brothers trophies

| Nickerson Trophy Youngest Skipper | | Danforth Trophy Middle of the Fleet | | Herold Jones Trophy Class D Overall | |
|---|---|---|---|---|---|
| 1971 | *Sarah Mead* | 1976 | *Eastward* | 1977 | *Anna B.* |
| 1972 | *Voyager* | 1977 | *Chrissy* | 1978 | *Phoenix* |
| 1973 | *Chance* | 1978 | *Chrissy* | 1980 | *Salatia* |
| 1974 | *Diana* | 1979 | *Sarah Mead* | 1981 | *Phoenix* |
| 1975 | *Rights of Man* | 1980 | *Kochab* | 1982 | *Phoenix* |
| 1976 | *David Major* | 1981 | *Freedom* | 1983 | *Liberty* |
| 1977 | *Edelweiss* | 1982 | *Christania* | | |
| 1978 | *Tannis* | 1983 | *Tannis* | | |
| 1979 | *Dictator* | | | | |
| 1980 | *Gladiator* | | | **Last-In Trophy** | |
| 1981 | *Loon* | | | | |
| 1982 | *Gladiator* | | | 1979 | *Fiddler's Green* |
| | | **Post Office Trophy** | | 1980 | *Edelweiss* |
| **Surprise Trophy** | | **Biggest Mistake** | | | |
| | | 1976 | *Departure* | | |
| 1975 | *Ray of Hope* | 1977 | *Loon* | | |
| | | 1978 | *Downeaster* | | |
| | | 1979 | *Calypso* | | |
| **Dr. Hahn Trophy** | | 1980 | *Surprise* | | |
| | | 1981 | *Ray of Hope* | | |
| 1974 | *Anna R.* | 1982 | *Ollie M.* | | |
| | | 1983 | *Headway* | | |

*Appendix* C

# *P*residents of the Friendship Sloop Society

| | |
|---|---|
| 1961-1963 | Bernard MacKenzie – *Voyager* |
| 1964 | Richard Swanson – *Jolly Buccaneer* |
| 1965 | Roger Duncan – *Eastward* |
| 1966-1967 | Robert Lash – *Gypsy* |
| 1968 | Roger Duncan – *Eastward* |
| 1969-1970 | George Morrill – *Sazerac* |
| 1971-1972 | William Pendleton – *Black Jack* |
| 1973-1974 | Frederick Brown – *Vida Mia* |
| 1975-1976 | Henry White – *Sarah Mead* |
| 1977-1978 | John Cronin – *Tannis* |
| 1979-1980 | Don Huston – *Eagle* |
| 1981-1982 | Alfred Beck – *Phoenix* |
| 1983-1984 | William Hadlock – *Heritage* |

# Bibliography

Albion, Baker and Labaree. *New England and the Sea*. Middletown: Wesleyan University Press, 1972.

Carrick, Robert W. and Henderson, Richard. *John G. Alden and His Yacht Designs*. Camden: International Marine Publishing Company, 1983.

Chapelle, Howard I. *American Fishing Schooners*. New York: W.W. Norton, 1973.

*American Sailing Craft*. Camden: International Marine Publishing Company, 1975.

*American Small Sailing Craft*. New York: W.W. Norton, 1951.

*National Watercraft Collection*. Camden: International Marine Publishing Company and Smithsonian Institution, 1976.

Clifford, Harold. *The Boothbay Region 1906-1960*. Cumberland Press, 1982.

*Charlie York*. Camden: International Marine Publishing Company, 1974.

Coffin, Robert P.T. *Kennebec: Cradle of Americans*. Boothbay: Downeast Enterprises, 1965.

Donham, G.M. *Maine Register*, 1895-6, 1903-4. Portland.

Goode, George Brown *et al*. *The Fisheries and Fishing Industry of the United States*. Washington: Smithsonian Institution, 1887.

Hatch, Louis. *Maine, A History*. Somersworth: New Hampshire Publishing Co., 1974.

Jones, Herold A., ed. *It's A Friendship*. Friendship: Friendship Sloop Society, 1965.

Jones, Herold. *Ships That Came Home*. Friendship: Friendship Sloop Society, 1961.

Morse, Ivan. *Friendship Long Island*. Friendship: Friendship Museum, 1974.

Munson, Gorham. *Penobscot*. Philadelphia: J.P. Lippincott and Co., 1959.

Richards, Joe. *Princess*. New York: David McKay, Inc., 1973.

Roberts, Albert *et al*. *Enduring Friendships*. Camden: International Marine Publishing Company, 1970.

Time-Life Books, Inc. *The Classic Boat*. Alexandria: Time-Life Books, Inc., 1977.

Wasson, G.S. and Colcord, L. *Sailing Days on the Penobscot*. Salem: Marine Research Society, 1932.


## PERIODICALS

Camden: *Down East* magazine, various issues (1969-1975).

*New England Magazine*, (February 1896).

Camden: *National Fisherman/Maine Coast Fisherman*, (July 1946) through September 1971).

Friendship: *Friendship Sloop Society yearbooks*, (1962-1984).

New York: *Harpers*, (August 1892 and November 1902).

*Outlook* (August 1903 and December 1906).

New York: *Rudder* (July and August 1946).

New York: *Yachting* (December 1924, December 1939, December 1946, May 1980, January 1933).

# Index